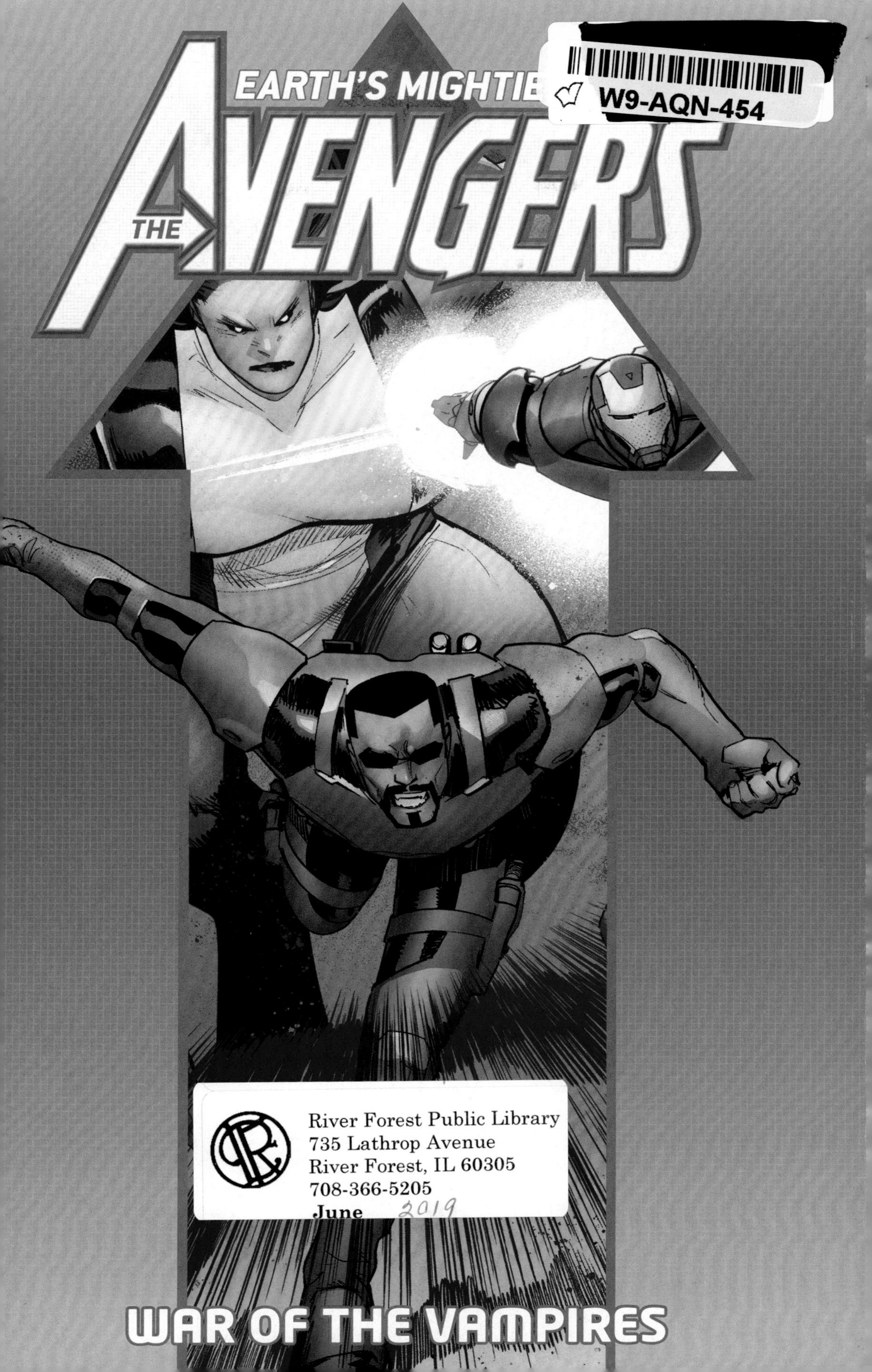
EARTH'S MIGHTIE
THE AVENGERS
WAR OF THE VAMPIRES

ON A DAY UNLIKE ANY OTHER, A DARK CELESTIAL INVASION LED IRON MAN, THOR AND CAPTAIN AMERICA TO RE-FORM THE AVENGERS, ADDING BLACK PANTHER, CAPTAIN MARVEL, SHE-HULK AND GHOST RIDER TO THEIR RANKS.

BUT ONE MILLION YEARS BEFORE THEM, A PREHISTORIC TEAM OF HEROES LED BY ODIN DEFENDED THE WORLD FROM ANY THREAT, NO MATTER HOW COLOSSAL. AND AMONG THEM WAS THE VERY FIRST IRON FIST...

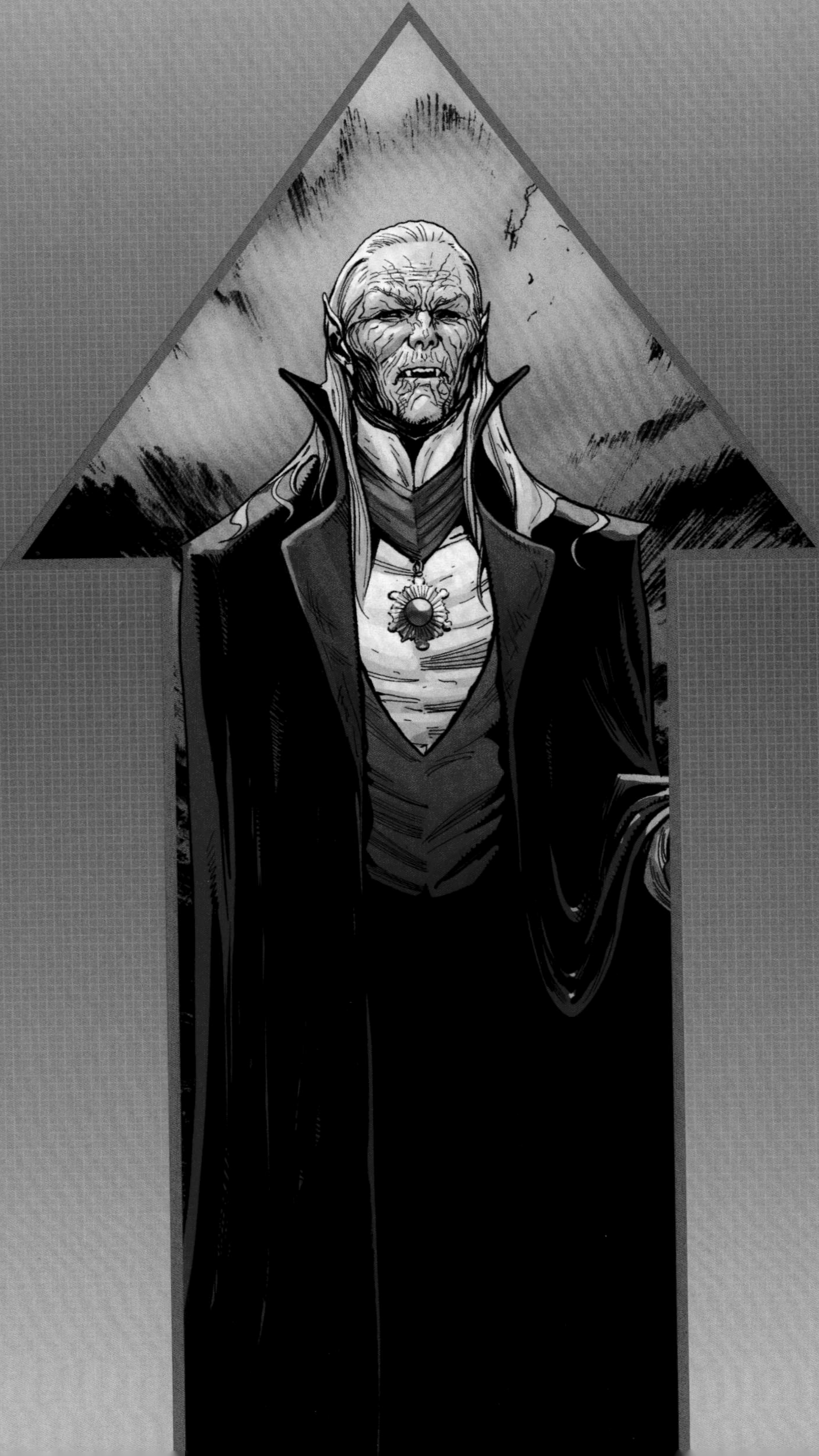

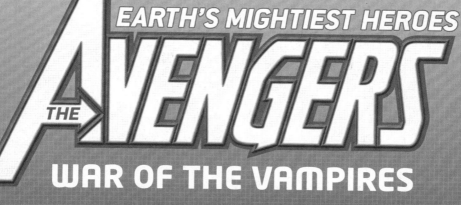

EARTH'S MIGHTIEST HEROES

THE AVENGERS

WAR OF THE VAMPIRES

JASON AARON
WRITER

AVENGERS #13

ANDREA SORRENTINO
ARTIST

JUSTIN PONSOR
& **ERICK ARCINIEGA**
COLOR ARTISTS

STEVE EPTING
COVER ART

AVENGERS #14-17

DAVID MARQUEZ
ARTIST

ERICK ARCINIEGA
WITH **JUSTIN PONSOR** [#14]
COLOR ARTISTS

DAVID MARQUEZ WITH **JUSTIN PONSOR** [#14-15]
& **MATTHEW WILSON** [#16-17]
COVER ART

VC'S CORY PETIT
LETTERER

ALANNA SMITH
ASSOCIATE EDITOR

TOM BREVOORT
EDITOR

AVENGERS CREATED BY **STAN LEE** & **JACK KIRBY**

COLLECTION EDITOR **JENNIFER GRÜNWALD**
ASSISTANT EDITOR **CAITLIN O'CONNELL**
ASSOCIATE MANAGING EDITOR **KATERI WOODY**
EDITOR, SPECIAL PROJECTS **MARK D. BEAZLEY**
VP PRODUCTION & SPECIAL PROJECTS **JEFF YOUNGQUIST**
SVP PRINT, SALES & MARKETING **DAVID GABRIEL**

BOOK DESIGNERS **SALENA MAHINA** & **MANNY MEDEROS**

EDITOR IN CHIEF **C.B. CEBULSKI**
CHIEF CREATIVE OFFICER **JOE QUESADA**
PRESIDENT **DAN BUCKLEY**
EXECUTIVE PRODUCER **ALAN FINE**

BY JASON AARON VOL. 3: WAR OF THE VAMPIRES. Contains material originally published in magazine form as AVENGERS #13-17. First printing 2019. ISBN 978-1-302-91461-5. Published by MARVEL WORLDWIDE, INC., a of MARVEL ENTERTAINMENT, LLC. OFFICE OF PUBLICATION: 135 West 50th Street, New York, NY 10020. © 2019 MARVEL No similarity between any of the names, characters, persons, and/or institutions in this magazine of any living or dead person or institution is intended, and any such similarity which may exist is purely coincidental. **Printed in Canada.** DAN BUCKLEY, President, Marvel Entertainment; JOHN NEE, Publisher; JOE QUESADA, tive Officer; TOM BREVOORT, SVP of Publishing; DAVID BOGART, Associate Publisher & SVP of Talent Affairs; DAVID GABRIEL, SVP of Sales & Marketing, Publishing; JEFF YOUNGQUIST, VP of Production & Special Projects; DAN cutive Director of Publishing Technology; ALEX MORALES, Director of Publishing Operations; DAN EDINGTON, Managing Editor; SUSAN CRESPI, Production Manager; STAN LEE, Chairman Emeritus. For information regarding in Marvel Comics or on Marvel.com, please contact Vit DeBellis, Custom Solutions & Integrated Advertising Manager, at vdebellis@marvel.com. For Marvel subscription inquiries, please call 888-511-5480. **Manufactured** 12/2019 and 5/14/2019 by SOLISCO PRINTERS, SCOTT, QC, CANADA.

5 4 3 2 1

13 THE GIRL WHO PUNCHED THE DRAGON

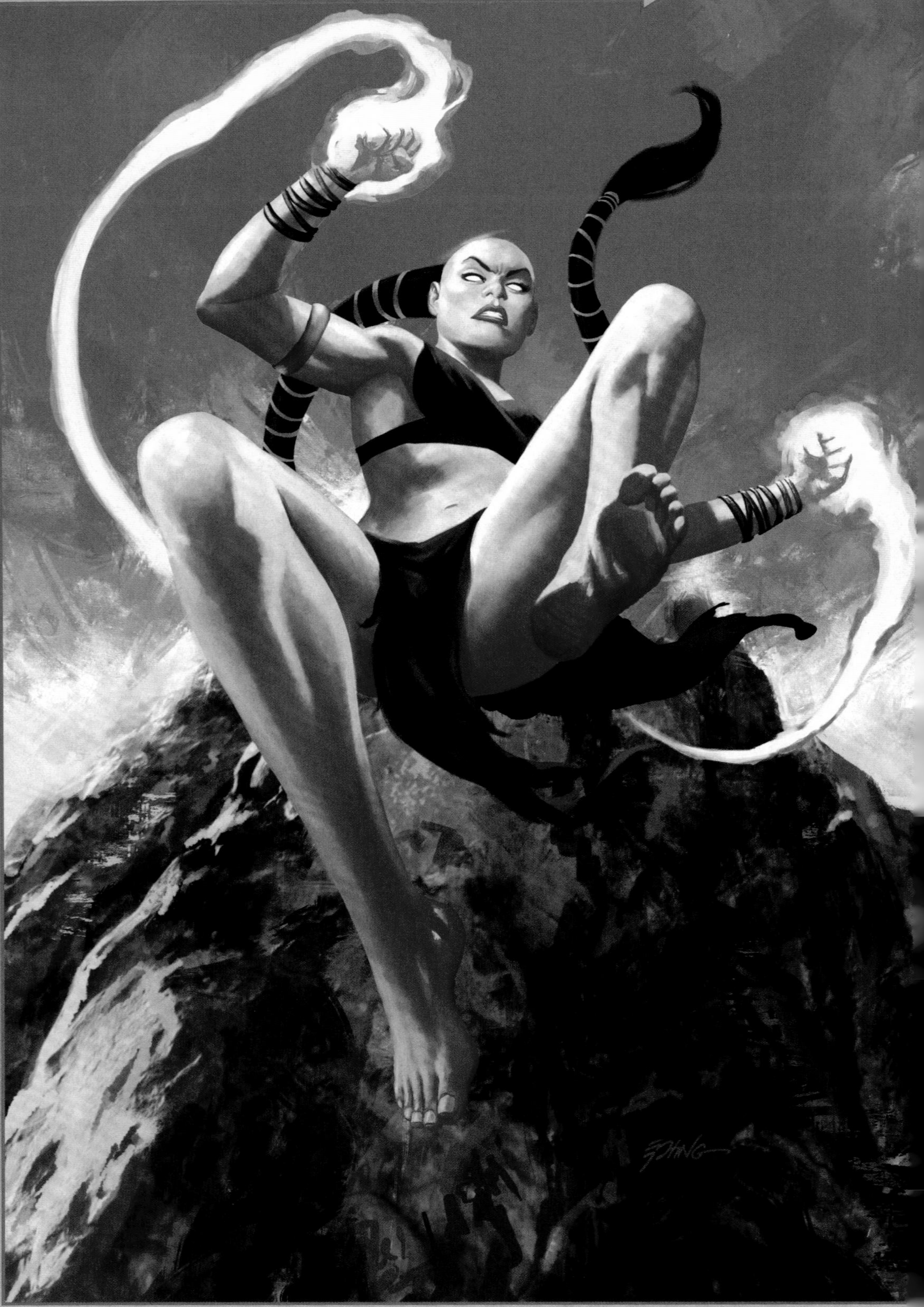

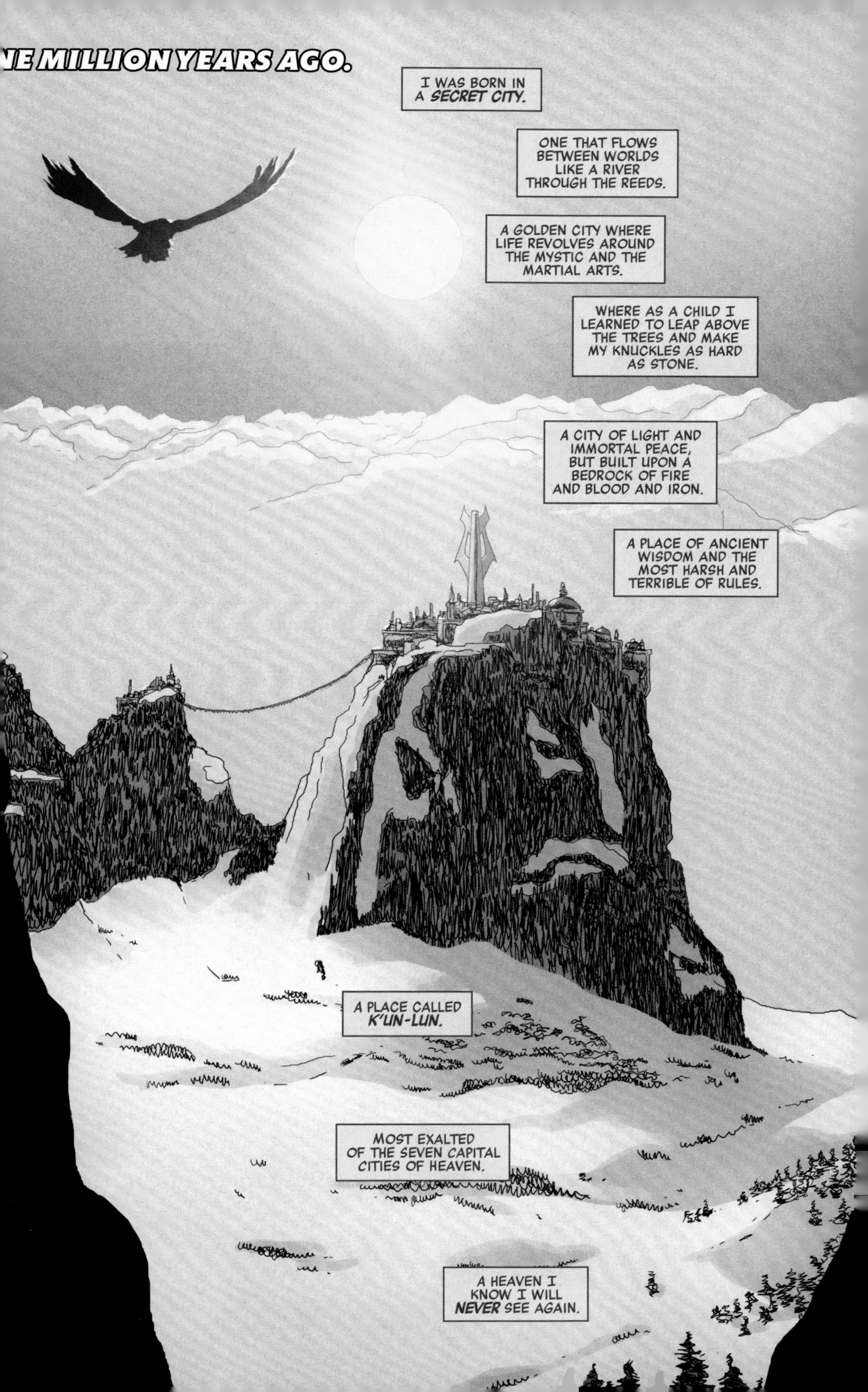
NE MILLION YEARS AGO.
I WAS BORN IN A SECRET CITY.
ONE THAT FLOWS BETWEEN WORLDS LIKE A RIVER THROUGH THE REEDS.
A GOLDEN CITY WHERE LIFE REVOLVES AROUND THE MYSTIC AND THE MARTIAL ARTS.
WHERE AS A CHILD I LEARNED TO LEAP ABOVE THE TREES AND MAKE MY KNUCKLES AS HARD AS STONE.
A CITY OF LIGHT AND IMMORTAL PEACE, BUT BUILT UPON A BEDROCK OF FIRE AND BLOOD AND IRON.
A PLACE OF ANCIENT WISDOM AND THE MOST HARSH AND TERRIBLE OF RULES.
A PLACE CALLED K'UN-LUN.
MOST EXALTED OF THE SEVEN CAPITAL CITIES OF HEAVEN.
A HEAVEN I KNOW I WILL NEVER SEE AGAIN.

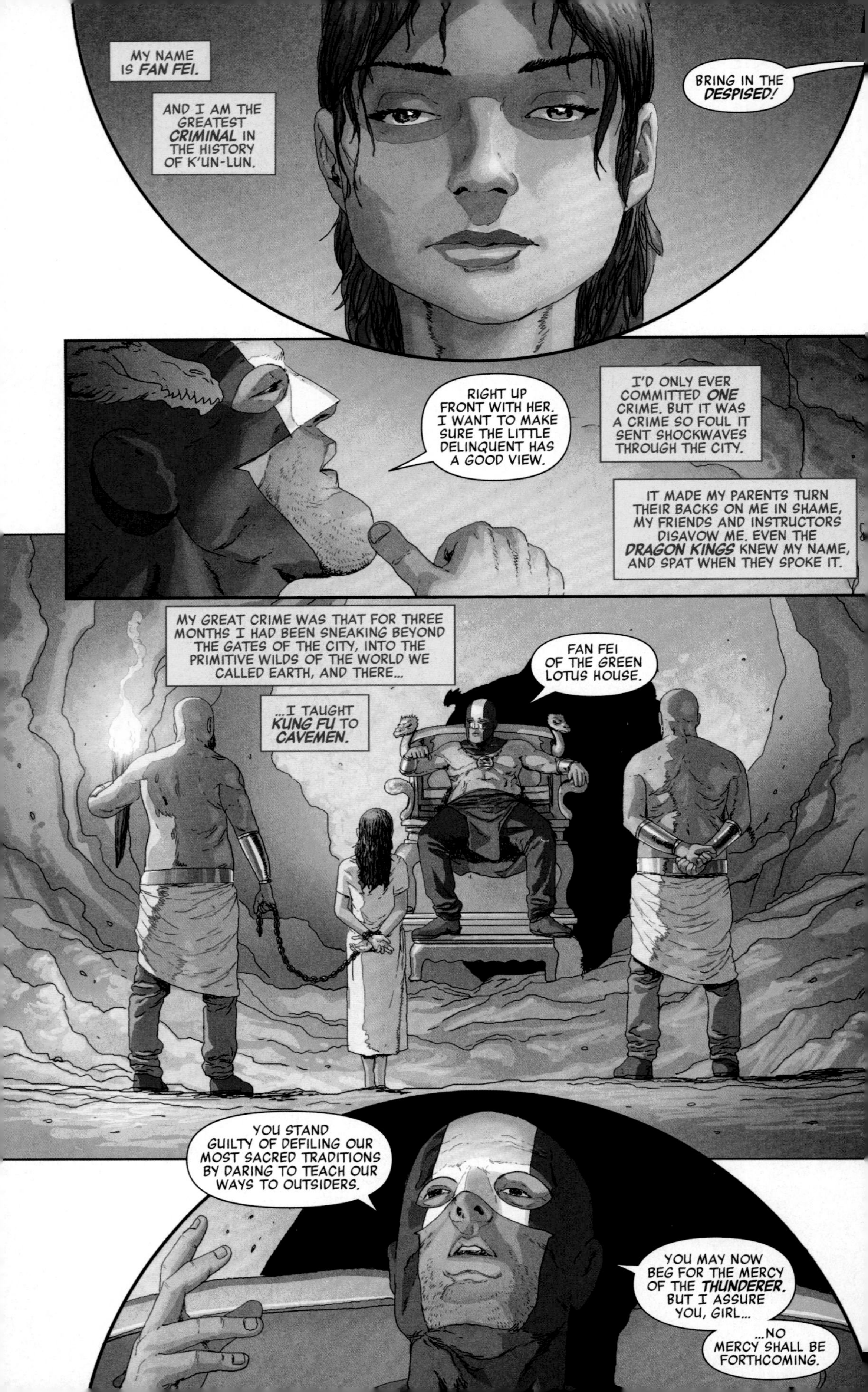

MY NAME IS FAN FEI.
AND I AM THE GREATEST CRIMINAL IN THE HISTORY OF K'UN-LUN.
BRING IN THE DESPISED!
RIGHT UP FRONT WITH HER. I WANT TO MAKE SURE THE LITTLE DELINQUENT HAS A GOOD VIEW.
I'D ONLY EVER COMMITTED ONE CRIME. BUT IT WAS A CRIME SO FOUL IT SENT SHOCKWAVES THROUGH THE CITY.
IT MADE MY PARENTS TURN THEIR BACKS ON ME IN SHAME, MY FRIENDS AND INSTRUCTORS DISAVOW ME. EVEN THE DRAGON KINGS KNEW MY NAME, AND SPAT WHEN THEY SPOKE IT.
MY GREAT CRIME WAS THAT FOR THREE MONTHS I HAD BEEN SNEAKING BEYOND THE GATES OF THE CITY, INTO THE PRIMITIVE WILDS OF THE WORLD WE CALLED EARTH, AND THERE...
...I TAUGHT KUNG FU TO CAVEMEN.
FAN FEI OF THE GREEN LOTUS HOUSE.
YOU STAND GUILTY OF DEFILING OUR MOST SACRED TRADITIONS BY DARING TO TEACH OUR WAYS TO OUTSIDERS.
YOU MAY NOW BEG FOR THE MERCY OF THE THUNDERER. BUT I ASSURE YOU, GIRL...
...NO MERCY SHALL BE FORTHCOMING.

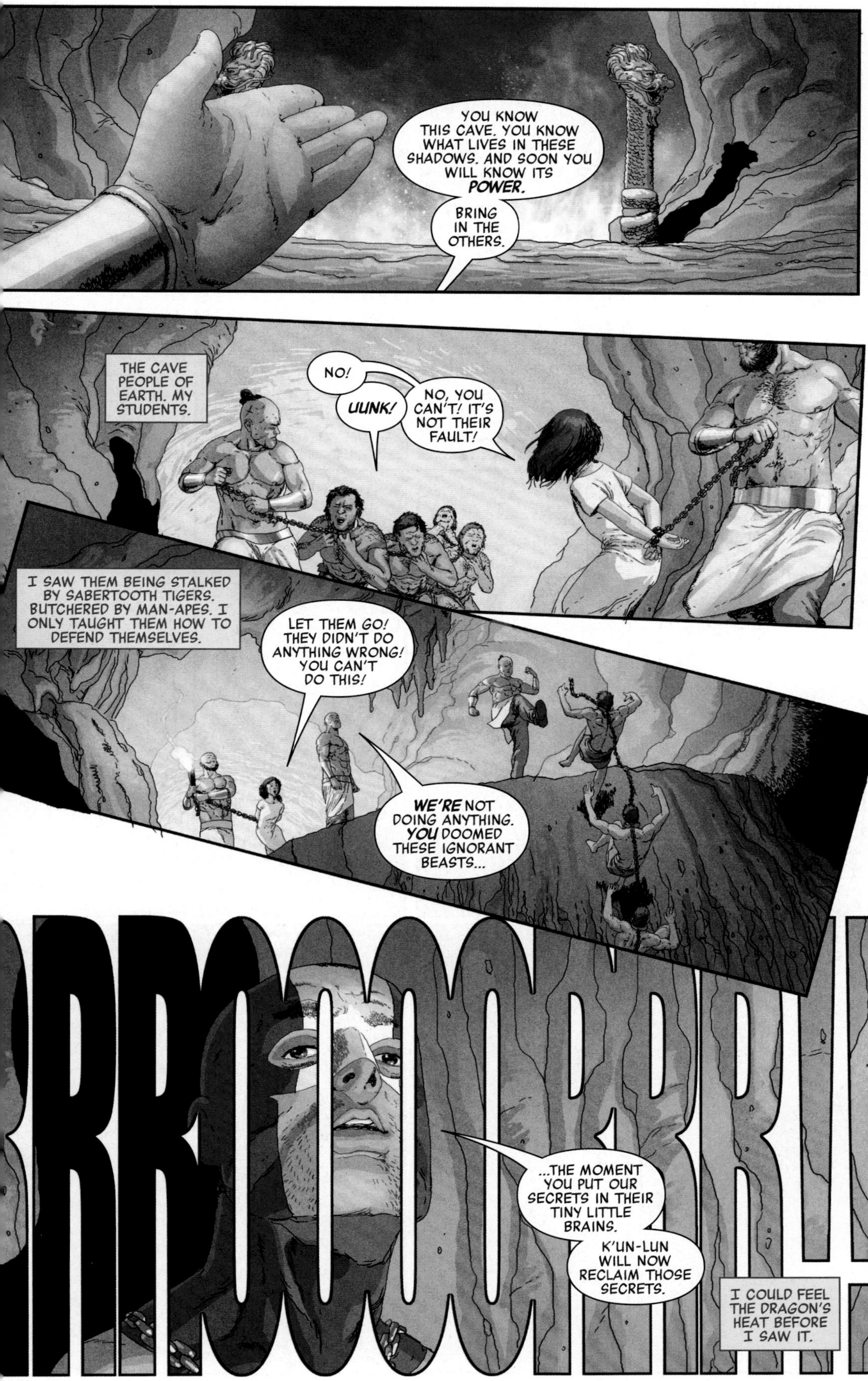
YOU KNOW THIS CAVE. YOU KNOW WHAT LIVES IN THESE SHADOWS. AND SOON YOU WILL KNOW ITS POWER.
BRING IN THE OTHERS.
THE CAVE PEOPLE OF EARTH. MY STUDENTS.
NO!
UUNK!
NO, YOU CAN'T! IT'S NOT THEIR FAULT!
I SAW THEM BEING STALKED BY SABERTOOTH TIGERS. BUTCHERED BY MAN-APES. I ONLY TAUGHT THEM HOW TO DEFEND THEMSELVES.
LET THEM GO! THEY DIDN'T DO ANYTHING WRONG! YOU CAN'T DO THIS!
WE'RE NOT DOING ANYTHING. YOU DOOMED THESE IGNORANT BEASTS...
...THE MOMENT YOU PUT OUR SECRETS IN THEIR TINY LITTLE BRAINS.
K'UN-LUN WILL NOW RECLAIM THOSE SECRETS.
I COULD FEEL THE DRAGON'S HEAT BEFORE I SAW IT.

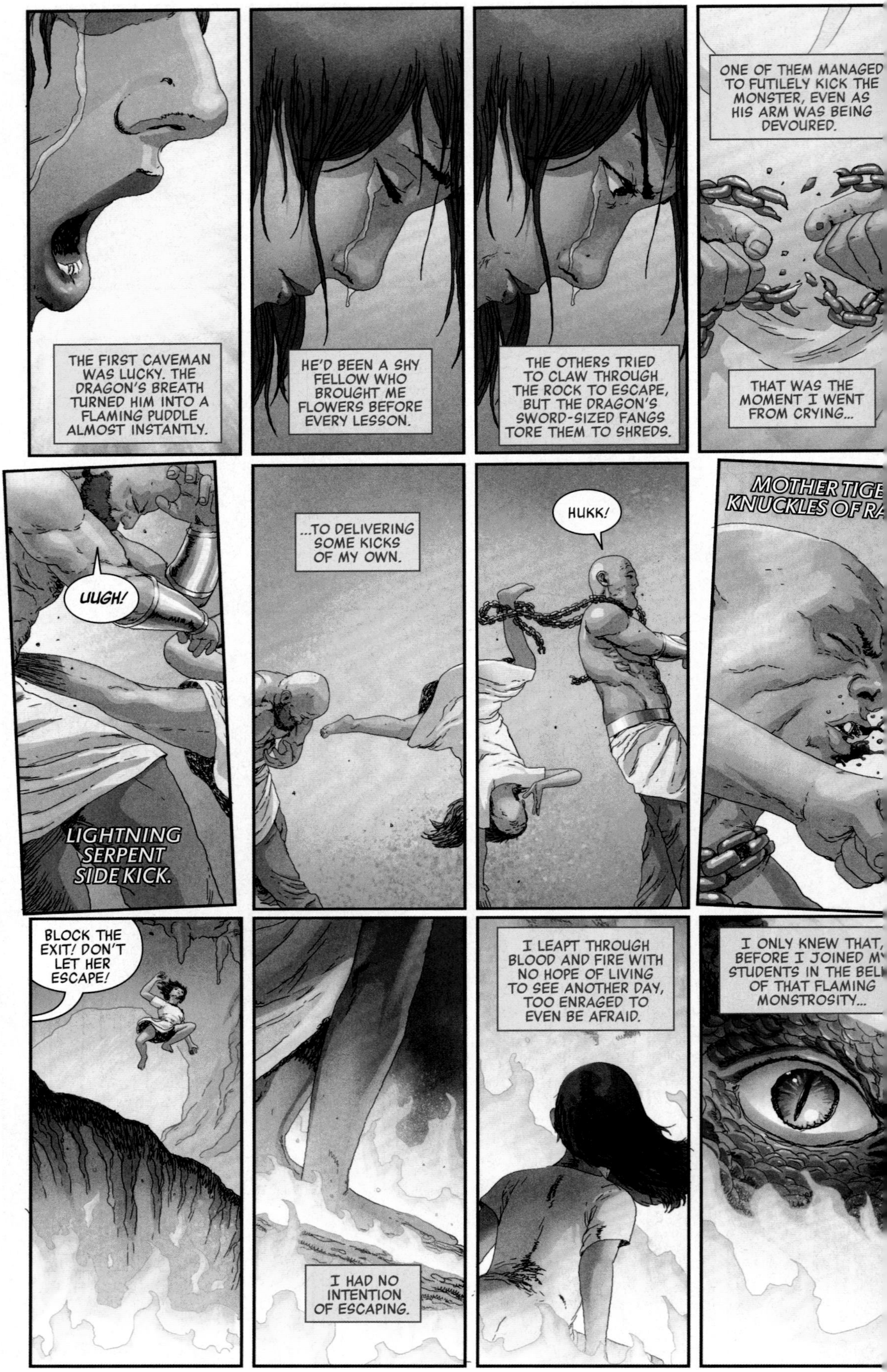
THE FIRST CAVEMAN WAS LUCKY. THE DRAGON'S BREATH TURNED HIM INTO A FLAMING PUDDLE ALMOST INSTANTLY.
HE'D BEEN A SHY FELLOW WHO BROUGHT ME FLOWERS BEFORE EVERY LESSON.
THE OTHERS TRIED TO CLAW THROUGH THE ROCK TO ESCAPE, BUT THE DRAGON'S SWORD-SIZED FANGS TORE THEM TO SHREDS.
ONE OF THEM MANAGED TO FUTILELY KICK THE MONSTER, EVEN AS HIS ARM WAS BEING DEVOURED.
THAT WAS THE MOMENT I WENT FROM CRYING...
UUGH!
LIGHTNING SERPENT SIDE KICK.
...TO DELIVERING SOME KICKS OF MY OWN.
HUKK!
MOTHER TIGE
KNUCKLES OF RA
BLOCK THE EXIT! DON'T LET HER ESCAPE!
I HAD NO INTENTION OF ESCAPING.
I LEAPT THROUGH BLOOD AND FIRE WITH NO HOPE OF LIVING TO SEE ANOTHER DAY, TOO ENRAGED TO EVEN BE AFRAID.
I ONLY KNEW THAT, BEFORE I JOINED M STUDENTS IN THE BEL OF THAT FLAMING MONSTROSITY...

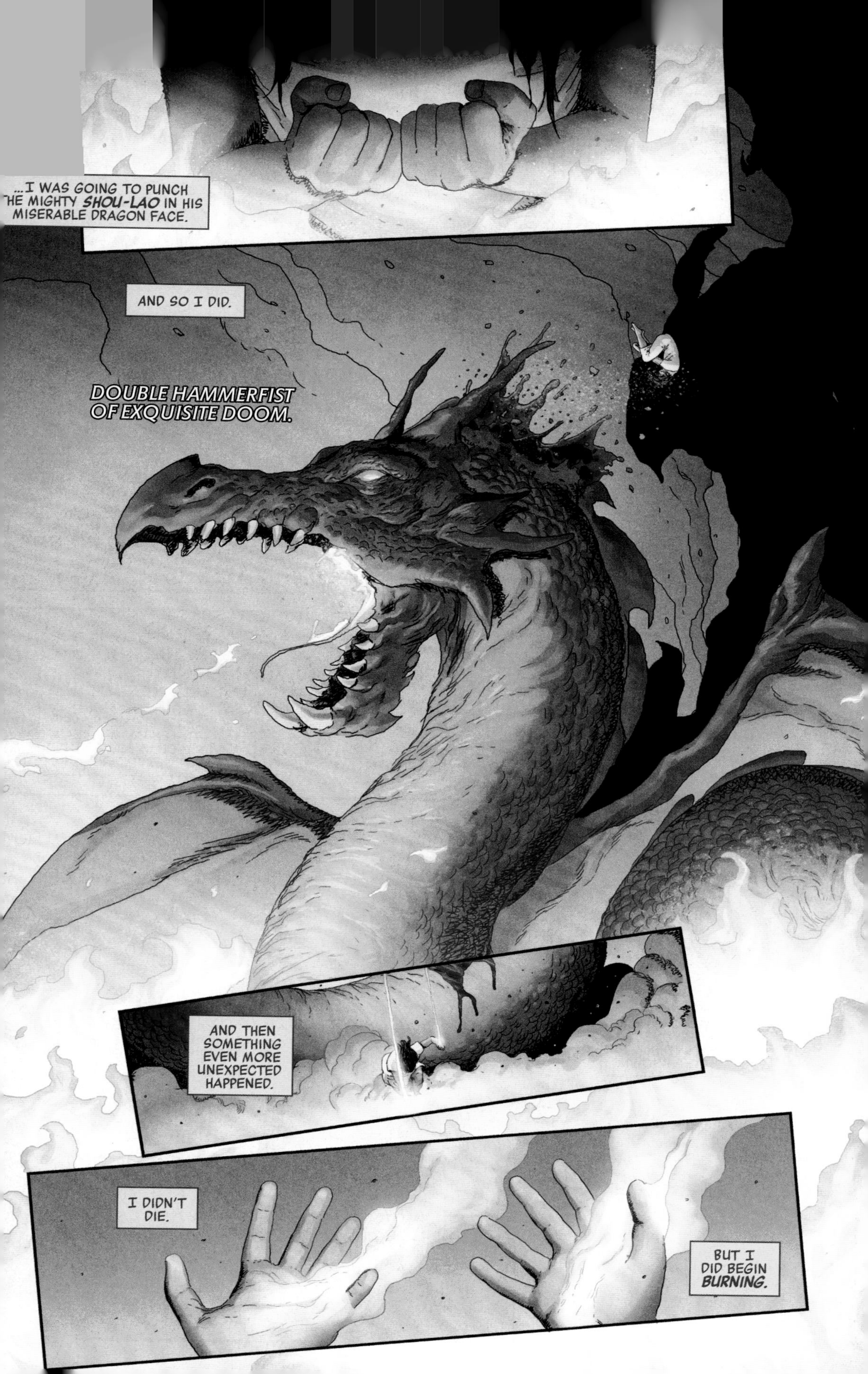
...I WAS GOING TO PUNCH THE MIGHTY SHOU-LAO IN HIS MISERABLE DRAGON FACE.
AND SO I DID.
DOUBLE HAMMERFIST OF EXQUISITE DOOM.
AND THEN SOMETHING EVEN MORE UNEXPECTED HAPPENED.
I DIDN'T DIE.
BUT I DID BEGIN BURNING.

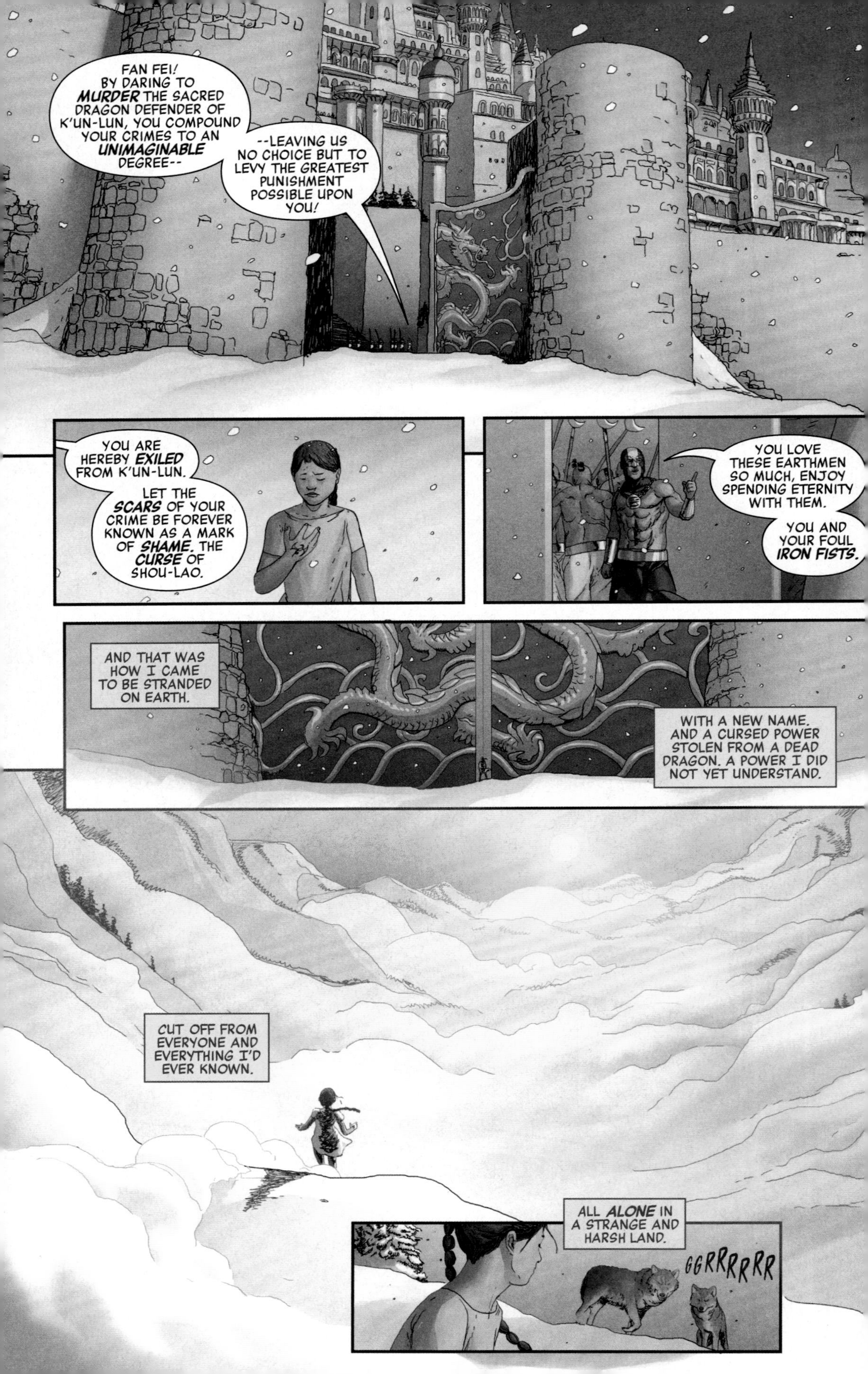
FAN FEI! BY DARING TO MURDER THE SACRED DRAGON DEFENDER OF K'UN-LUN, YOU COMPOUND YOUR CRIMES TO AN UNIMAGINABLE DEGREE--
--LEAVING US NO CHOICE BUT TO LEVY THE GREATEST PUNISHMENT POSSIBLE UPON YOU!
YOU ARE HEREBY EXILED FROM K'UN-LUN.
LET THE SCARS OF YOUR CRIME BE FOREVER KNOWN AS A MARK OF SHAME. THE CURSE OF SHOU-LAO.
YOU LOVE THESE EARTHMEN SO MUCH, ENJOY SPENDING ETERNITY WITH THEM.
YOU AND YOUR FOUL IRON FISTS.
AND THAT WAS HOW I CAME TO BE STRANDED ON EARTH.
WITH A NEW NAME. AND A CURSED POWER STOLEN FROM A DEAD DRAGON. A POWER I DID NOT YET UNDERSTAND.
CUT OFF FROM EVERYONE AND EVERYTHING I'D EVER KNOWN.
ALL ALONE IN A STRANGE AND HARSH LAND.
GGRRRRRR

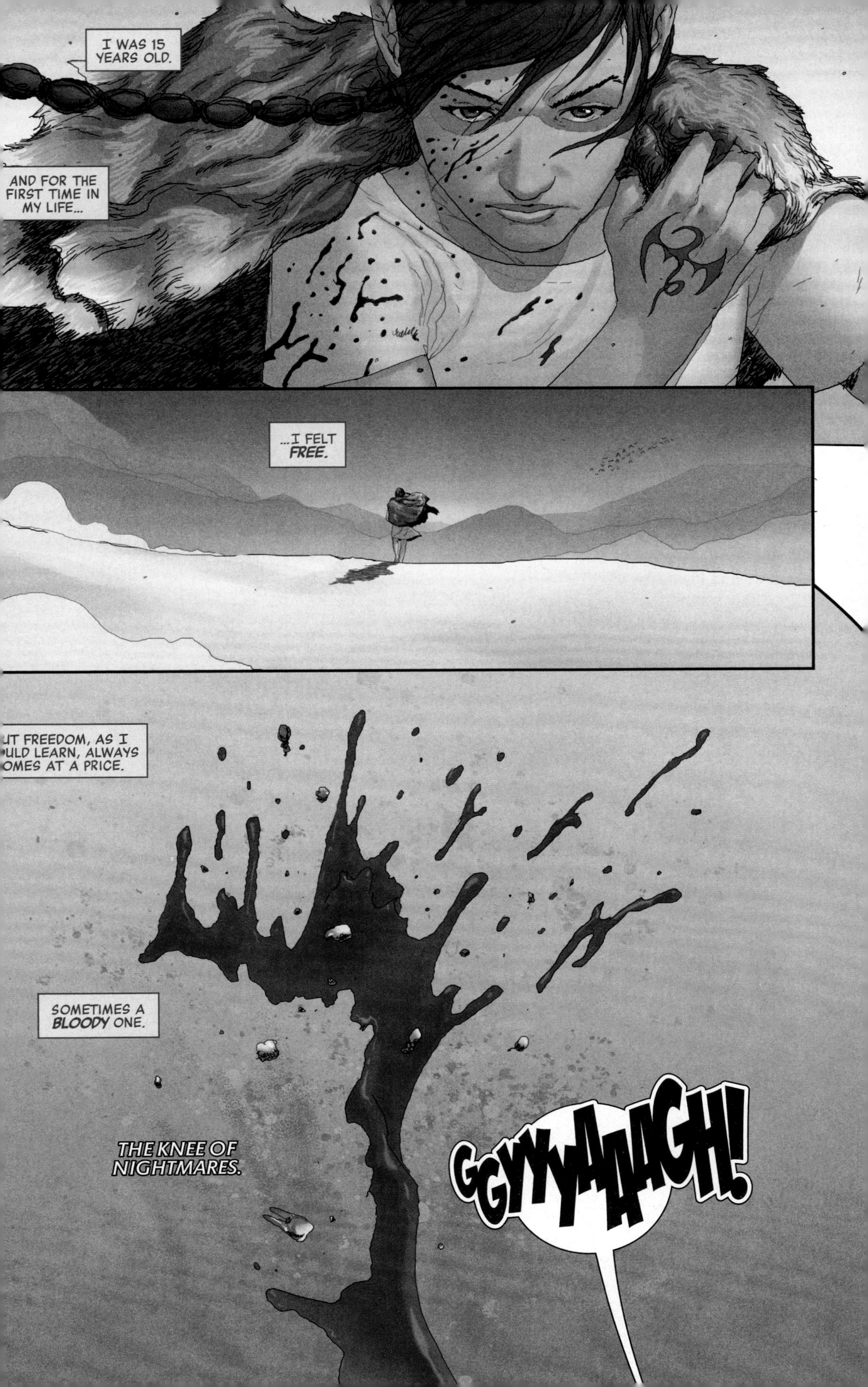
I WAS 15 YEARS OLD.
AND FOR THE FIRST TIME IN MY LIFE...
...I FELT FREE.
UT FREEDOM, AS I
ULD LEARN, ALWAYS
OMES AT A PRICE.
SOMETIMES A BLOODY ONE.
THE KNEE OF NIGHTMARES.
GGYYYAAAAGH!

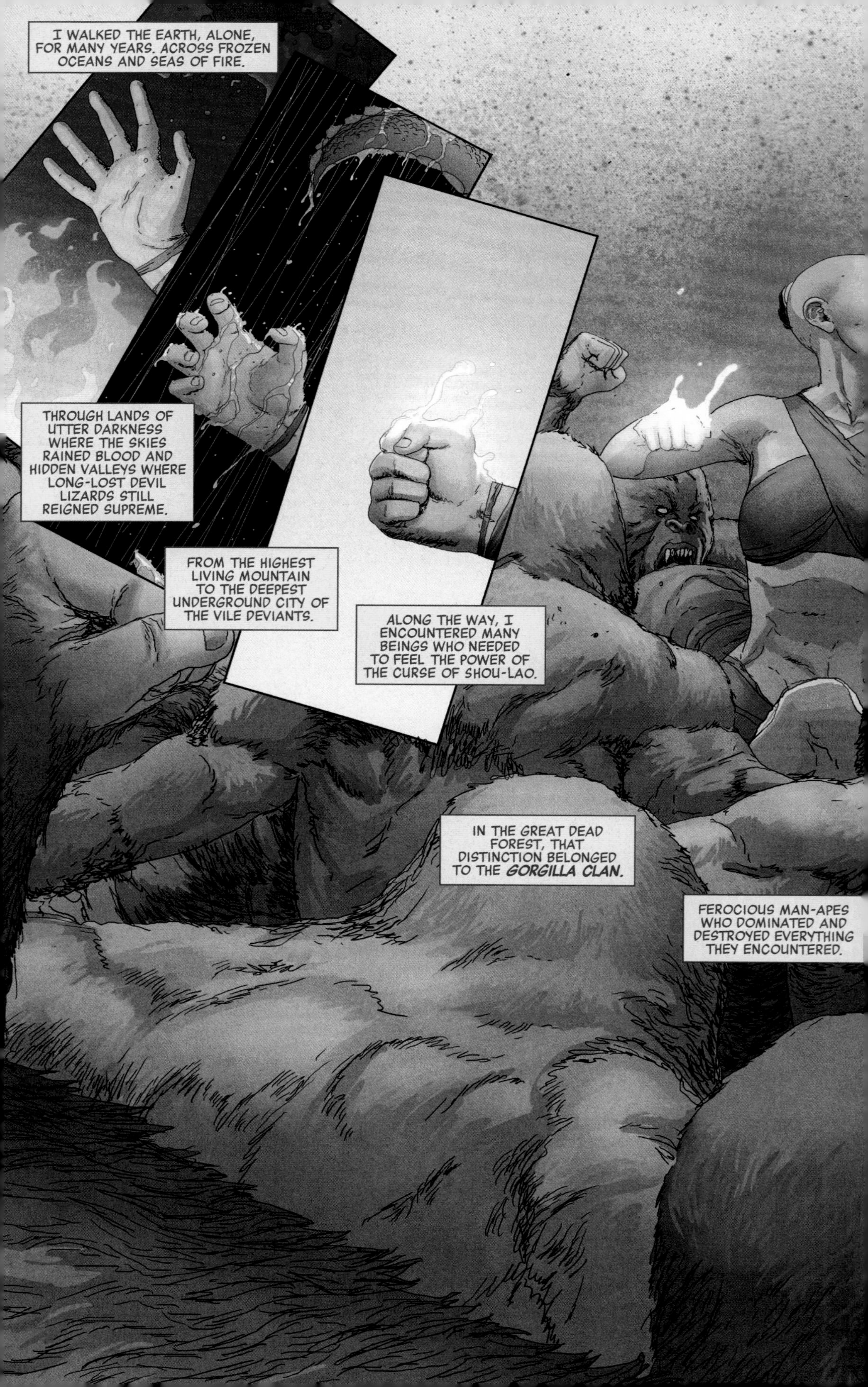
I WALKED THE EARTH, ALONE, FOR MANY YEARS. ACROSS FROZEN OCEANS AND SEAS OF FIRE.
THROUGH LANDS OF UTTER DARKNESS WHERE THE SKIES RAINED BLOOD AND HIDDEN VALLEYS WHERE LONG-LOST DEVIL LIZARDS STILL REIGNED SUPREME.
FROM THE HIGHEST LIVING MOUNTAIN TO THE DEEPEST UNDERGROUND CITY OF THE VILE DEVIANTS.
ALONG THE WAY, I ENCOUNTERED MANY BEINGS WHO NEEDED TO FEEL THE POWER OF THE CURSE OF SHOU-LAO.
IN THE GREAT DEAD FOREST, THAT DISTINCTION BELONGED TO THE ***GORGILLA CLAN.***
FEROCIOUS MAN-APES WHO DOMINATED AND DESTROYED EVERYTHING THEY ENCOUNTERED.

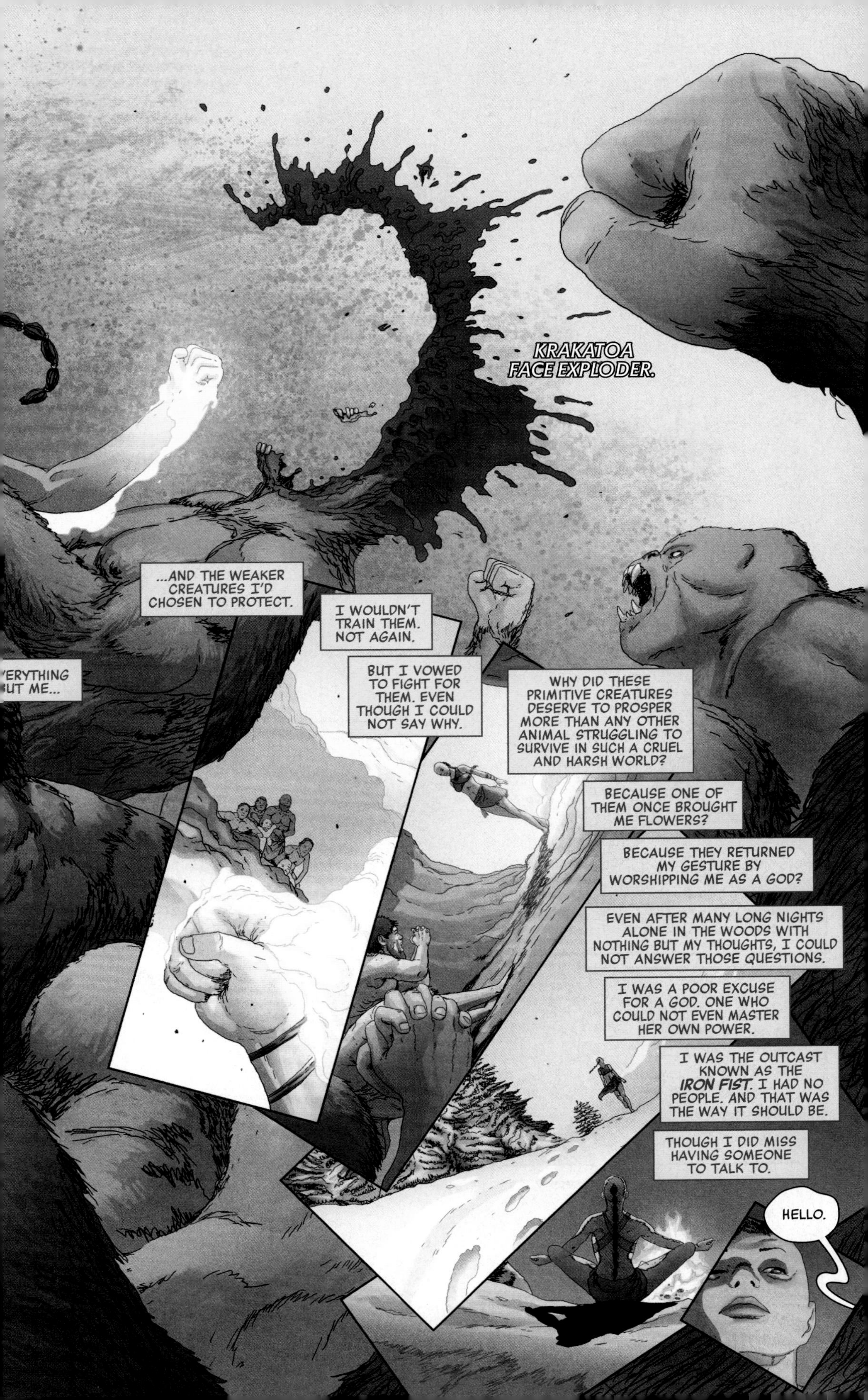

KRAKATOA FACE EXPLODER.
...AND THE WEAKER CREATURES I'D CHOSEN TO PROTECT.
I WOULDN'T TRAIN THEM. NOT AGAIN.
BUT I VOWED TO FIGHT FOR THEM. EVEN THOUGH I COULD NOT SAY WHY.
WHY DID THESE PRIMITIVE CREATURES DESERVE TO PROSPER MORE THAN ANY OTHER ANIMAL STRUGGLING TO SURVIVE IN SUCH A CRUEL AND HARSH WORLD?
BECAUSE ONE OF THEM ONCE BROUGHT ME FLOWERS?
BECAUSE THEY RETURNED MY GESTURE BY WORSHIPPING ME AS A GOD?
EVEN AFTER MANY LONG NIGHTS ALONE IN THE WOODS WITH NOTHING BUT MY THOUGHTS, I COULD NOT ANSWER THOSE QUESTIONS.
I WAS A POOR EXCUSE FOR A GOD. ONE WHO COULD NOT EVEN MASTER HER OWN POWER.
I WAS THE OUTCAST KNOWN AS THE IRON FIST. I HAD NO PEOPLE. AND THAT WAS THE WAY IT SHOULD BE.
THOUGH I DID MISS HAVING SOMEONE TO TALK TO.
HELLO.

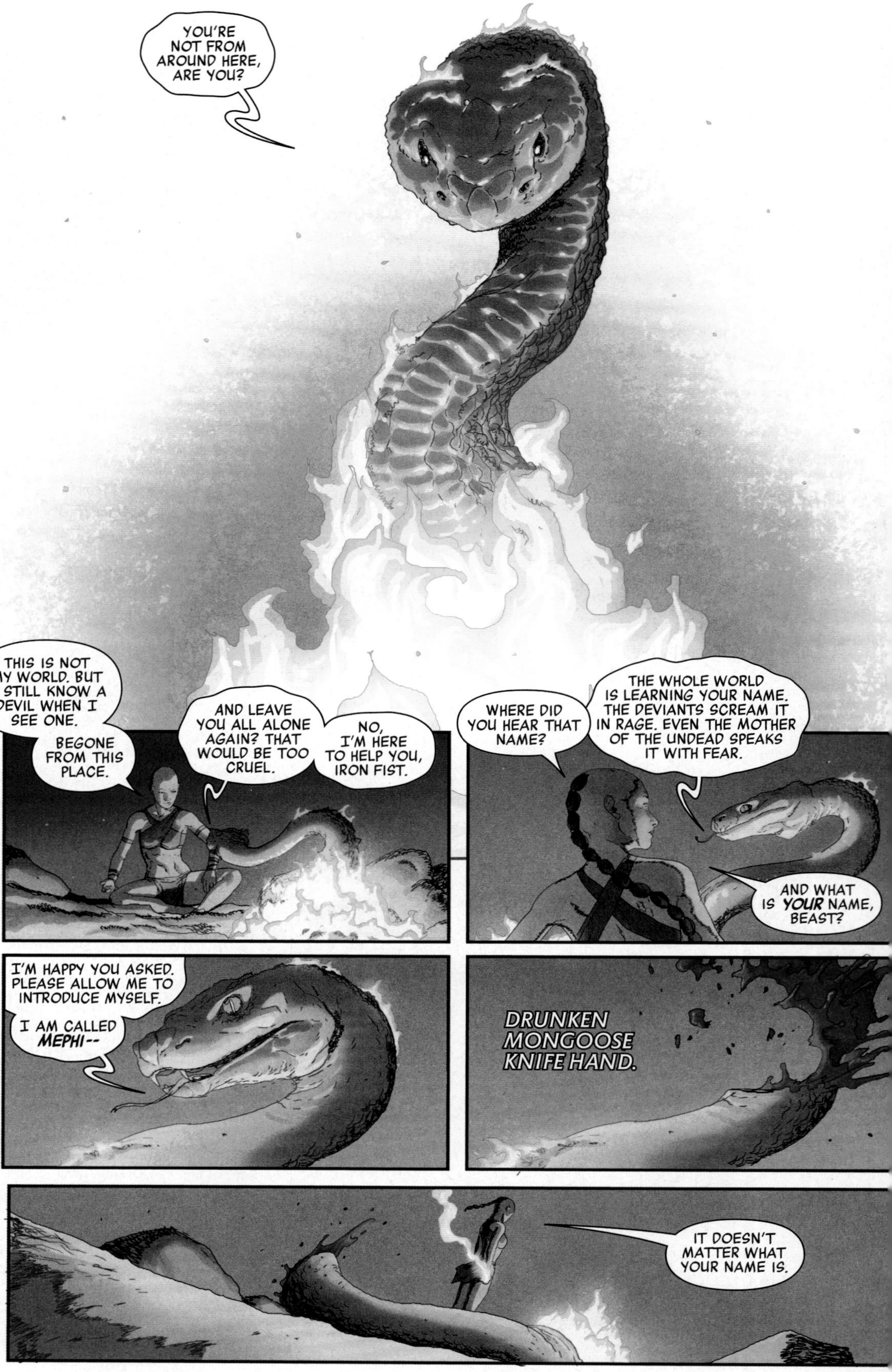
YOU'RE NOT FROM AROUND HERE, ARE YOU?
THIS IS NOT MY WORLD. BUT I STILL KNOW A DEVIL WHEN I SEE ONE.
BEGONE FROM THIS PLACE.
NO, I'M HERE TO HELP YOU, IRON FIST.
AND LEAVE YOU ALL ALONE AGAIN? THAT WOULD BE TOO CRUEL.
WHERE DID YOU HEAR THAT NAME?
THE WHOLE WORLD IS LEARNING YOUR NAME. THE DEVIANTS SCREAM IT IN RAGE. EVEN THE MOTHER OF THE UNDEAD SPEAKS IT WITH FEAR.
AND WHAT IS YOUR NAME, BEAST?
I'M HAPPY YOU ASKED. PLEASE ALLOW ME TO INTRODUCE MYSELF.
I AM CALLED MEPHI--
DRUNKEN MONGOOSE KNIFE HAND.
IT DOESN'T MATTER WHAT YOUR NAME IS.

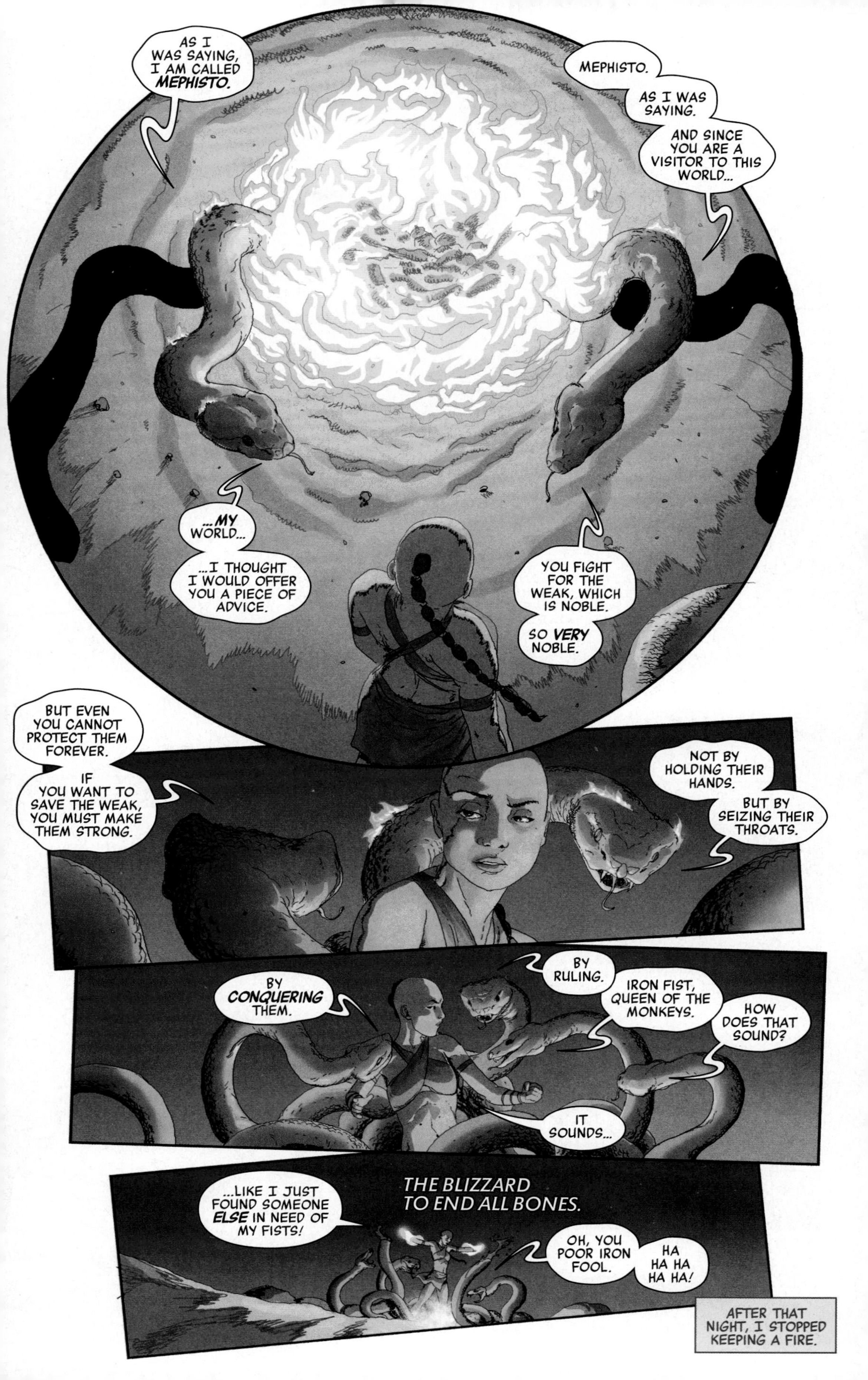
AS I WAS SAYING, I AM CALLED MEPHISTO.
MEPHISTO.
AS I WAS SAYING.
AND SINCE YOU ARE A VISITOR TO THIS WORLD...
...MY WORLD...
...I THOUGHT I WOULD OFFER YOU A PIECE OF ADVICE.
YOU FIGHT FOR THE WEAK, WHICH IS NOBLE.
SO VERY NOBLE.
BUT EVEN YOU CANNOT PROTECT THEM FOREVER.
IF YOU WANT TO SAVE THE WEAK, YOU MUST MAKE THEM STRONG.
NOT BY HOLDING THEIR HANDS.
BUT BY SEIZING THEIR THROATS.
BY CONQUERING THEM.
BY RULING.
IRON FIST, QUEEN OF THE MONKEYS.
HOW DOES THAT SOUND?
IT SOUNDS...
...LIKE I JUST FOUND SOMEONE ELSE IN NEED OF MY FISTS!
THE BLIZZARD TO END ALL BONES.
OH, YOU POOR IRON FOOL.
HA HA HA HA HA!
AFTER THAT NIGHT, I STOPPED KEEPING A FIRE.

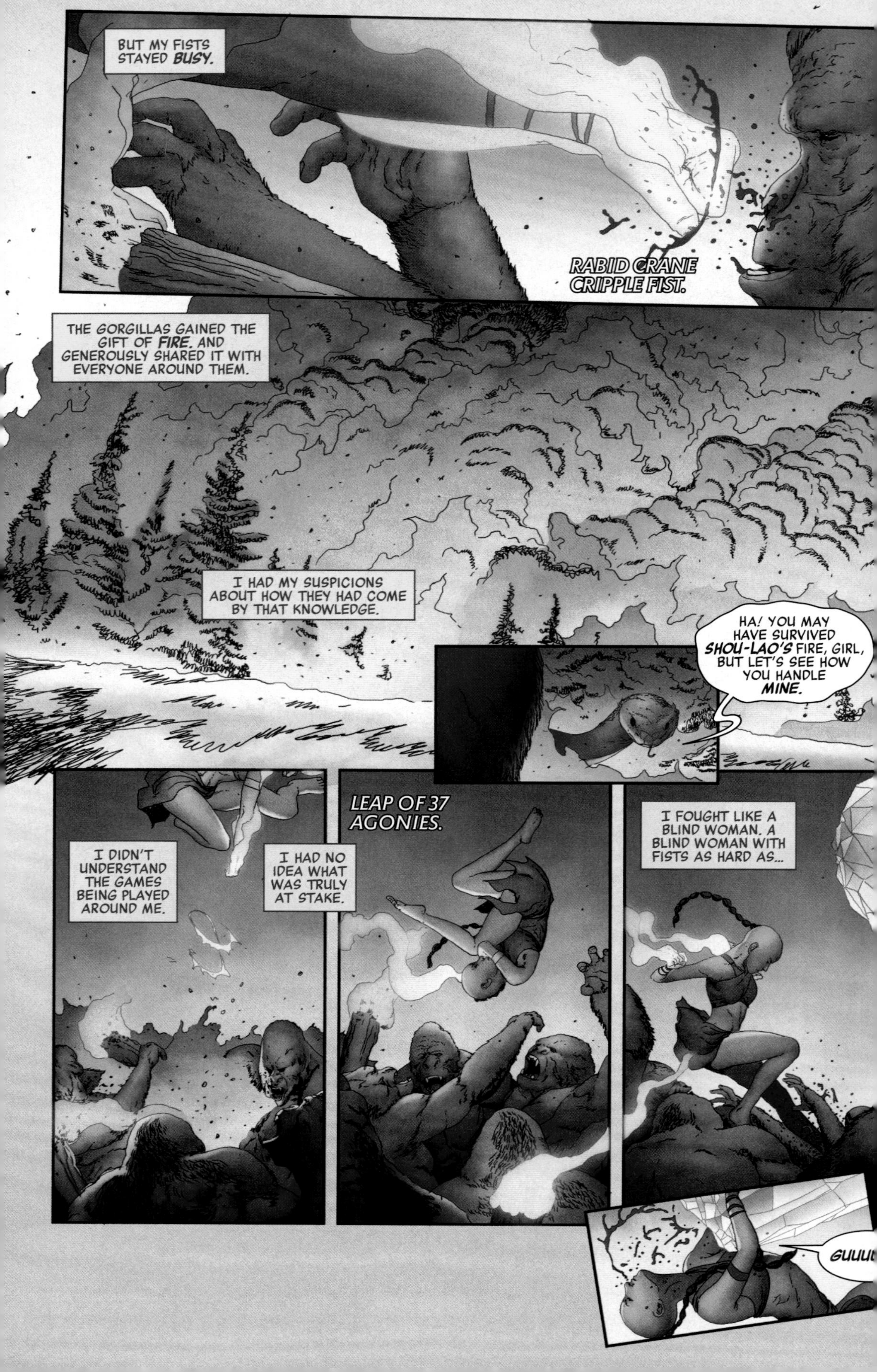
BUT MY FISTS STAYED BUSY.
RABID CRANE CRIPPLE FIST.
THE GORGILLAS GAINED THE GIFT OF FIRE. AND GENEROUSLY SHARED IT WITH EVERYONE AROUND THEM.
I HAD MY SUSPICIONS ABOUT HOW THEY HAD COME BY THAT KNOWLEDGE.
HA! YOU MAY HAVE SURVIVED SHOU-LAO'S FIRE, GIRL, BUT LET'S SEE HOW YOU HANDLE MINE.
I DIDN'T UNDERSTAND THE GAMES BEING PLAYED AROUND ME.
I HAD NO IDEA WHAT WAS TRULY AT STAKE.
LEAP OF 37 AGONIES.
I FOUGHT LIKE A BLIND WOMAN. A BLIND WOMAN WITH FISTS AS HARD AS...
GUUU

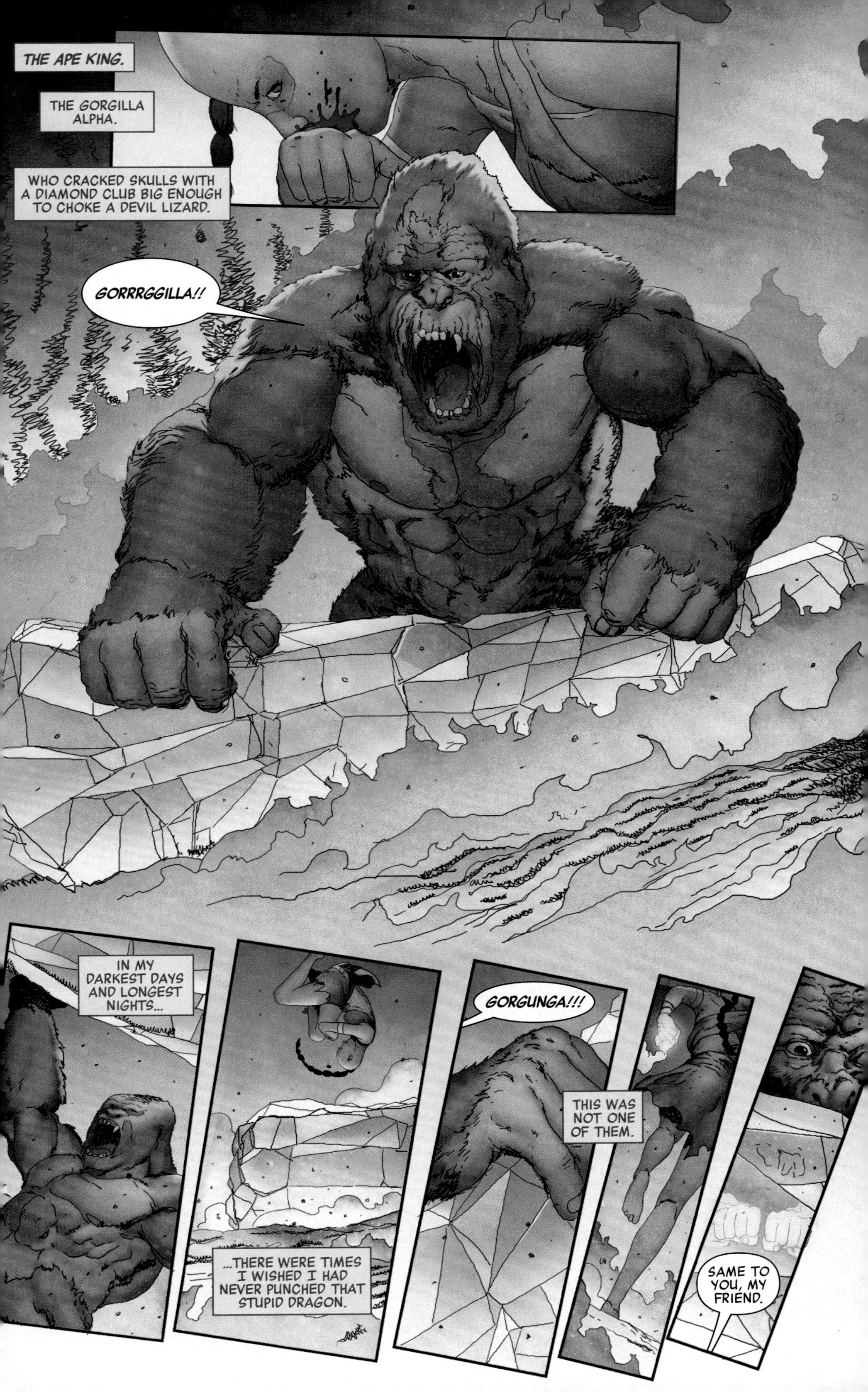
THE APE KING.
THE GORGILLA ALPHA.
WHO CRACKED SKULLS WITH A DIAMOND CLUB BIG ENOUGH TO CHOKE A DEVIL LIZARD.
GORRRGGILLA!!
IN MY DARKEST DAYS AND LONGEST NIGHTS...
...THERE WERE TIMES I WISHED I HAD NEVER PUNCHED THAT STUPID DRAGON.
GORGUNGA!!!
THIS WAS NOT ONE OF THEM.
SAME TO YOU, MY FRIEND.

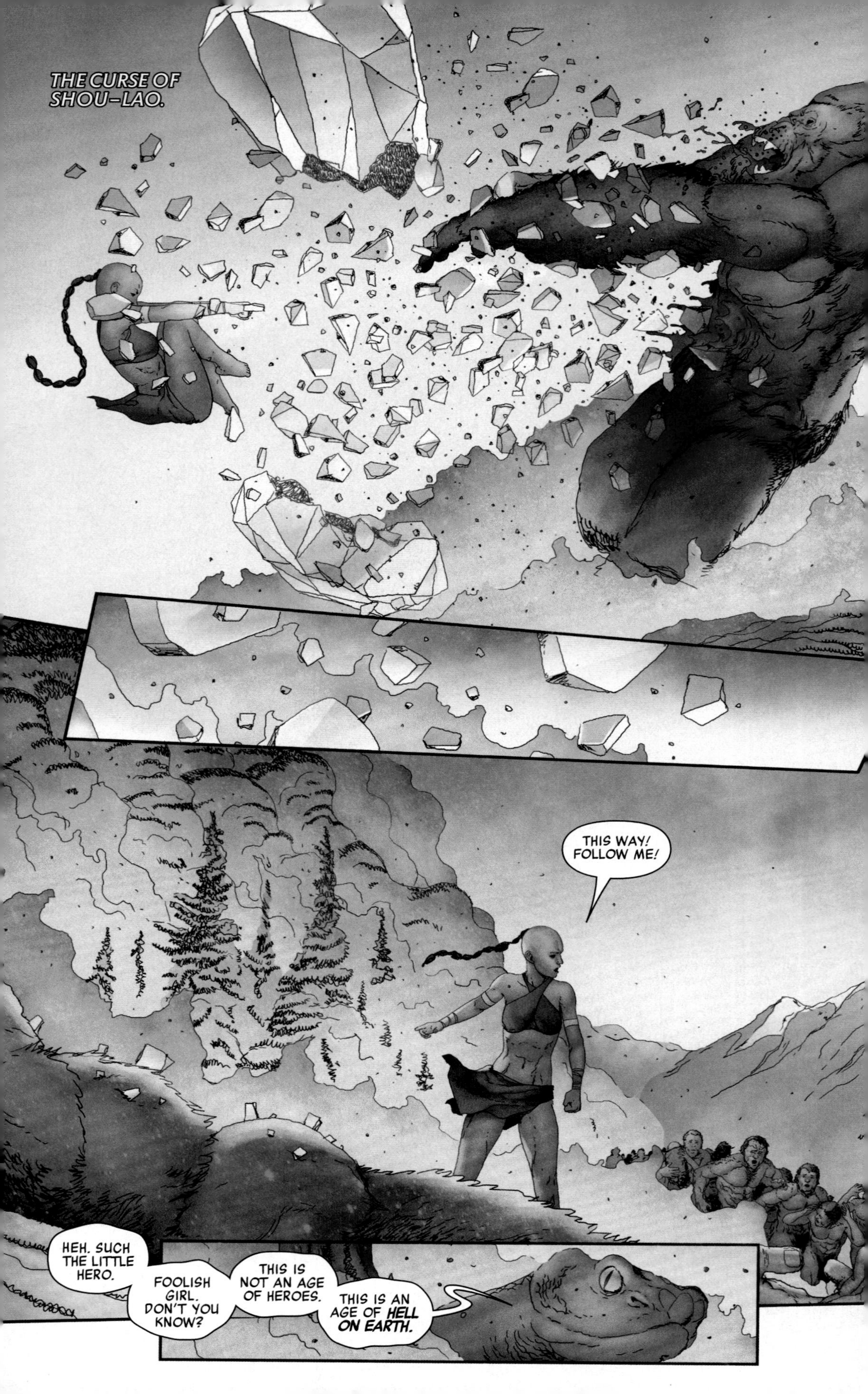
THE CURSE OF SHOU-LAO.
THIS WAY! FOLLOW ME!
HEH. SUCH THE LITTLE HERO.
FOOLISH GIRL. DON'T YOU KNOW?
THIS IS NOT AN AGE OF HEROES.
THIS IS AN AGE OF HELL ON EARTH.

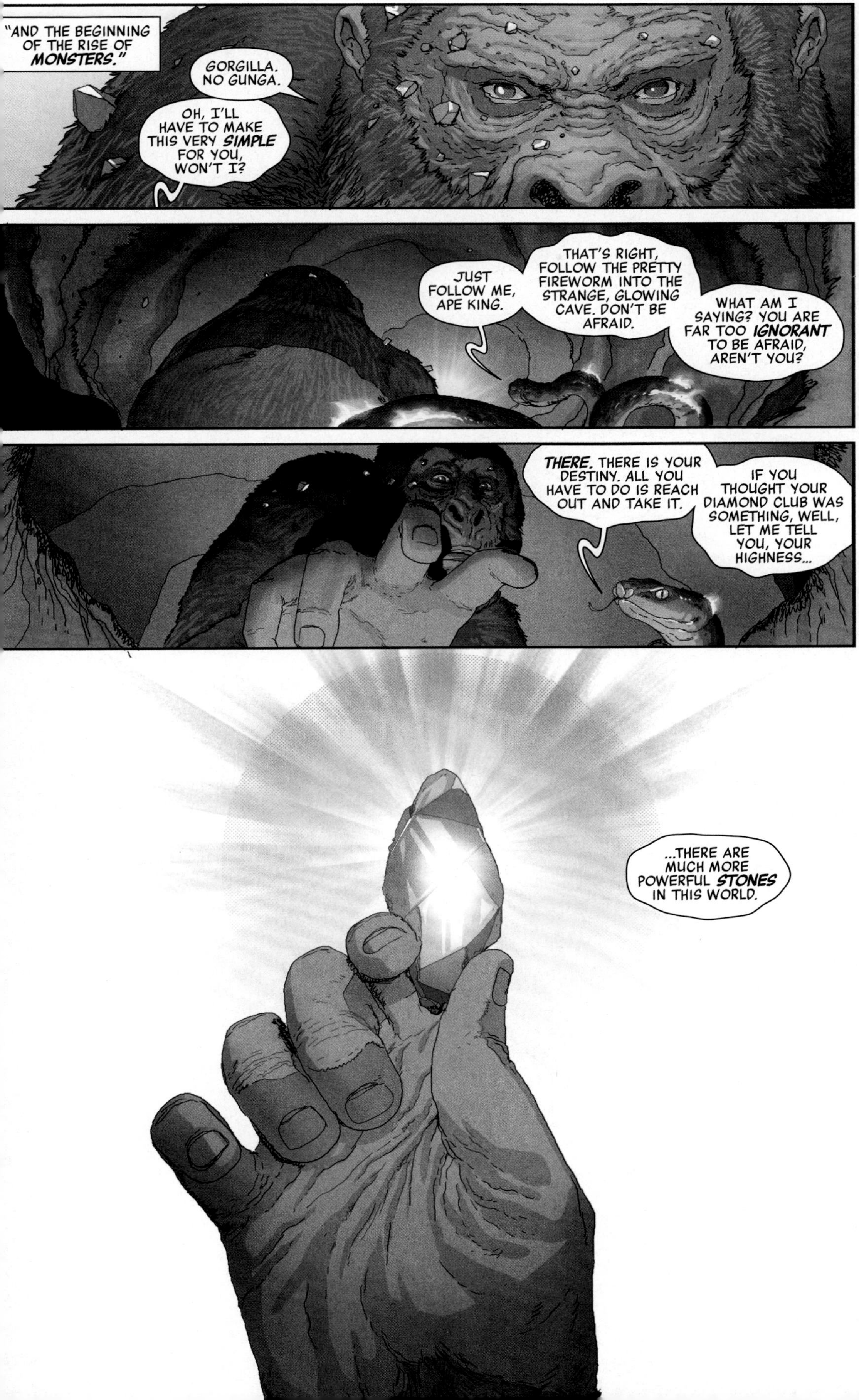
"AND THE BEGINNING OF THE RISE OF MONSTERS."
GORGILLA. NO GUNGA.
OH, I'LL HAVE TO MAKE THIS VERY SIMPLE FOR YOU, WON'T I?
JUST FOLLOW ME, APE KING.
THAT'S RIGHT, FOLLOW THE PRETTY FIREWORM INTO THE STRANGE, GLOWING CAVE. DON'T BE AFRAID.
WHAT AM I SAYING? YOU ARE FAR TOO IGNORANT TO BE AFRAID, AREN'T YOU?
THERE. THERE IS YOUR DESTINY. ALL YOU HAVE TO DO IS REACH OUT AND TAKE IT.
IF YOU THOUGHT YOUR DIAMOND CLUB WAS SOMETHING, WELL, LET ME TELL YOU, YOUR HIGHNESS...
...THERE ARE MUCH MORE POWERFUL STONES IN THIS WORLD.

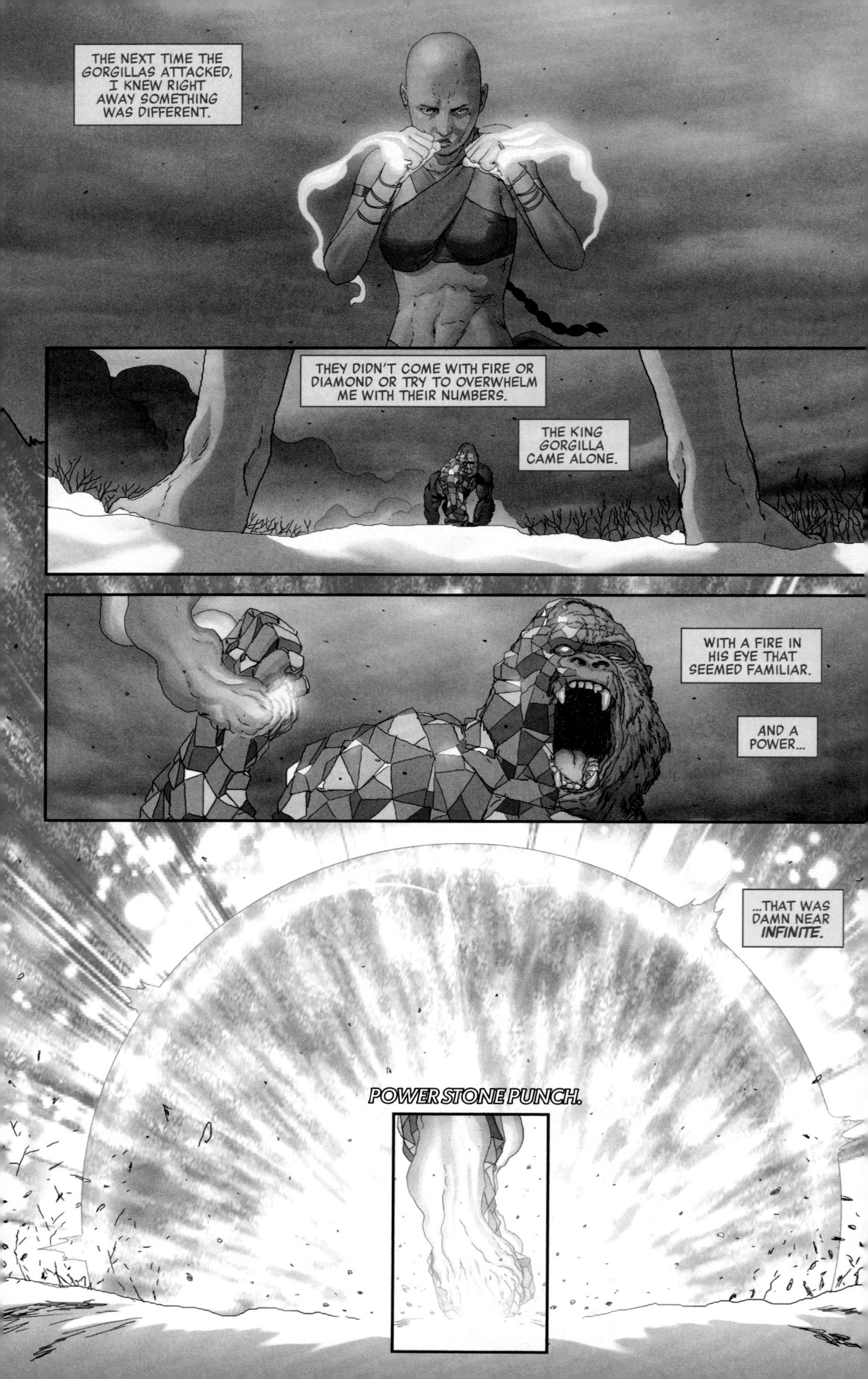
THE NEXT TIME THE GORGILLAS ATTACKED, I KNEW RIGHT AWAY SOMETHING WAS DIFFERENT.
THEY DIDN'T COME WITH FIRE OR DIAMOND OR TRY TO OVERWHELM ME WITH THEIR NUMBERS.
THE KING GORGILLA CAME ALONE.
WITH A FIRE IN HIS EYE THAT SEEMED FAMILIAR.
AND A POWER...
...THAT WAS DAMN NEAR *INFINITE.*
POWER STONE PUNCH.

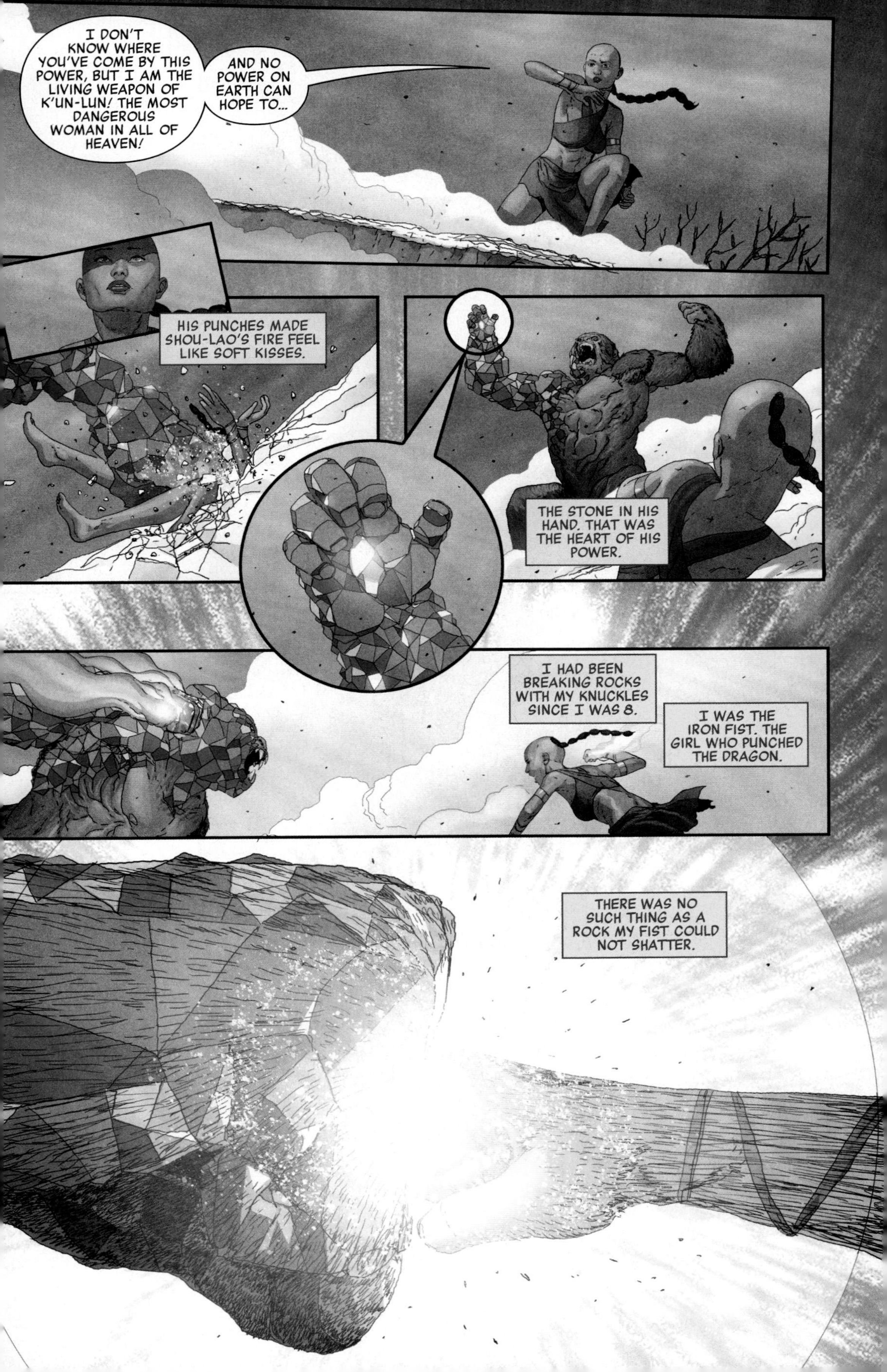
I DON'T KNOW WHERE YOU'VE COME BY THIS POWER, BUT I AM THE LIVING WEAPON OF K'UN-LUN! THE MOST DANGEROUS WOMAN IN ALL OF HEAVEN!
AND NO POWER ON EARTH CAN HOPE TO...
HIS PUNCHES MADE SHOU-LAO'S FIRE FEEL LIKE SOFT KISSES.
THE STONE IN HIS HAND. THAT WAS THE HEART OF HIS POWER.
I HAD BEEN BREAKING ROCKS WITH MY KNUCKLES SINCE I WAS 8.
I WAS THE IRON FIST. THE GIRL WHO PUNCHED THE DRAGON.
THERE WAS NO SUCH THING AS A ROCK MY FIST COULD NOT SHATTER.

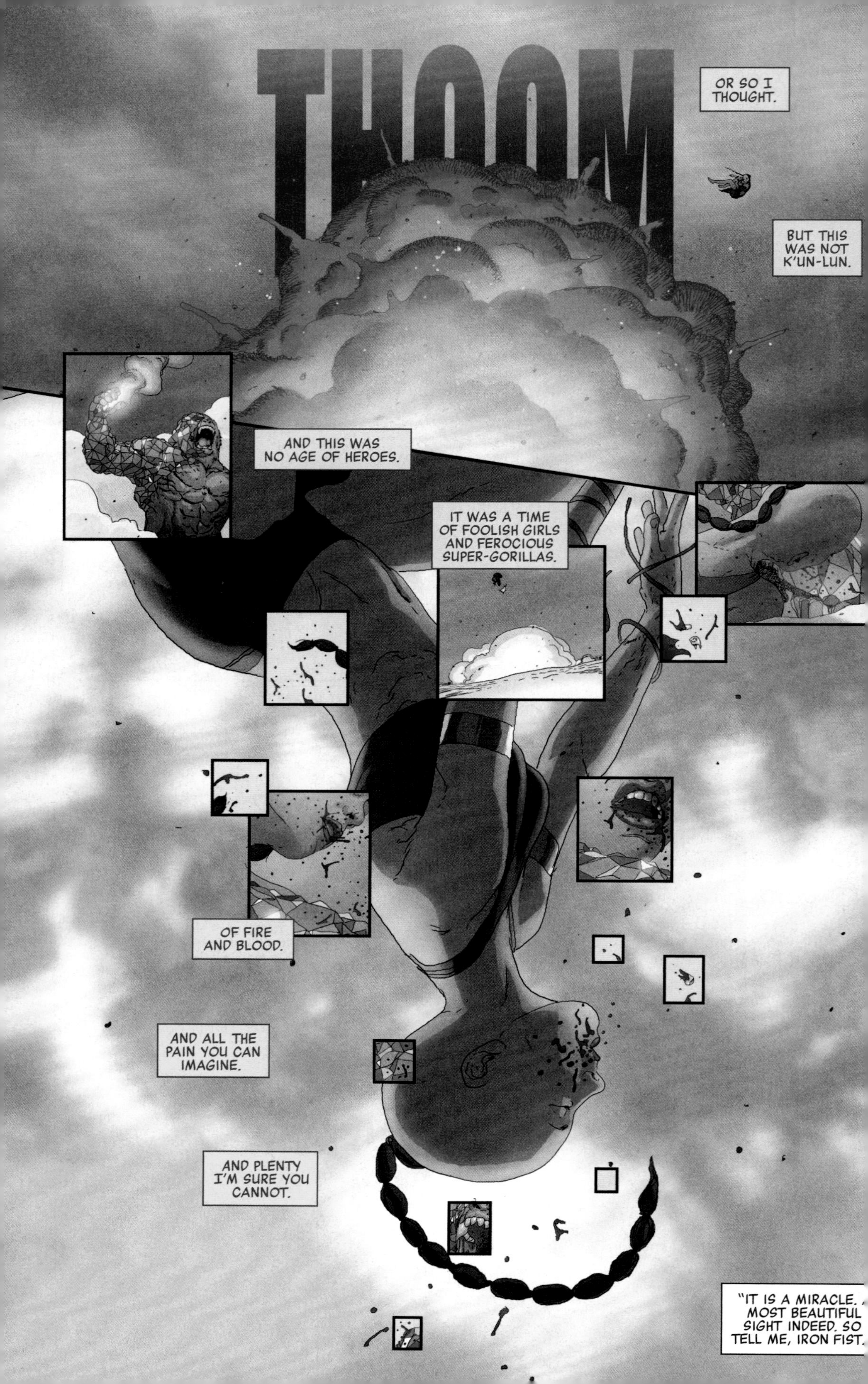
THOOM
OR SO I THOUGHT.
BUT THIS WAS NOT K'UN-LUN.
AND THIS WAS NO AGE OF HEROES.
IT WAS A TIME OF FOOLISH GIRLS AND FEROCIOUS SUPER-GORILLAS.
OF FIRE AND BLOOD.
AND ALL THE PAIN YOU CAN IMAGINE.
AND PLENTY I'M SURE YOU CANNOT.
"IT IS A MIRACLE. MOST BEAUTIFUL SIGHT INDEED. SO TELL ME, IRON FIST.

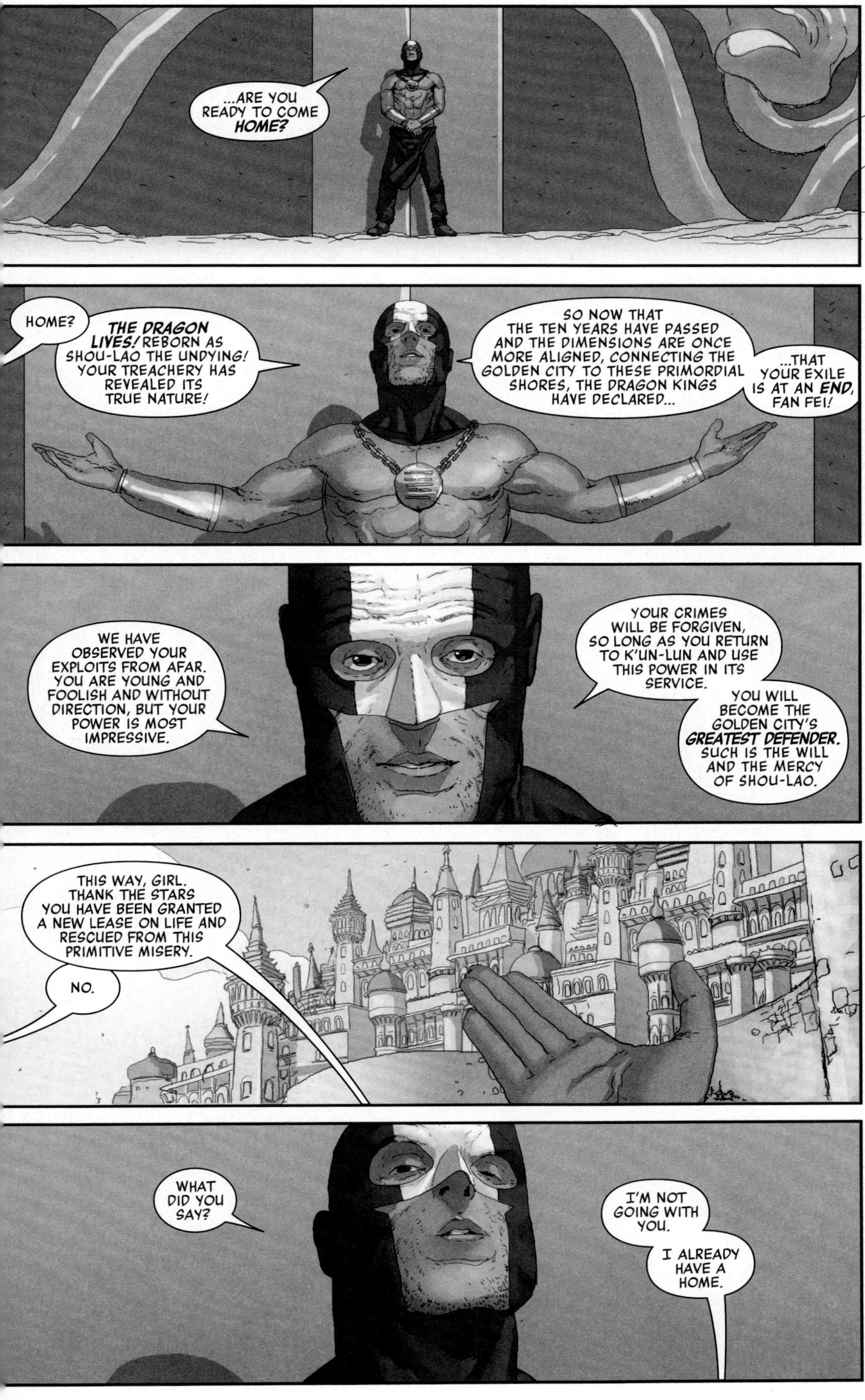
...ARE YOU READY TO COME HOME?
HOME?
THE DRAGON LIVES! REBORN AS SHOU-LAO THE UNDYING! YOUR TREACHERY HAS REVEALED ITS TRUE NATURE!
SO NOW THAT THE TEN YEARS HAVE PASSED AND THE DIMENSIONS ARE ONCE MORE ALIGNED, CONNECTING THE GOLDEN CITY TO THESE PRIMORDIAL SHORES, THE DRAGON KINGS HAVE DECLARED...
...THAT YOUR EXILE IS AT AN END, FAN FEI!
WE HAVE OBSERVED YOUR EXPLOITS FROM AFAR. YOU ARE YOUNG AND FOOLISH AND WITHOUT DIRECTION, BUT YOUR POWER IS MOST IMPRESSIVE.
YOUR CRIMES WILL BE FORGIVEN, SO LONG AS YOU RETURN TO K'UN-LUN AND USE THIS POWER IN ITS SERVICE.
YOU WILL BECOME THE GOLDEN CITY'S GREATEST DEFENDER. SUCH IS THE WILL AND THE MERCY OF SHOU-LAO.
THIS WAY, GIRL. THANK THE STARS YOU HAVE BEEN GRANTED A NEW LEASE ON LIFE AND RESCUED FROM THIS PRIMITIVE MISERY.
NO.
WHAT DID YOU SAY?
I'M NOT GOING WITH YOU.
I ALREADY HAVE A HOME.

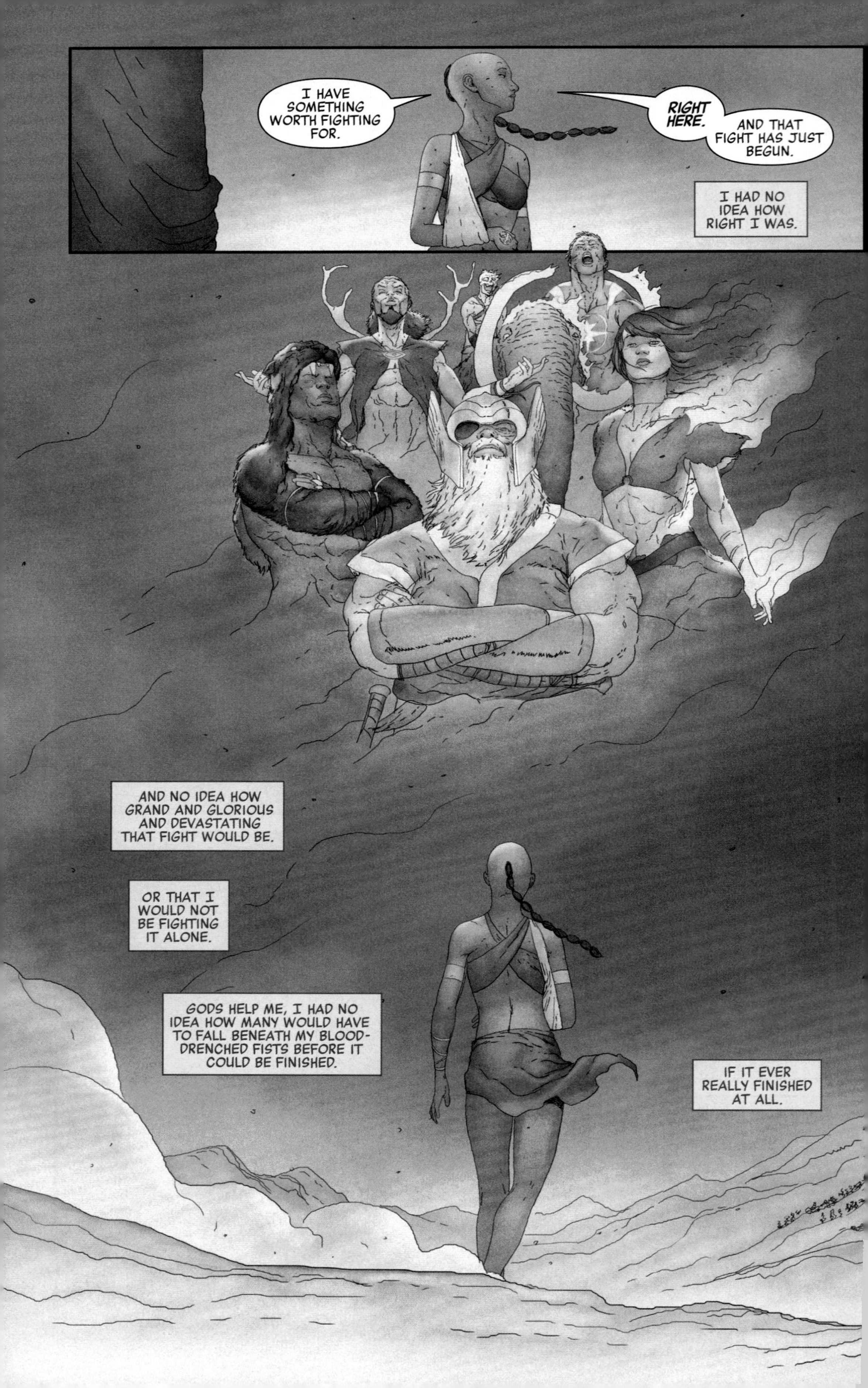
I HAVE SOMETHING WORTH FIGHTING FOR.
RIGHT HERE.
AND THAT FIGHT HAS JUST BEGUN.
I HAD NO IDEA HOW RIGHT I WAS.
AND NO IDEA HOW GRAND AND GLORIOUS AND DEVASTATING THAT FIGHT WOULD BE.
OR THAT I WOULD NOT BE FIGHTING IT ALONE.
GODS HELP ME, I HAD NO IDEA HOW MANY WOULD HAVE TO FALL BENEATH MY BLOOD-DRENCHED FISTS BEFORE IT COULD BE FINISHED.
IF IT EVER REALLY FINISHED AT ALL.

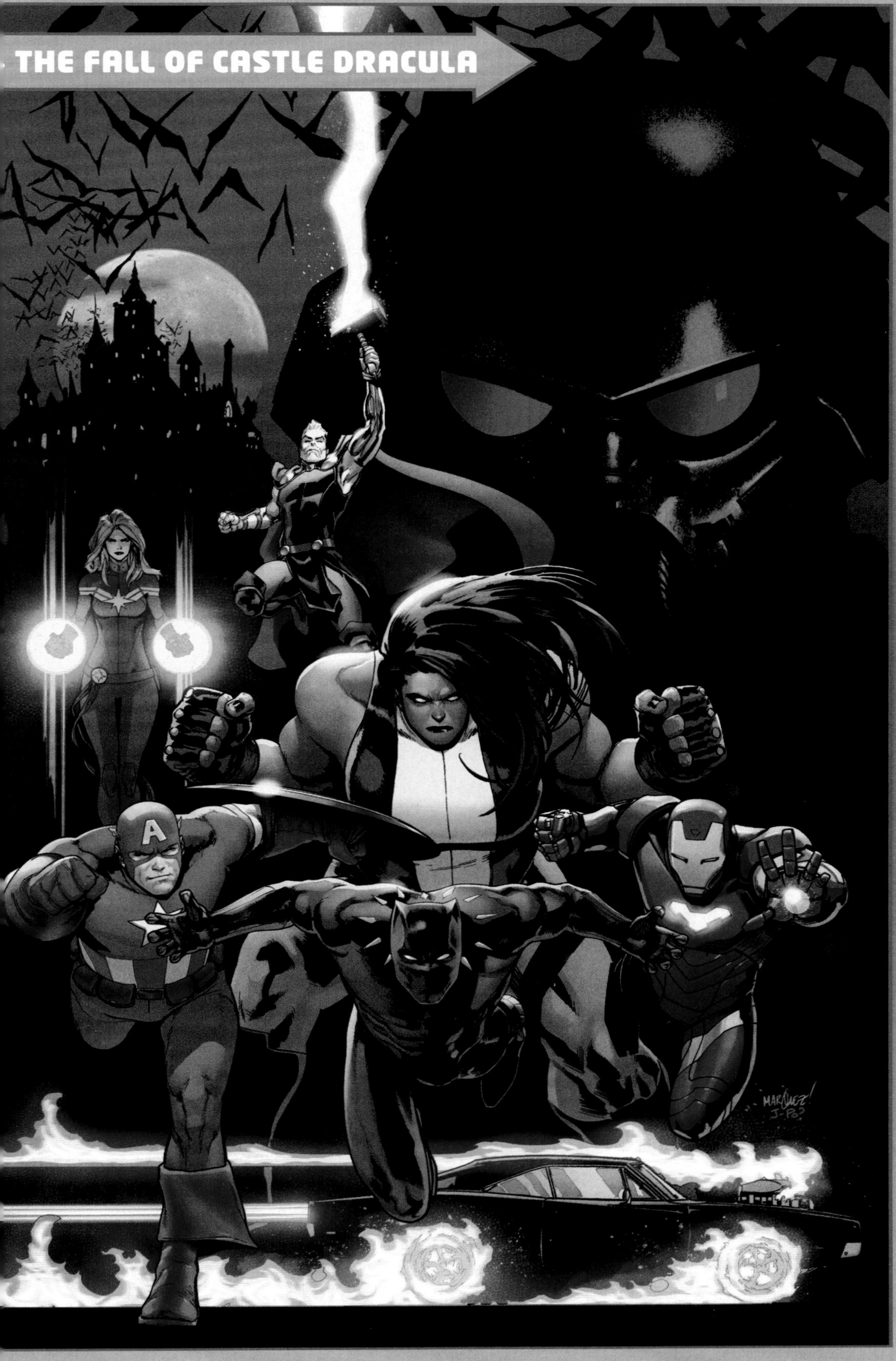
THE FALL OF CASTLE DRACULA

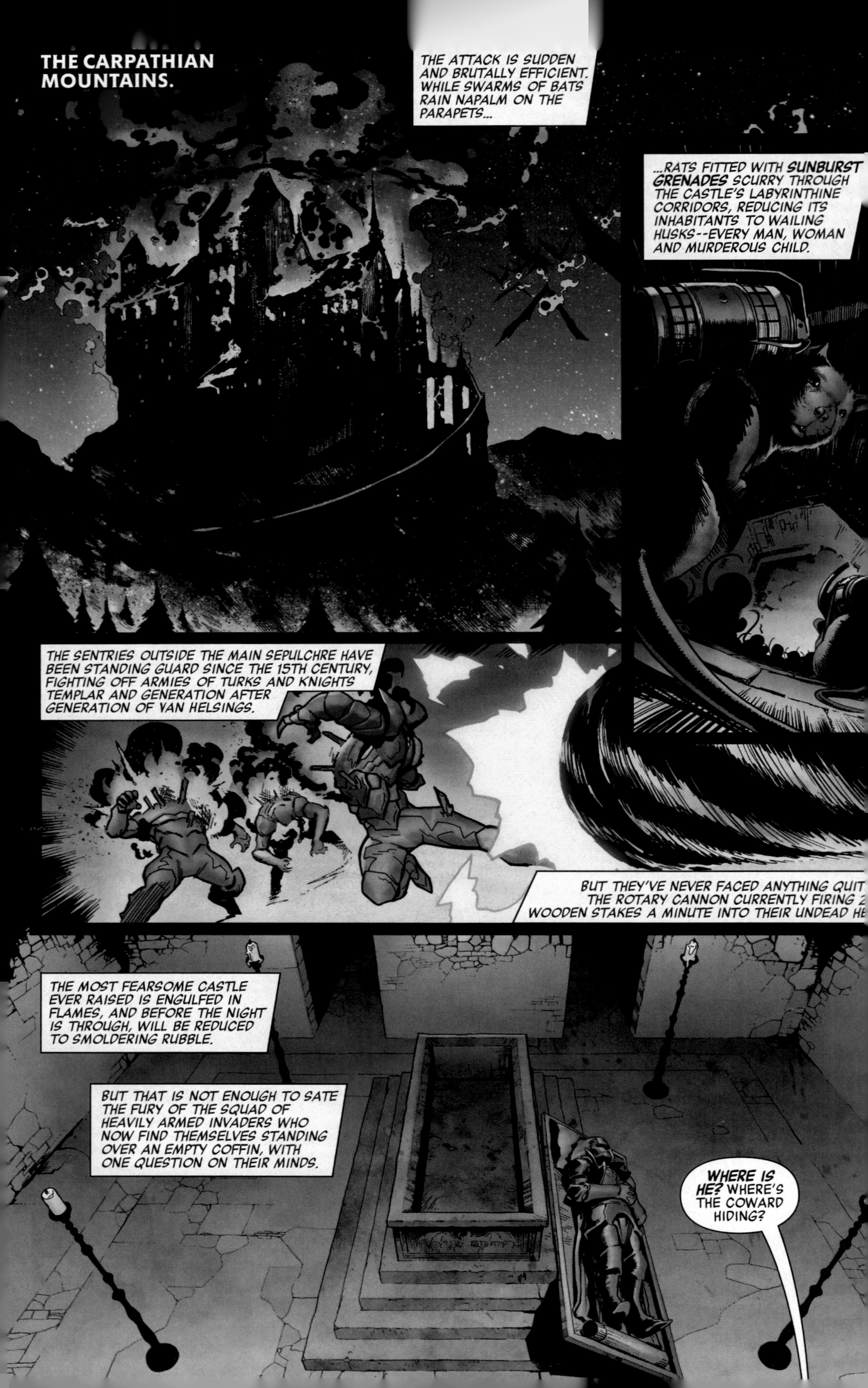
THE CARPATHIAN MOUNTAINS.
THE ATTACK IS SUDDEN AND BRUTALLY EFFICIENT. WHILE SWARMS OF BATS RAIN NAPALM ON THE PARAPETS...
...RATS FITTED WITH SUNBURST GRENADES SCURRY THROUGH THE CASTLE'S LABYRINTHINE CORRIDORS, REDUCING ITS INHABITANTS TO WAILING HUSKS--EVERY MAN, WOMAN AND MURDEROUS CHILD.
THE SENTRIES OUTSIDE THE MAIN SEPULCHRE HAVE BEEN STANDING GUARD SINCE THE 15TH CENTURY, FIGHTING OFF ARMIES OF TURKS AND KNIGHTS TEMPLAR AND GENERATION AFTER GENERATION OF VAN HELSINGS.
BUT THEY'VE NEVER FACED ANYTHING QUIT THE ROTARY CANNON CURRENTLY FIRING 2 WOODEN STAKES A MINUTE INTO THEIR UNDEAD HE
THE MOST FEARSOME CASTLE EVER RAISED IS ENGULFED IN FLAMES, AND BEFORE THE NIGHT IS THROUGH, WILL BE REDUCED TO SMOLDERING RUBBLE.
BUT THAT IS NOT ENOUGH TO SATE THE FURY OF THE SQUAD OF HEAVILY ARMED INVADERS WHO NOW FIND THEMSELVES STANDING OVER AN EMPTY COFFIN, WITH ONE QUESTION ON THEIR MINDS.
WHERE IS HE? WHERE'S THE COWARD HIDING?

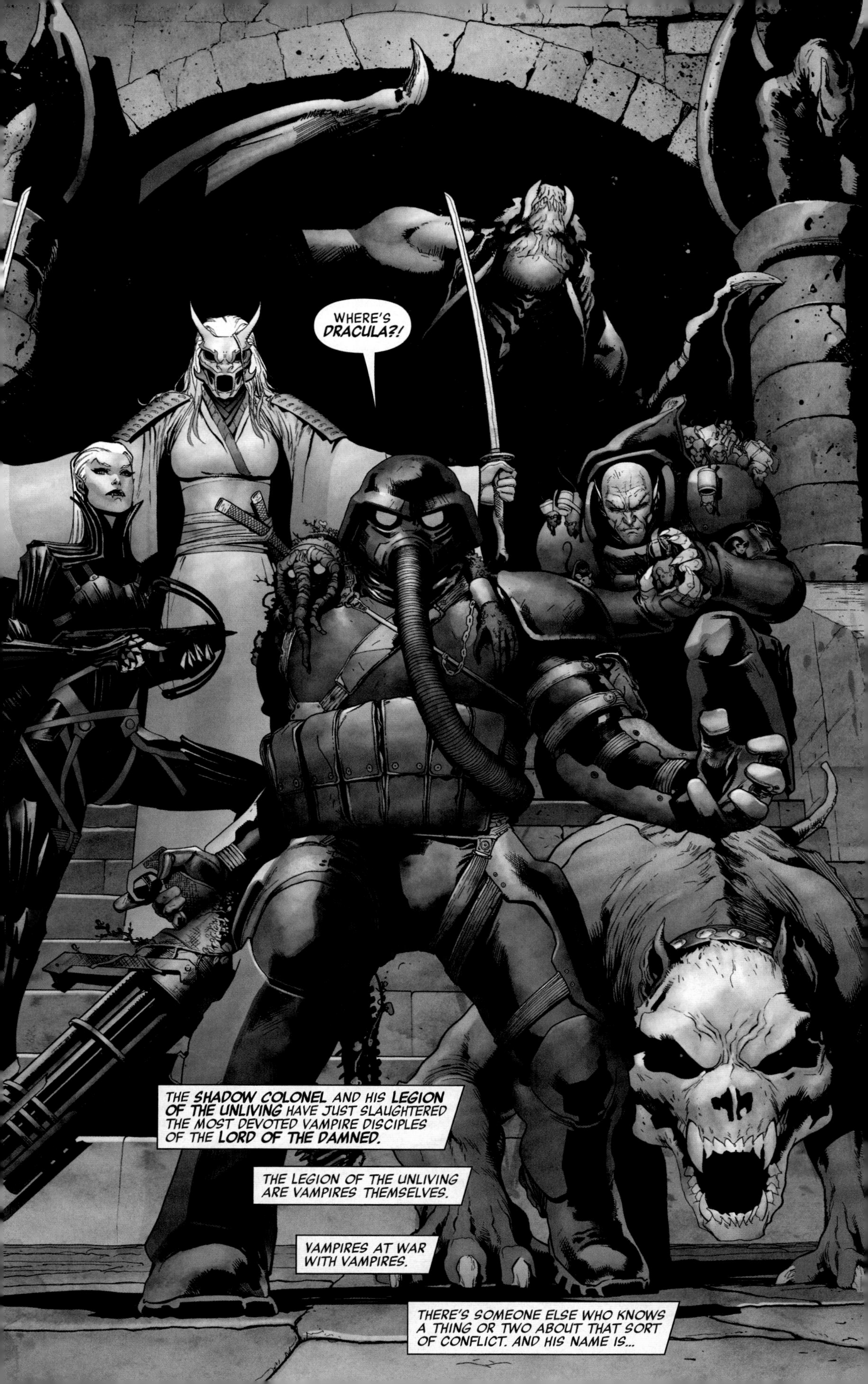
WHERE'S DRACULA?!
THE SHADOW COLONEL AND HIS LEGION OF THE UNLIVING HAVE JUST SLAUGHTERED THE MOST DEVOTED VAMPIRE DISCIPLES OF THE LORD OF THE DAMNED.
THE LEGION OF THE UNLIVING ARE VAMPIRES THEMSELVES.
VAMPIRES AT WAR WITH VAMPIRES.
THERE'S SOMEONE ELSE WHO KNOWS A THING OR TWO ABOUT THAT SORT OF CONFLICT. AND HIS NAME IS...

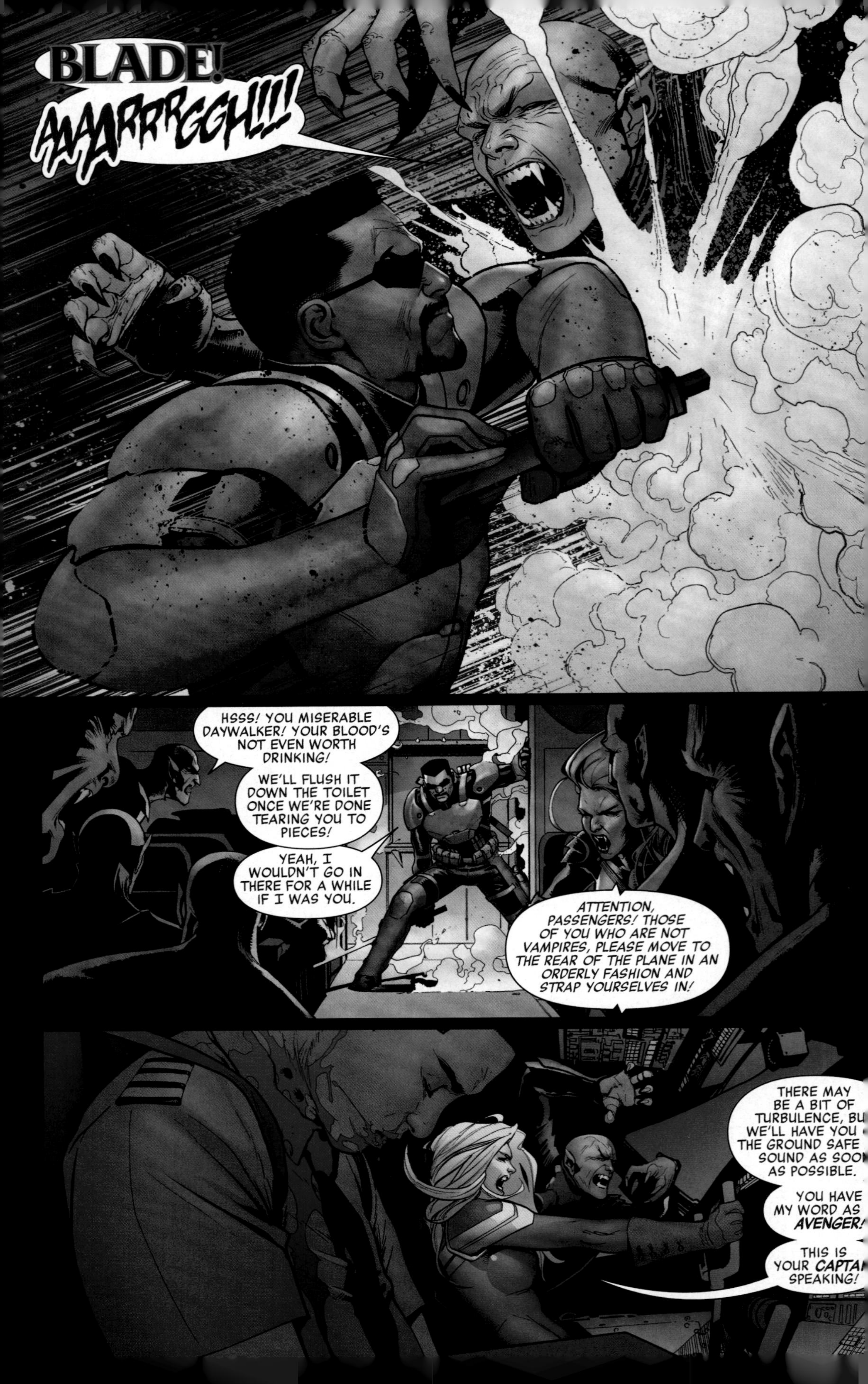
BLADE!
AAAARRRGGH!!!
HSSS! YOU MISERABLE DAYWALKER! YOUR BLOOD'S NOT EVEN WORTH DRINKING!
WE'LL FLUSH IT DOWN THE TOILET ONCE WE'RE DONE TEARING YOU TO PIECES!
YEAH, I WOULDN'T GO IN THERE FOR A WHILE IF I WAS YOU.
ATTENTION, PASSENGERS! THOSE OF YOU WHO ARE NOT VAMPIRES, PLEASE MOVE TO THE REAR OF THE PLANE IN AN ORDERLY FASHION AND STRAP YOURSELVES IN!
THIS IS YOUR CAPTA SPEAKING!
THERE MAY BE A BIT OF TURBULENCE, BU WE'LL HAVE YOU THE GROUND SAFE SOUND AS SOO AS POSSIBLE.
YOU HAVE MY WORD AS AVENGER!

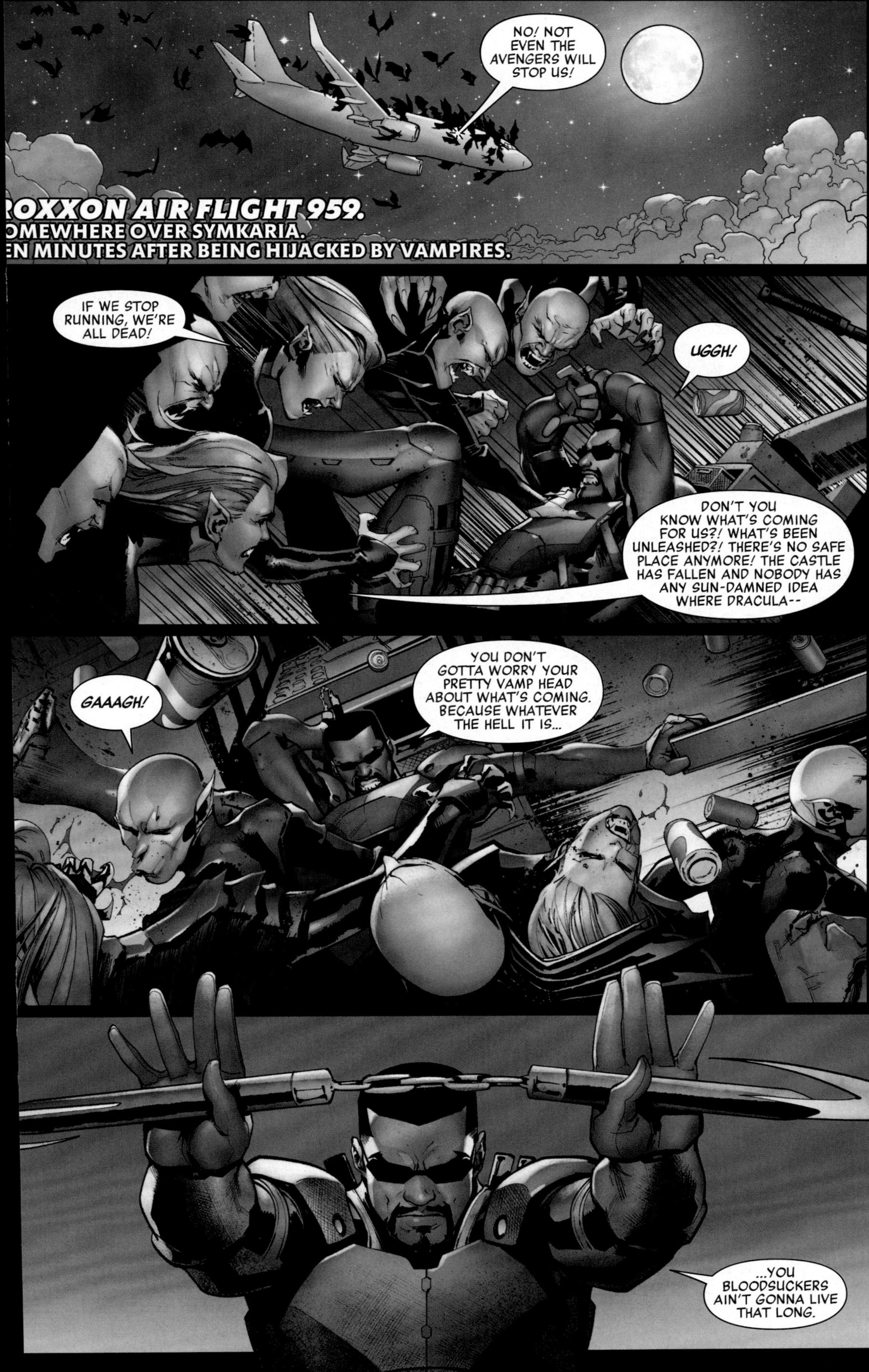
NO! NOT EVEN THE AVENGERS WILL STOP US!
ROXXON AIR FLIGHT 959.
OMEWHERE OVER SYMKARIA.
EN MINUTES AFTER BEING HIJACKED BY VAMPIRES.
IF WE STOP RUNNING, WE'RE ALL DEAD!
UGGH!
DON'T YOU KNOW WHAT'S COMING FOR US?! WHAT'S BEEN UNLEASHED?! THERE'S NO SAFE PLACE ANYMORE! THE CASTLE HAS FALLEN AND NOBODY HAS ANY SUN-DAMNED IDEA WHERE DRACULA--
GAAAGH!
YOU DON'T GOTTA WORRY YOUR PRETTY VAMP HEAD ABOUT WHAT'S COMING. BECAUSE WHATEVER THE HELL IT IS...
...YOU BLOODSUCKERS AIN'T GONNA LIVE THAT LONG.

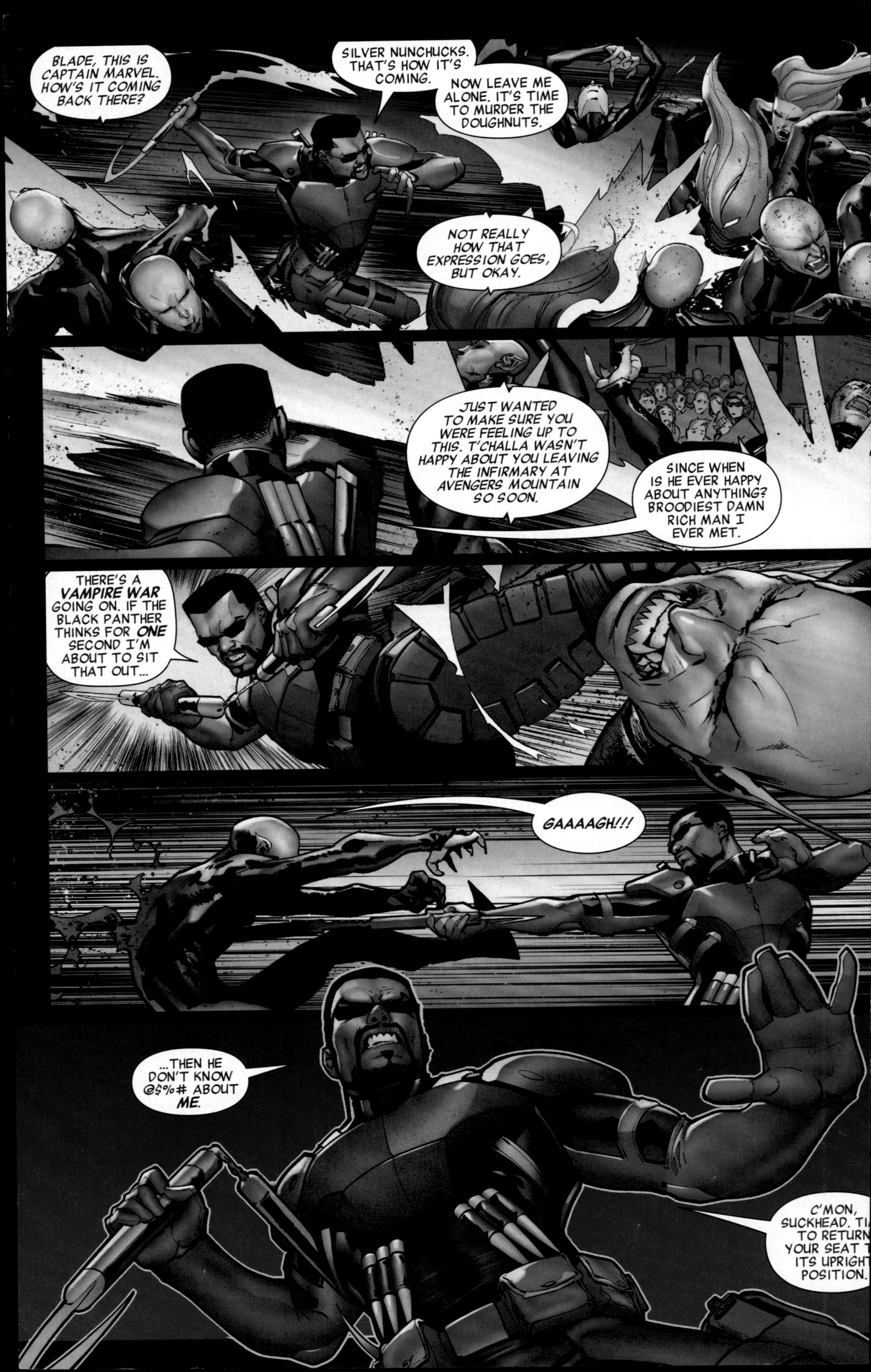
BLADE, THIS IS CAPTAIN MARVEL. HOW'S IT COMING BACK THERE?
SILVER NUNCHUCKS. THAT'S HOW IT'S COMING.
NOW LEAVE ME ALONE. IT'S TIME TO MURDER THE DOUGHNUTS.
NOT REALLY HOW THAT EXPRESSION GOES, BUT OKAY.
JUST WANTED TO MAKE SURE YOU WERE FEELING UP TO THIS. T'CHALLA WASN'T HAPPY ABOUT YOU LEAVING THE INFIRMARY AT AVENGERS MOUNTAIN SO SOON.
SINCE WHEN IS HE EVER HAPPY ABOUT ANYTHING? BROODIEST DAMN RICH MAN I EVER MET.
THERE'S A VAMPIRE WAR GOING ON. IF THE BLACK PANTHER THINKS FOR ONE SECOND I'M ABOUT TO SIT THAT OUT...
GAAAAGH!!!
...THEN HE DON'T KNOW @$%# ABOUT ME.
C'MON, SUCKHEAD. TI TO RETURN YOUR SEAT T ITS UPRIGH POSITION.

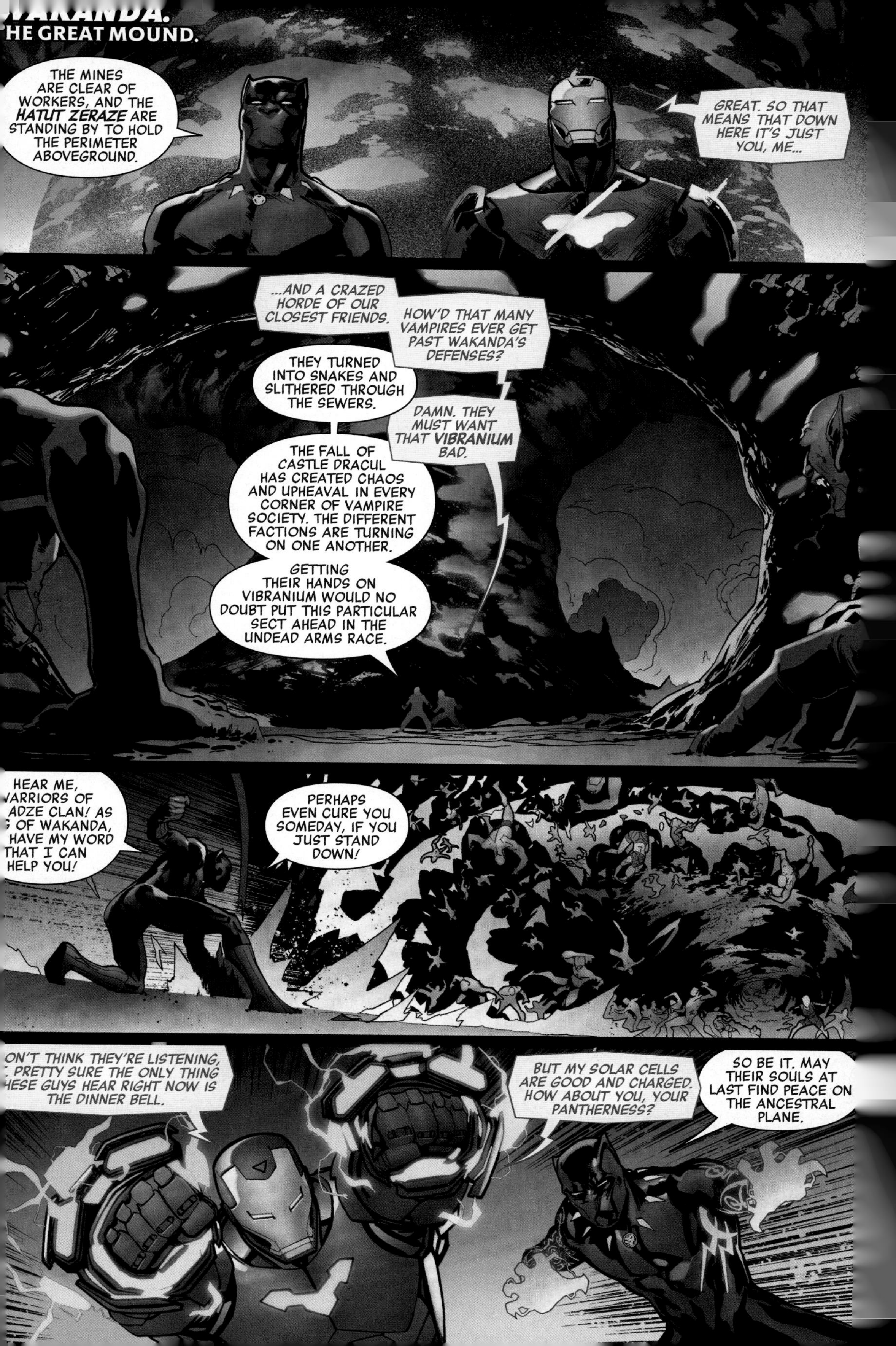

AKANDA.
HE GREAT MOUND.
THE MINES ARE CLEAR OF WORKERS, AND THE HATUT ZERAZE ARE STANDING BY TO HOLD THE PERIMETER ABOVEGROUND.
GREAT. SO THAT MEANS THAT DOWN HERE IT'S JUST YOU, ME...
...AND A CRAZED HORDE OF OUR CLOSEST FRIENDS.
HOW'D THAT MANY VAMPIRES EVER GET PAST WAKANDA'S DEFENSES?
THEY TURNED INTO SNAKES AND SLITHERED THROUGH THE SEWERS.
DAMN. THEY MUST WANT THAT VIBRANIUM BAD.
THE FALL OF CASTLE DRACUL HAS CREATED CHAOS AND UPHEAVAL IN EVERY CORNER OF VAMPIRE SOCIETY. THE DIFFERENT FACTIONS ARE TURNING ON ONE ANOTHER.
GETTING THEIR HANDS ON VIBRANIUM WOULD NO DOUBT PUT THIS PARTICULAR SECT AHEAD IN THE UNDEAD ARMS RACE.
HEAR ME, VARRIORS OF ADZE CLAN! AS OF WAKANDA, HAVE MY WORD THAT I CAN HELP YOU!
PERHAPS EVEN CURE YOU SOMEDAY, IF YOU JUST STAND DOWN!
ON'T THINK THEY'RE LISTENING, PRETTY SURE THE ONLY THING HESE GUYS HEAR RIGHT NOW IS THE DINNER BELL.
BUT MY SOLAR CELLS ARE GOOD AND CHARGED. HOW ABOUT YOU, YOUR PANTHERNESS?
SO BE IT. MAY THEIR SOULS AT LAST FIND PEACE ON THE ANCESTRAL PLANE.

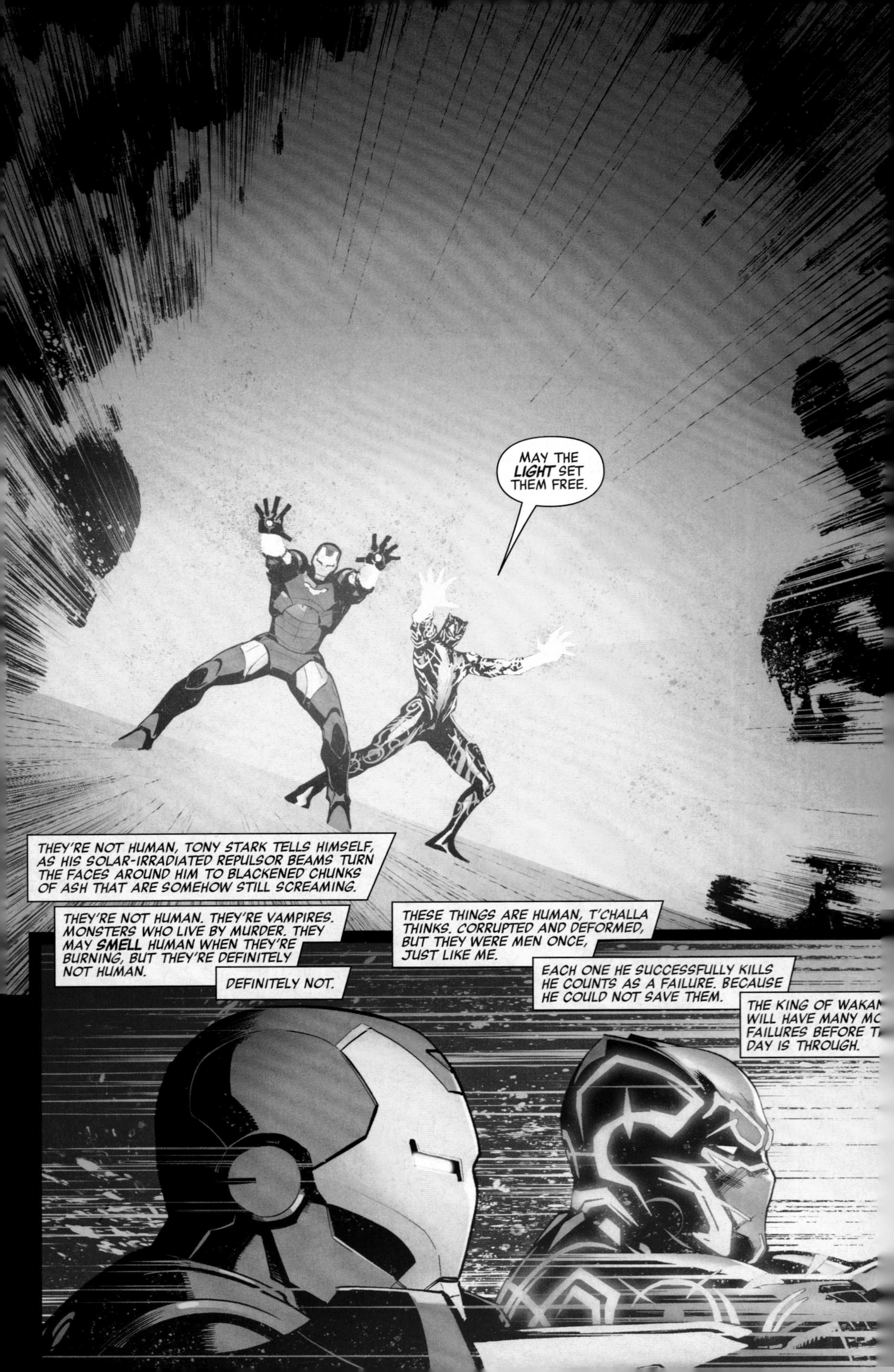
MAY THE LIGHT SET THEM FREE.
THEY'RE NOT HUMAN, TONY STARK TELLS HIMSELF, AS HIS SOLAR-IRRADIATED REPULSOR BEAMS TURN THE FACES AROUND HIM TO BLACKENED CHUNKS OF ASH THAT ARE SOMEHOW STILL SCREAMING.
THEY'RE NOT HUMAN. THEY'RE VAMPIRES. MONSTERS WHO LIVE BY MURDER. THEY MAY SMELL HUMAN WHEN THEY'RE BURNING, BUT THEY'RE DEFINITELY NOT HUMAN.
DEFINITELY NOT.
THESE THINGS ARE HUMAN, T'CHALLA THINKS. CORRUPTED AND DEFORMED, BUT THEY WERE MEN ONCE, JUST LIKE ME.
EACH ONE HE SUCCESSFULLY KILLS HE COUNTS AS A FAILURE. BECAUSE HE COULD NOT SAVE THEM.
THE KING OF WAKAN
WILL HAVE MANY MO
FAILURES BEFORE T
DAY IS THROUGH.

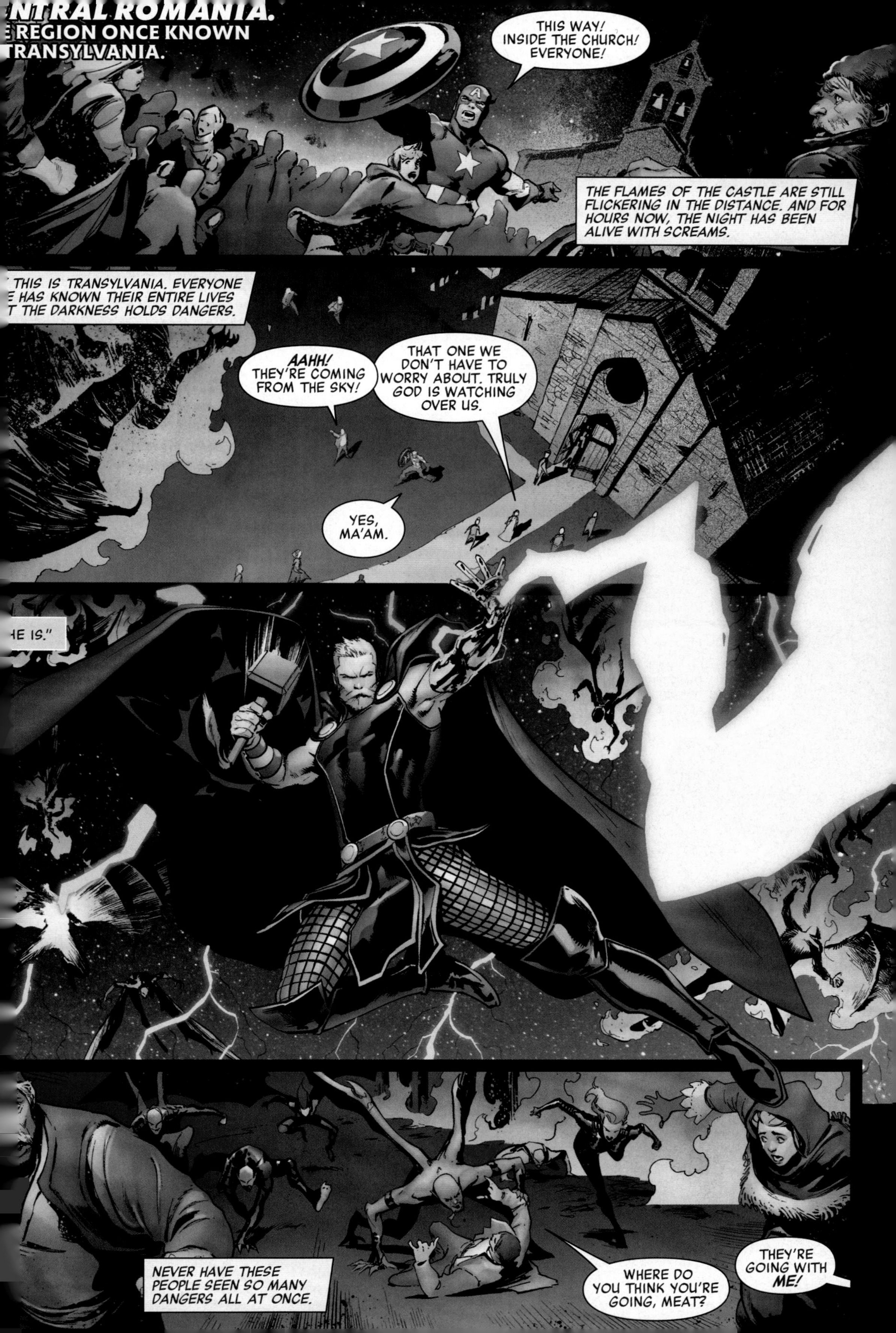
NTRAL ROMANIA.
E REGION ONCE KNOWN
TRANSYLVANIA.
THIS WAY! INSIDE THE CHURCH! EVERYONE!
THE FLAMES OF THE CASTLE ARE STILL FLICKERING IN THE DISTANCE. AND FOR HOURS NOW, THE NIGHT HAS BEEN ALIVE WITH SCREAMS.
THIS IS TRANSYLVANIA. EVERYONE E HAS KNOWN THEIR ENTIRE LIVES T THE DARKNESS HOLDS DANGERS.
AAHH! THEY'RE COMING FROM THE SKY!
THAT ONE WE DON'T HAVE TO WORRY ABOUT. TRULY GOD IS WATCHING OVER US.
YES, MA'AM.
HE IS."
NEVER HAVE THESE PEOPLE SEEN SO MANY DANGERS ALL AT ONCE.
WHERE DO YOU THINK YOU'RE GOING, MEAT?
THEY'RE GOING WITH ME!

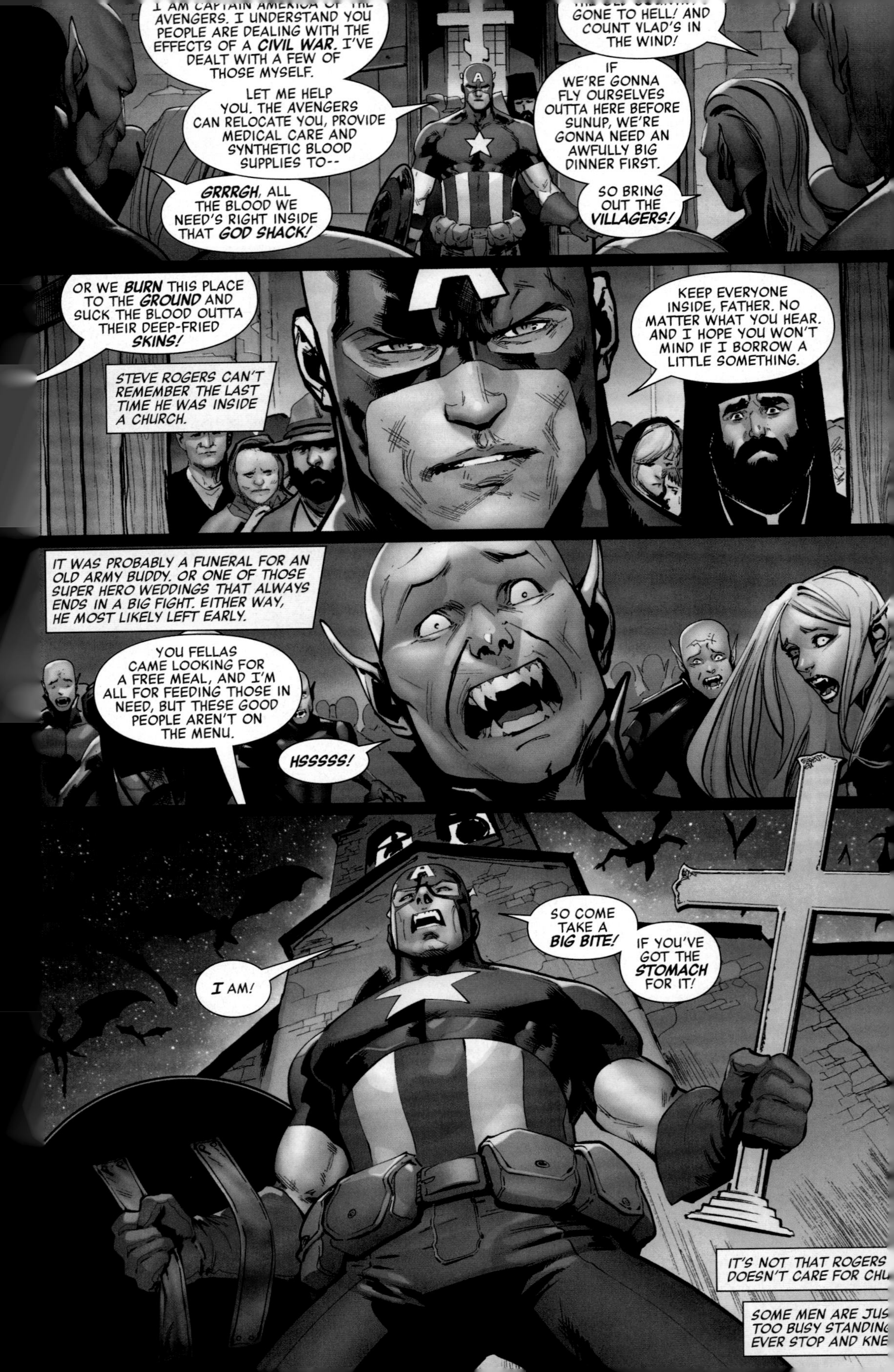

I AM CAPTAIN AMERICA OF THE AVENGERS. I UNDERSTAND YOU PEOPLE ARE DEALING WITH THE EFFECTS OF A CIVIL WAR. I'VE DEALT WITH A FEW OF THOSE MYSELF.
LET ME HELP YOU. THE AVENGERS CAN RELOCATE YOU, PROVIDE MEDICAL CARE AND SYNTHETIC BLOOD SUPPLIES TO--
GONE TO HELL! AND COUNT VLAD'S IN THE WIND!
IF WE'RE GONNA FLY OURSELVES OUTTA HERE BEFORE SUNUP, WE'RE GONNA NEED AN AWFULLY BIG DINNER FIRST.
SO BRING OUT THE VILLAGERS!
GRRRGH, ALL THE BLOOD WE NEED'S RIGHT INSIDE THAT GOD SHACK!
OR WE BURN THIS PLACE TO THE GROUND AND SUCK THE BLOOD OUTTA THEIR DEEP-FRIED SKINS!
STEVE ROGERS CAN'T REMEMBER THE LAST TIME HE WAS INSIDE A CHURCH.
KEEP EVERYONE INSIDE, FATHER. NO MATTER WHAT YOU HEAR. AND I HOPE YOU WON'T MIND IF I BORROW A LITTLE SOMETHING.
IT WAS PROBABLY A FUNERAL FOR AN OLD ARMY BUDDY. OR ONE OF THOSE SUPER HERO WEDDINGS THAT ALWAYS ENDS IN A BIG FIGHT. EITHER WAY, HE MOST LIKELY LEFT EARLY.
YOU FELLAS CAME LOOKING FOR A FREE MEAL, AND I'M ALL FOR FEEDING THOSE IN NEED, BUT THESE GOOD PEOPLE AREN'T ON THE MENU.
HSSSSS!
SO COME TAKE A BIG BITE!
I AM!
IF YOU'VE GOT THE STOMACH FOR IT!
IT'S NOT THAT ROGERS DOESN'T CARE FOR CHU
SOME MEN ARE JUS TOO BUSY STANDING EVER STOP AND KNE

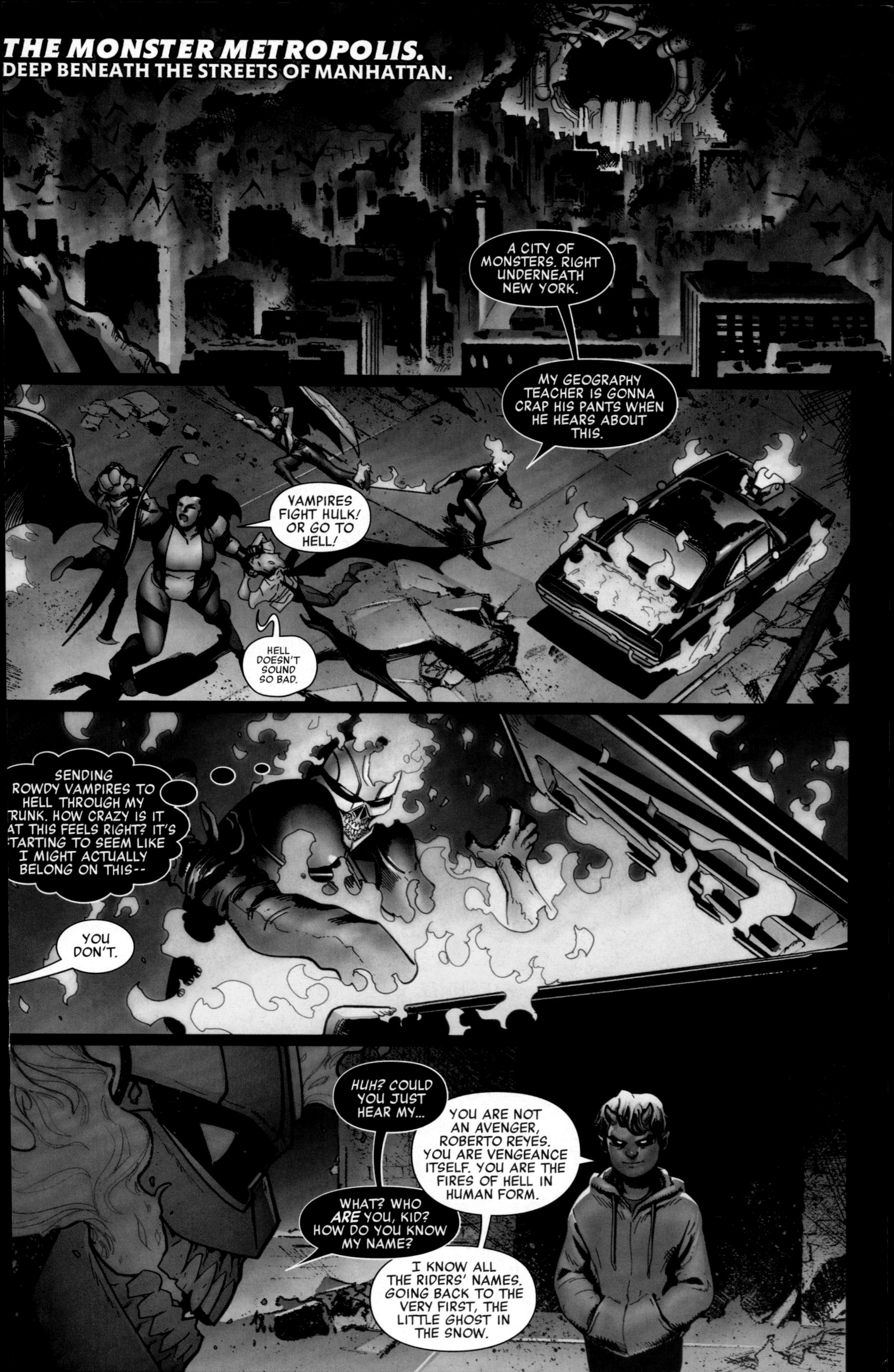
THE MONSTER METROPOLIS.
DEEP BENEATH THE STREETS OF MANHATTAN.
A CITY OF MONSTERS. RIGHT UNDERNEATH NEW YORK.
MY GEOGRAPHY TEACHER IS GONNA CRAP HIS PANTS WHEN HE HEARS ABOUT THIS.
VAMPIRES FIGHT HULK! OR GO TO HELL!
HELL DOESN'T SOUND SO BAD.
SENDING ROWDY VAMPIRES TO HELL THROUGH MY TRUNK. HOW CRAZY IS IT AT THIS FEELS RIGHT? IT'S TARTING TO SEEM LIKE I MIGHT ACTUALLY BELONG ON THIS--
YOU DON'T.
HUH? COULD YOU JUST HEAR MY...
YOU ARE NOT AN AVENGER, ROBERTO REYES. YOU ARE VENGEANCE ITSELF. YOU ARE THE FIRES OF HELL IN HUMAN FORM.
WHAT? WHO ARE YOU, KID? HOW DO YOU KNOW MY NAME?
I KNOW ALL THE RIDERS' NAMES. GOING BACK TO THE VERY FIRST, THE LITTLE GHOST IN THE SNOW.

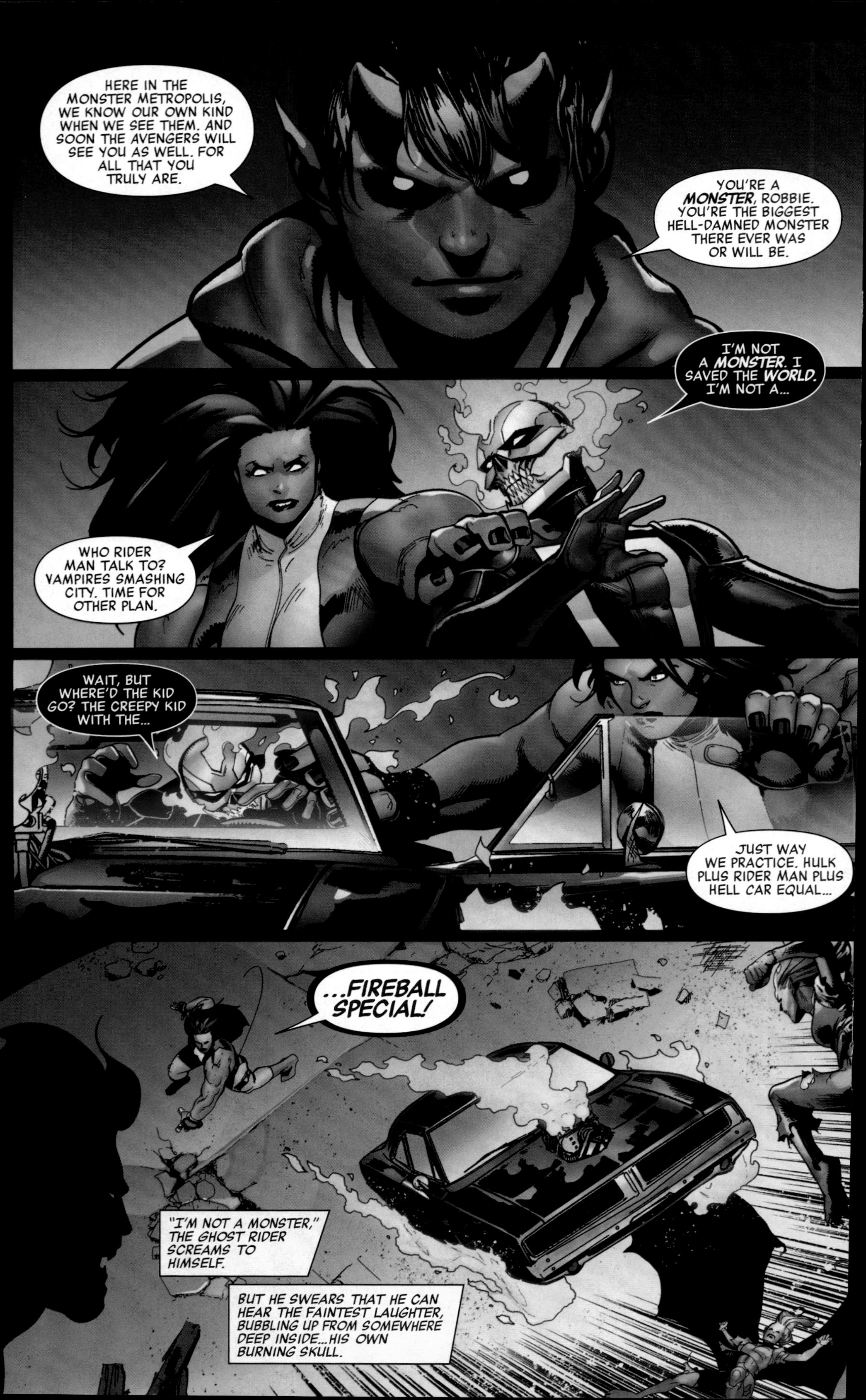
HERE IN THE MONSTER METROPOLIS, WE KNOW OUR OWN KIND WHEN WE SEE THEM. AND SOON THE AVENGERS WILL SEE YOU AS WELL. FOR ALL THAT YOU TRULY ARE.
YOU'RE A *MONSTER*, ROBBIE. YOU'RE THE BIGGEST HELL-DAMNED MONSTER THERE EVER WAS OR WILL BE.
I'M NOT A *MONSTER*. I SAVED THE *WORLD*. I'M NOT A...
WHO RIDER MAN TALK TO? VAMPIRES SMASHING CITY. TIME FOR OTHER PLAN.
WAIT, BUT WHERE'D THE KID GO? THE CREEPY KID WITH THE...
JUST WAY WE PRACTICE. HULK PLUS RIDER MAN PLUS HELL CAR EQUAL...
...FIREBALL SPECIAL!
"I'M NOT A MONSTER," THE GHOST RIDER SCREAMS TO HIMSELF.
BUT HE SWEARS THAT HE CAN HEAR THE FAINTEST LAUGHTER, BUBBLING UP FROM SOMEWHERE DEEP INSIDE...HIS OWN BURNING SKULL.

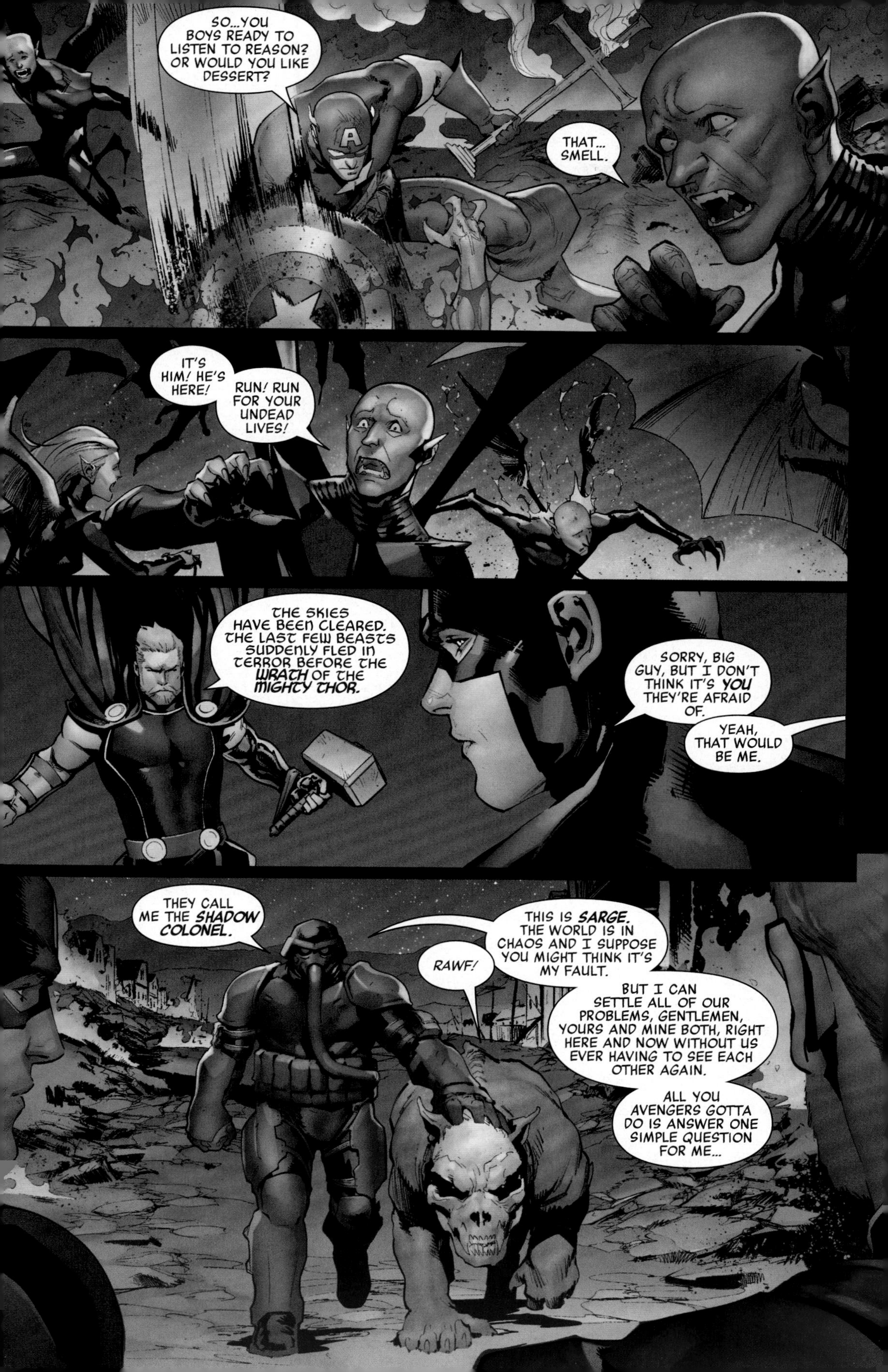

SO...YOU BOYS READY TO LISTEN TO REASON? OR WOULD YOU LIKE DESSERT?
THAT... SMELL.
IT'S HIM! HE'S HERE!
RUN! RUN FOR YOUR UNDEAD LIVES!
THE SKIES HAVE BEEN CLEARED. THE LAST FEW BEASTS SUDDENLY FLED IN TERROR BEFORE THE WRATH OF THE MIGHTY THOR.
SORRY, BIG GUY, BUT I DON'T THINK IT'S YOU THEY'RE AFRAID OF.
YEAH, THAT WOULD BE ME.
THEY CALL ME THE SHADOW COLONEL.
THIS IS SARGE. THE WORLD IS IN CHAOS AND I SUPPOSE YOU MIGHT THINK IT'S MY FAULT.
RAWF!
BUT I CAN SETTLE ALL OF OUR PROBLEMS, GENTLEMEN, YOURS AND MINE BOTH, RIGHT HERE AND NOW WITHOUT US EVER HAVING TO SEE EACH OTHER AGAIN.
ALL YOU AVENGERS GOTTA DO IS ANSWER ONE SIMPLE QUESTION FOR ME...

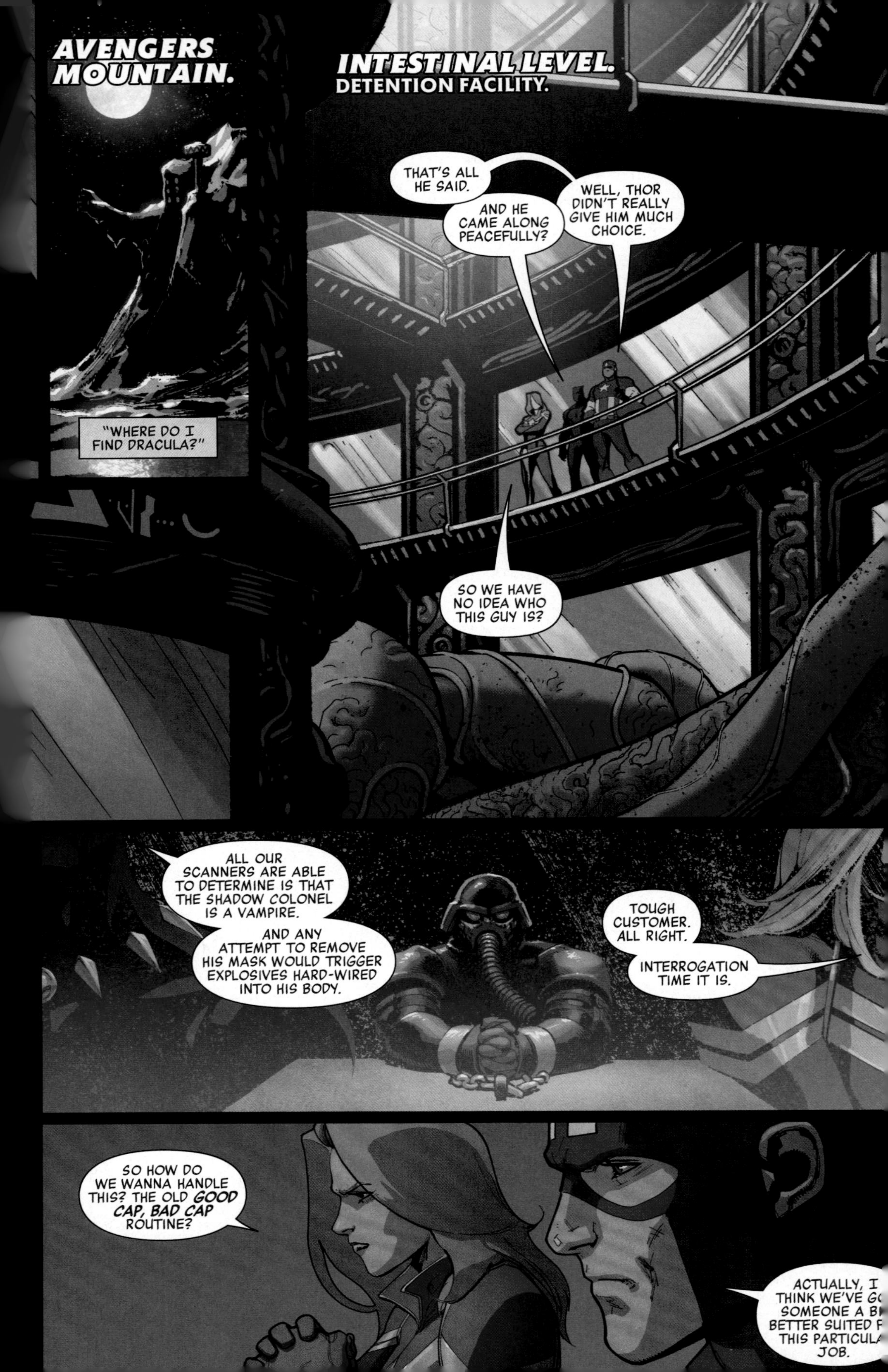

AVENGERS MOUNTAIN.
"WHERE DO I FIND DRACULA?"
INTESTINAL LEVEL. DETENTION FACILITY.
THAT'S ALL HE SAID.
AND HE CAME ALONG PEACEFULLY?
WELL, THOR DIDN'T REALLY GIVE HIM MUCH CHOICE.
SO WE HAVE NO IDEA WHO THIS GUY IS?
ALL OUR SCANNERS ARE ABLE TO DETERMINE IS THAT THE SHADOW COLONEL IS A VAMPIRE.
AND ANY ATTEMPT TO REMOVE HIS MASK WOULD TRIGGER EXPLOSIVES HARD-WIRED INTO HIS BODY.
TOUGH CUSTOMER. ALL RIGHT.
INTERROGATION TIME IT IS.
SO HOW DO WE WANNA HANDLE THIS? THE OLD *GOOD CAP, BAD CAP* ROUTINE?
ACTUALLY, I THINK WE'VE G SOMEONE A BI BETTER SUITED F THIS PARTICULA JOB.

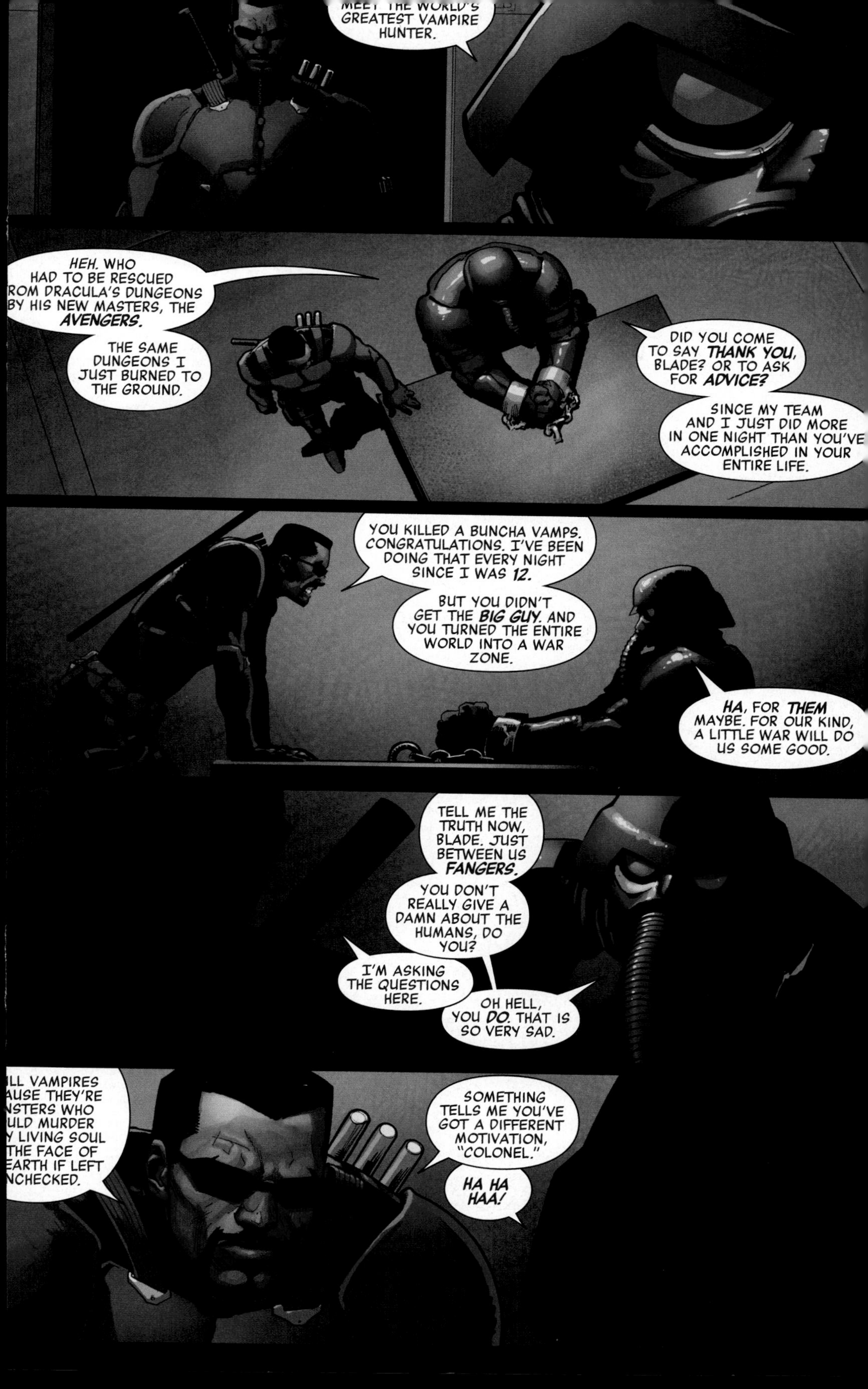

MEET THE WORLD'S GREATEST VAMPIRE HUNTER.
HEH. WHO HAD TO BE RESCUED FROM DRACULA'S DUNGEONS BY HIS NEW MASTERS, THE AVENGERS.
THE SAME DUNGEONS I JUST BURNED TO THE GROUND.
DID YOU COME TO SAY THANK YOU, BLADE? OR TO ASK FOR ADVICE?
SINCE MY TEAM AND I JUST DID MORE IN ONE NIGHT THAN YOU'VE ACCOMPLISHED IN YOUR ENTIRE LIFE.
YOU KILLED A BUNCHA VAMPS. CONGRATULATIONS. I'VE BEEN DOING THAT EVERY NIGHT SINCE I WAS 12.
BUT YOU DIDN'T GET THE BIG GUY. AND YOU TURNED THE ENTIRE WORLD INTO A WAR ZONE.
HA, FOR THEM MAYBE. FOR OUR KIND, A LITTLE WAR WILL DO US SOME GOOD.
TELL ME THE TRUTH NOW, BLADE. JUST BETWEEN US FANGERS.
YOU DON'T REALLY GIVE A DAMN ABOUT THE HUMANS, DO YOU?
I'M ASKING THE QUESTIONS HERE.
OH HELL, YOU DO. THAT IS SO VERY SAD.
LL VAMPIRES AUSE THEY'RE NSTERS WHO ULD MURDER LIVING SOUL THE FACE OF EARTH IF LEFT NCHECKED.
SOMETHING TELLS ME YOU'VE GOT A DIFFERENT MOTIVATION, "COLONEL."
HA HA HAA!

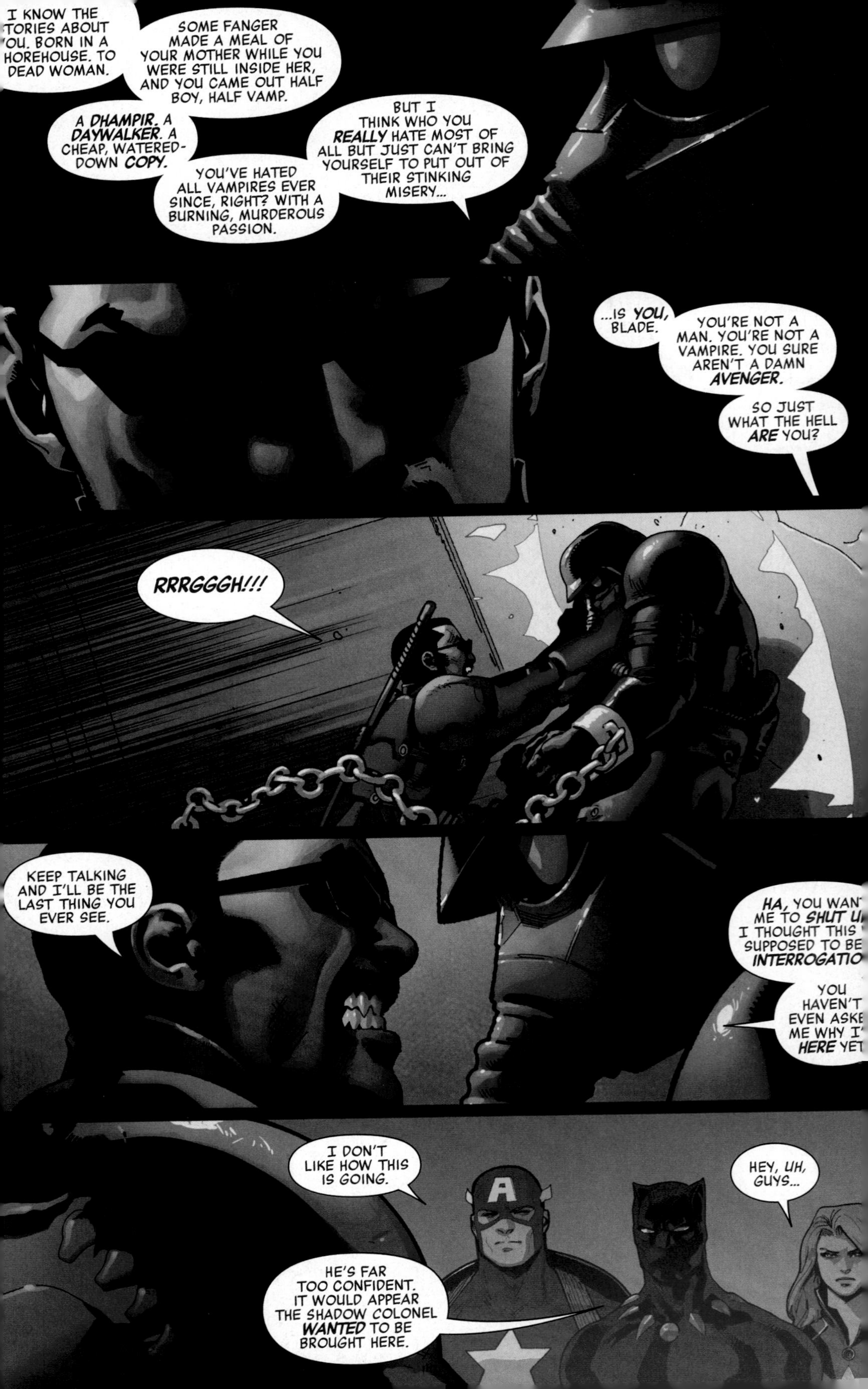
I KNOW THE
TORIES ABOUT
OU. BORN IN A
HOREHOUSE. TO
DEAD WOMAN.
SOME FANGER MADE A MEAL OF YOUR MOTHER WHILE YOU WERE STILL INSIDE HER, AND YOU CAME OUT HALF BOY, HALF VAMP.
A DHAMPIR. A DAYWALKER. A CHEAP, WATERED-DOWN COPY.
YOU'VE HATED ALL VAMPIRES EVER SINCE, RIGHT? WITH A BURNING, MURDEROUS PASSION.
BUT I THINK WHO YOU REALLY HATE MOST OF ALL BUT JUST CAN'T BRING YOURSELF TO PUT OUT OF THEIR STINKING MISERY...
...IS YOU, BLADE.
YOU'RE NOT A MAN. YOU'RE NOT A VAMPIRE. YOU SURE AREN'T A DAMN AVENGER.
SO JUST WHAT THE HELL ARE YOU?
RRRGGGH!!!
KEEP TALKING AND I'LL BE THE LAST THING YOU EVER SEE.
HA, YOU WANT
ME TO SHUT U
I THOUGHT THIS
SUPPOSED TO BE
INTERROGATIO
YOU
HAVEN'T
EVEN ASKE
ME WHY I'
HERE YET
I DON'T LIKE HOW THIS IS GOING.
HEY, UH, GUYS...
HE'S FAR TOO CONFIDENT. IT WOULD APPEAR THE SHADOW COLONEL WANTED TO BE BROUGHT HERE.

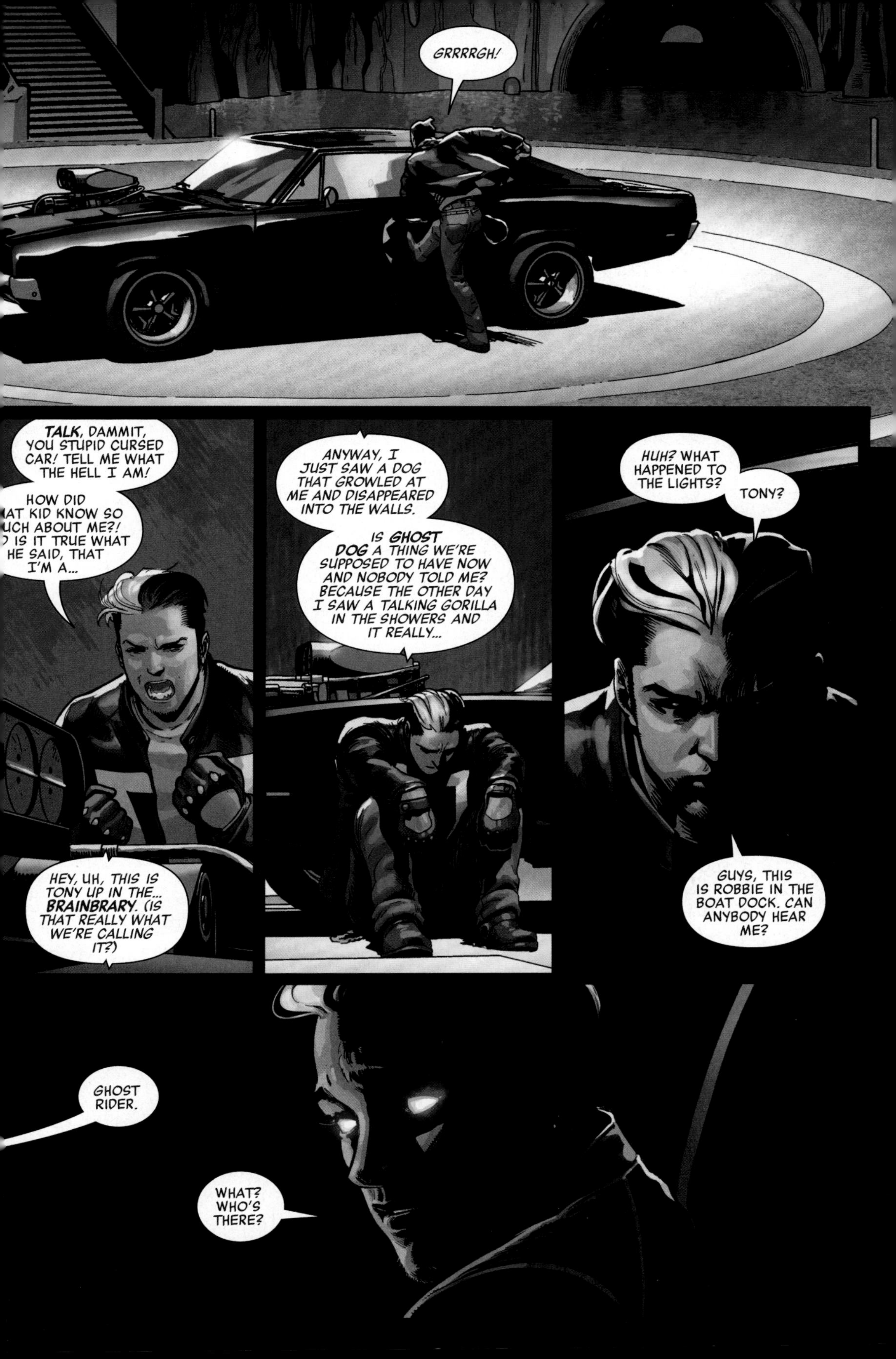
GRRRRGH!
TALK, DAMMIT, YOU STUPID CURSED CAR! TELL ME WHAT THE HELL I AM!
HOW DID
AT KID KNOW SO
UCH ABOUT ME?!
D IS IT TRUE WHAT HE SAID, THAT I'M A...
HEY, UH, THIS IS TONY UP IN THE... BRAINBRARY. (IS THAT REALLY WHAT WE'RE CALLING IT?)
ANYWAY, I JUST SAW A DOG THAT GROWLED AT ME AND DISAPPEARED INTO THE WALLS.
IS GHOST DOG A THING WE'RE SUPPOSED TO HAVE NOW AND NOBODY TOLD ME? BECAUSE THE OTHER DAY I SAW A TALKING GORILLA IN THE SHOWERS AND IT REALLY...
HUH? WHAT HAPPENED TO THE LIGHTS?
TONY?
GUYS, THIS IS ROBBIE IN THE BOAT DOCK. CAN ANYBODY HEAR ME?
GHOST RIDER.
WHAT? WHO'S THERE?

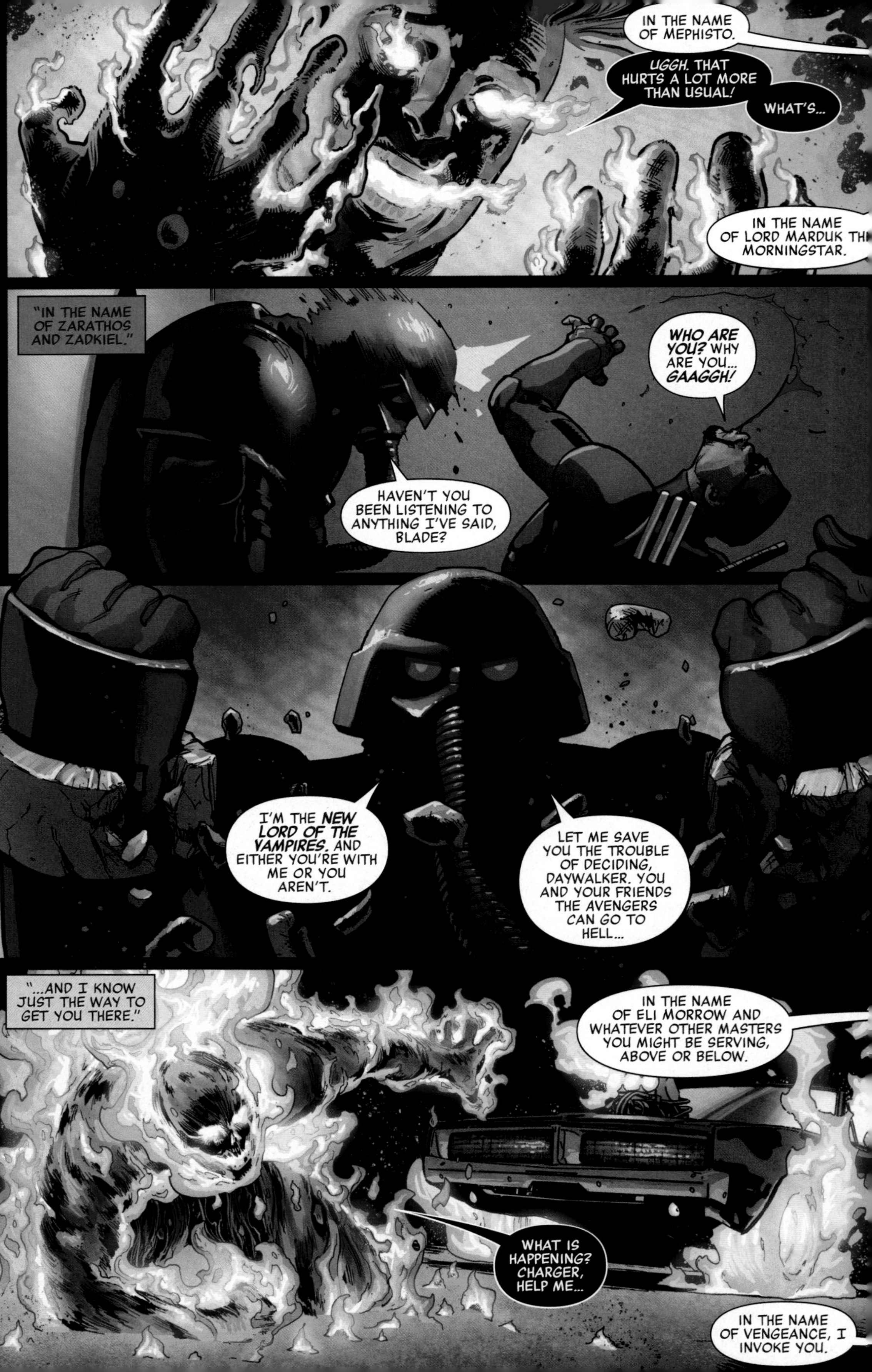
IN THE NAME OF MEPHISTO.
UGGH. THAT HURTS A LOT MORE THAN USUAL!
WHAT'S...
IN THE NAME OF LORD MARDUK TH MORNINGSTAR.
"IN THE NAME OF ZARATHOS AND ZADKIEL."
WHO ARE YOU? WHY ARE YOU... GAAGGH!
HAVEN'T YOU BEEN LISTENING TO ANYTHING I'VE SAID, BLADE?
I'M THE NEW LORD OF THE VAMPIRES. AND EITHER YOU'RE WITH ME OR YOU AREN'T.
LET ME SAVE YOU THE TROUBLE OF DECIDING, DAYWALKER. YOU AND YOUR FRIENDS THE AVENGERS CAN GO TO HELL...
"...AND I KNOW JUST THE WAY TO GET YOU THERE."
IN THE NAME OF ELI MORROW AND WHATEVER OTHER MASTERS YOU MIGHT BE SERVING, ABOVE OR BELOW.
WHAT IS HAPPENING? CHARGER, HELP ME...
IN THE NAME OF VENGEANCE, I INVOKE YOU.

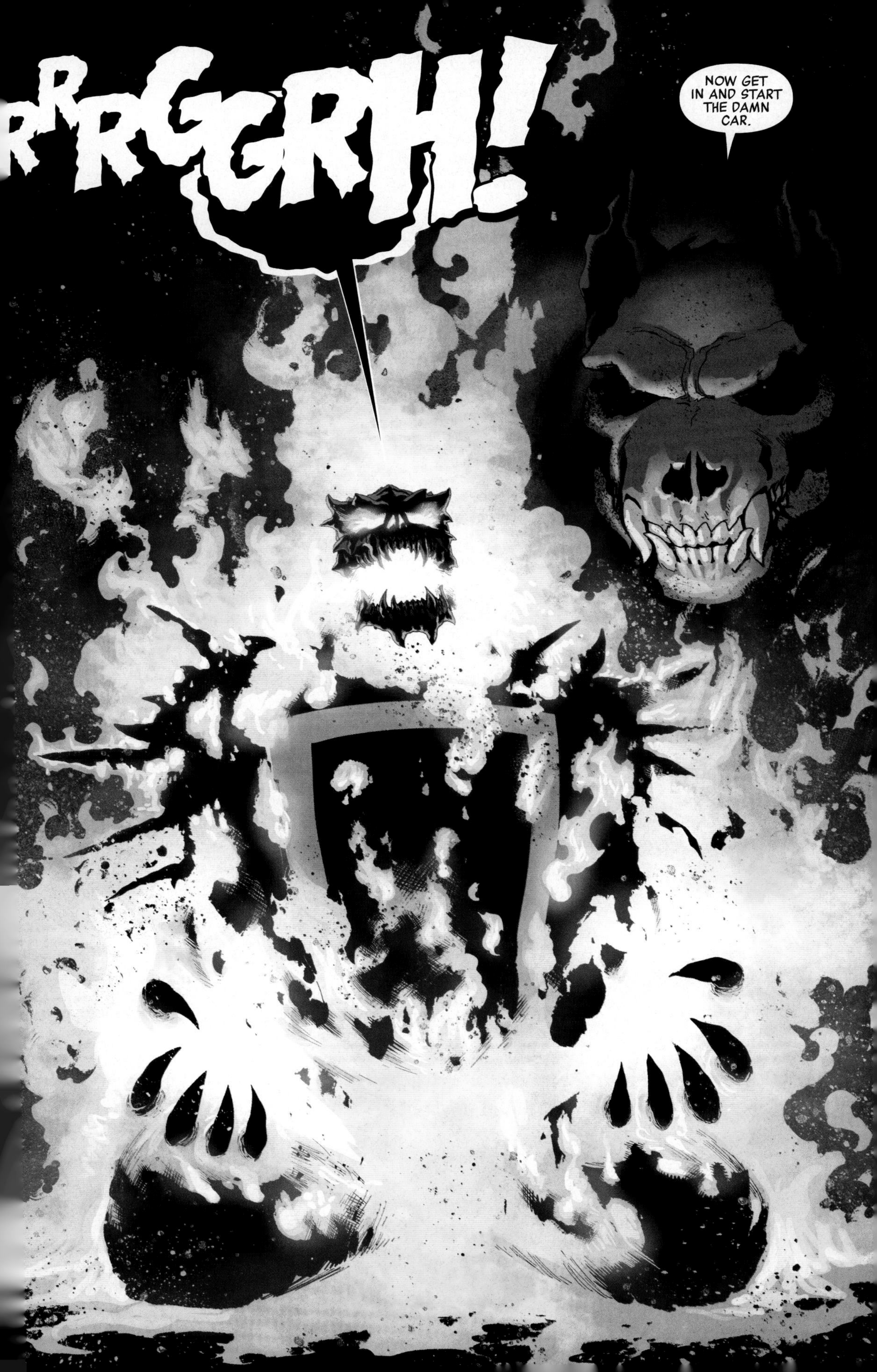
RRRGGRH!
NOW GET IN AND START THE DAMN CAR.

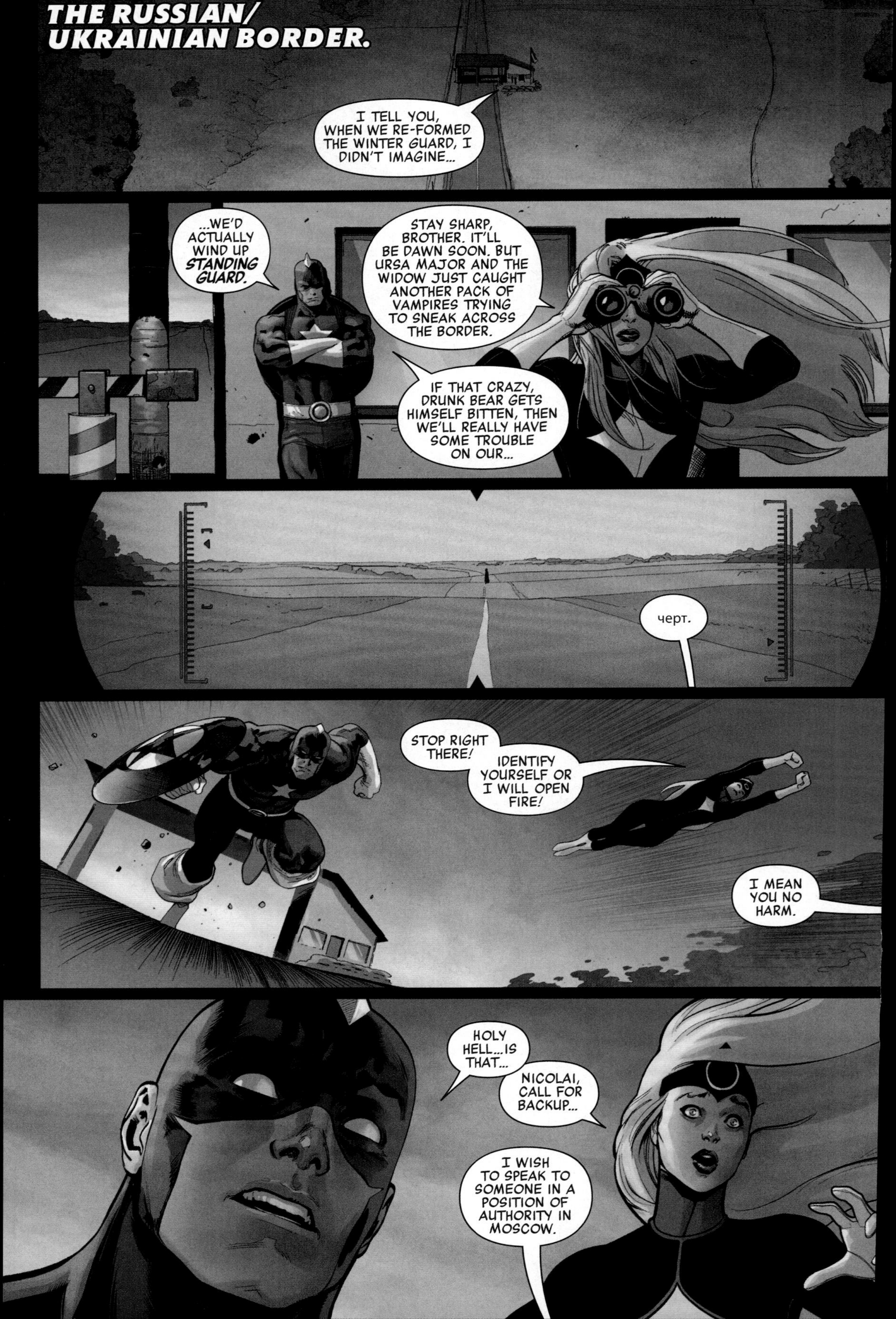
THE RUSSIAN/ UKRAINIAN BORDER.
I TELL YOU, WHEN WE RE-FORMED THE WINTER GUARD, I DIDN'T IMAGINE...
...WE'D ACTUALLY WIND UP STANDING GUARD.
STAY SHARP, BROTHER. IT'LL BE DAWN SOON. BUT URSA MAJOR AND THE WIDOW JUST CAUGHT ANOTHER PACK OF VAMPIRES TRYING TO SNEAK ACROSS THE BORDER.
IF THAT CRAZY, DRUNK BEAR GETS HIMSELF BITTEN, THEN WE'LL REALLY HAVE SOME TROUBLE ON OUR...
черт.
STOP RIGHT THERE!
IDENTIFY YOURSELF OR I WILL OPEN FIRE!
I MEAN YOU NO HARM.
HOLY HELL...IS THAT...
NICOLAI, CALL FOR BACKUP...
I WISH TO SPEAK TO SOMEONE IN A POSITION OF AUTHORITY IN MOSCOW.

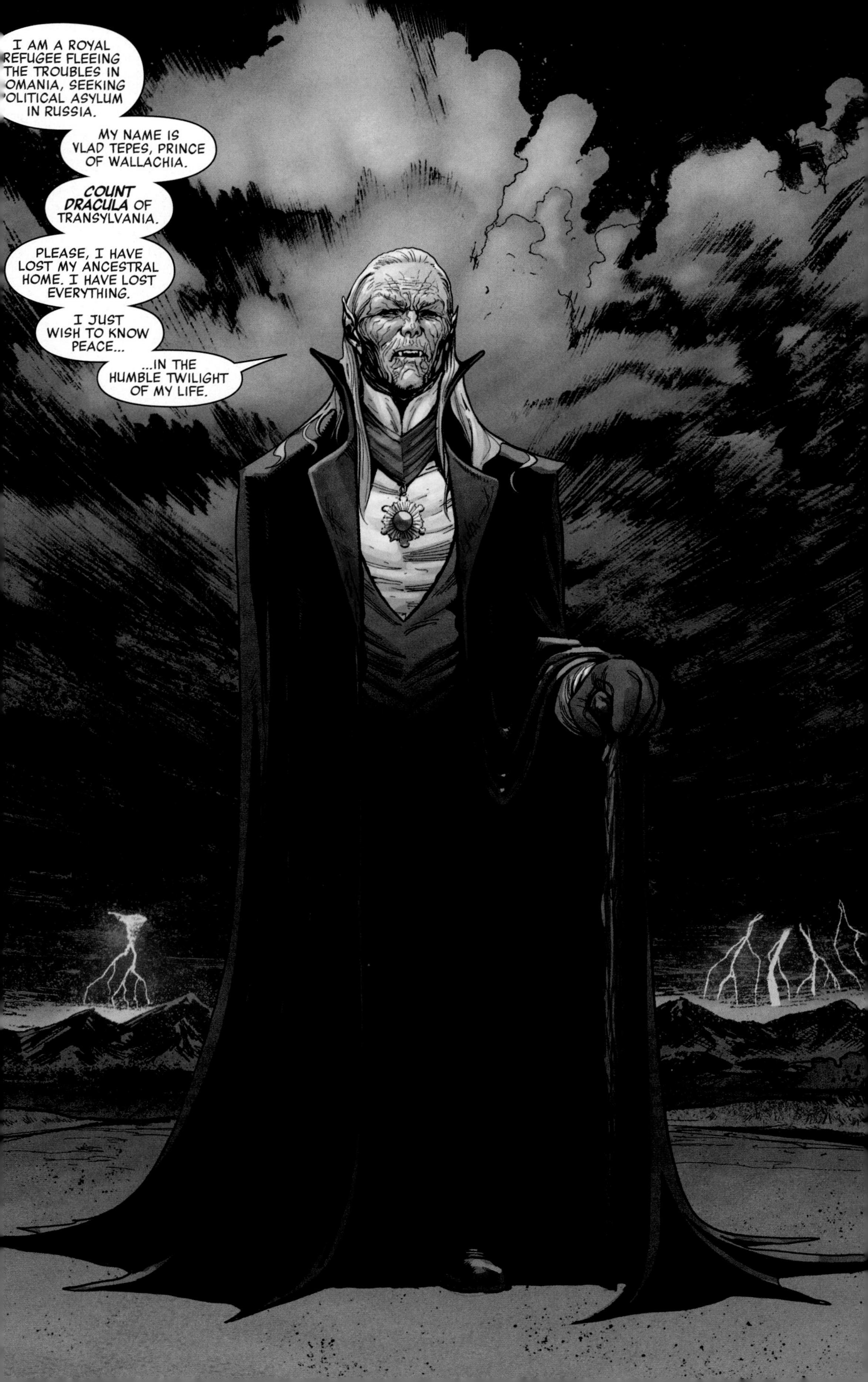
I AM A ROYAL REFUGEE FLEEING THE TROUBLES IN OMANIA, SEEKING POLITICAL ASYLUM IN RUSSIA.
MY NAME IS VLAD TEPES, PRINCE OF WALLACHIA.
COUNT DRACULA OF TRANSYLVANIA.
PLEASE, I HAVE LOST MY ANCESTRAL HOME. I HAVE LOST EVERYTHING.
I JUST WISH TO KNOW PEACE...
...IN THE HUMBLE TWILIGHT OF MY LIFE.

15 THE BATTLE FOR THE THRONE OF THE DAMNED

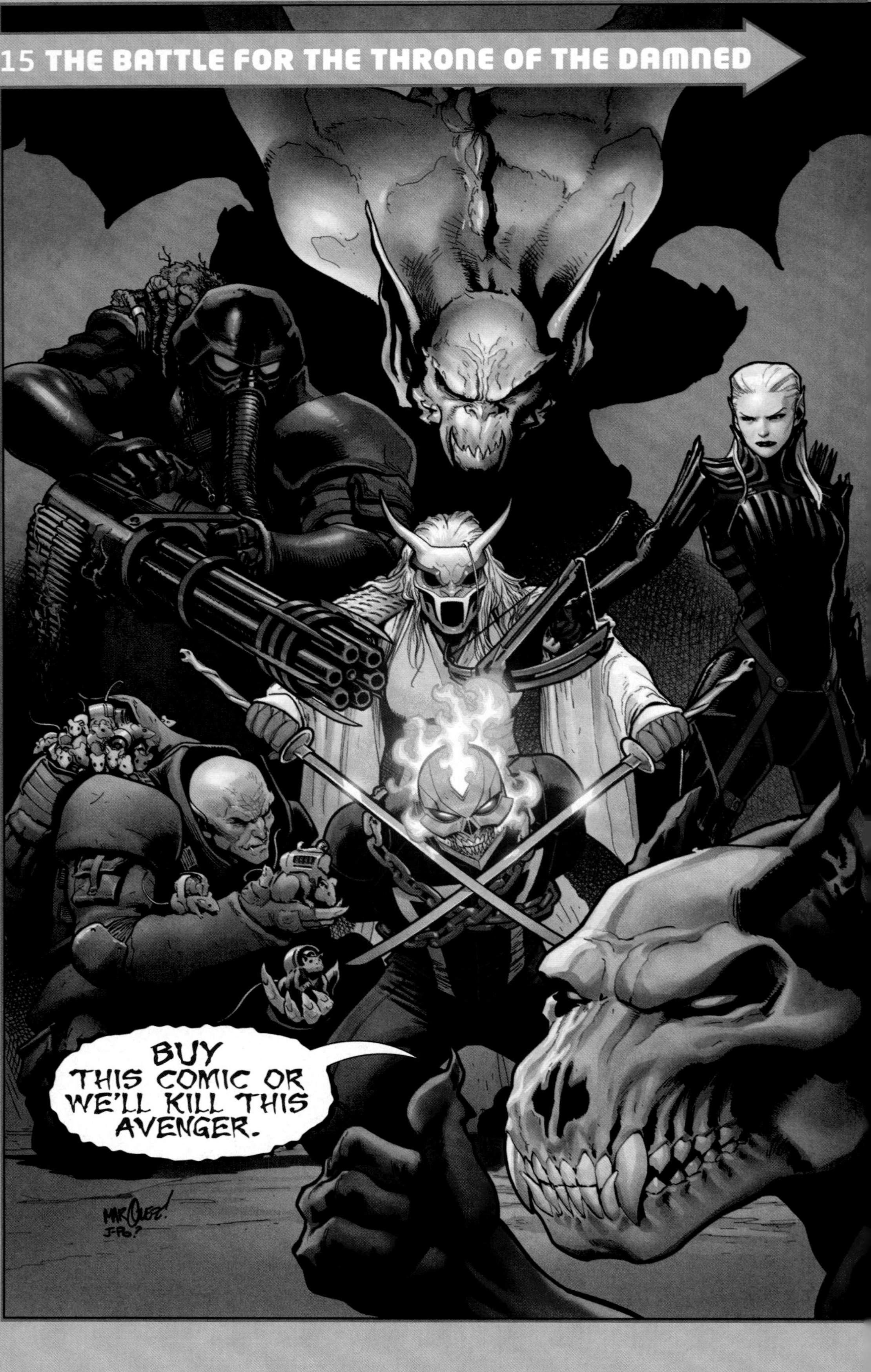
BUY THIS COMIC OR WE'LL KILL THIS AVENGER.

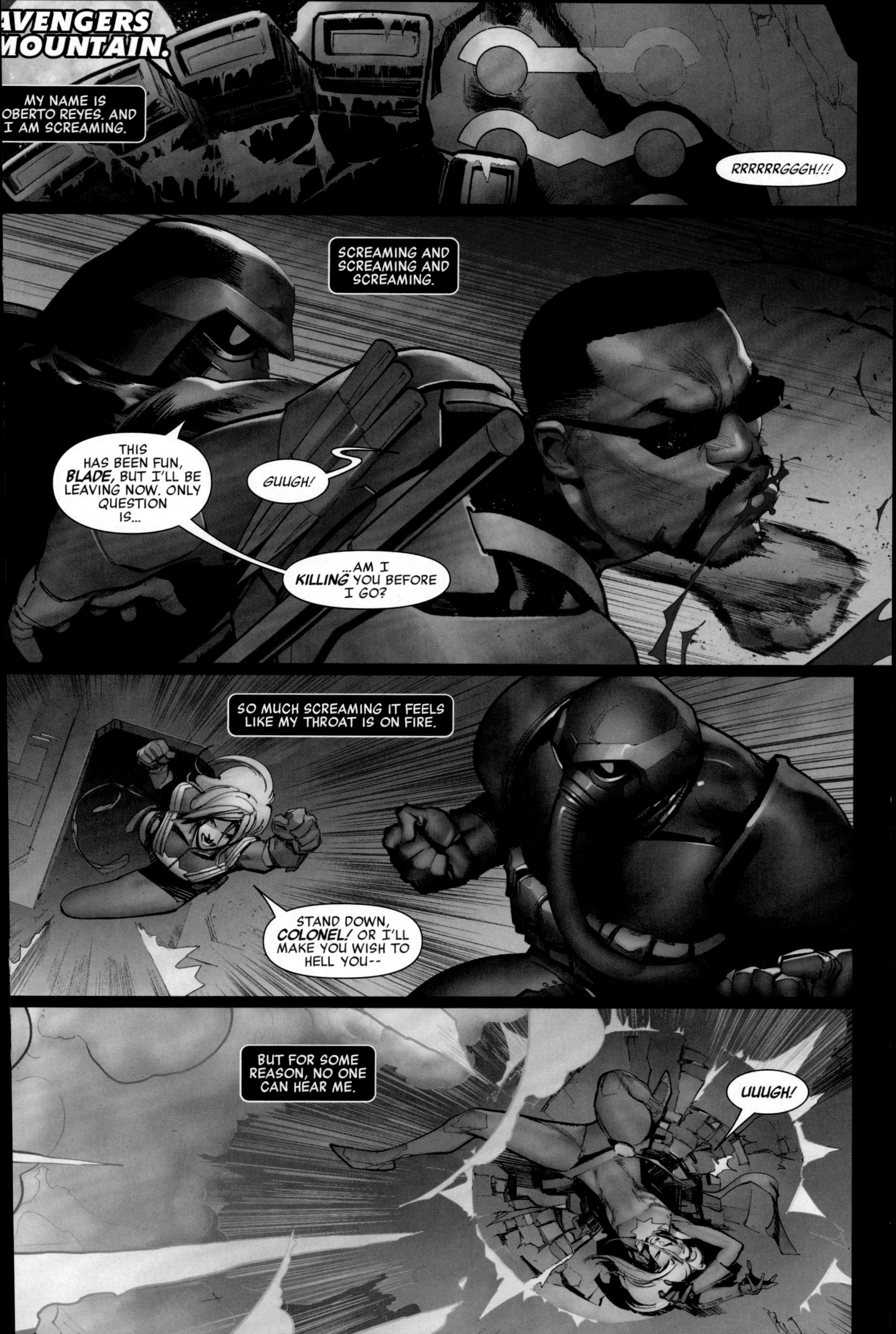
AVENGERS MOUNTAIN.
MY NAME IS OBERTO REYES. AND I AM SCREAMING.
RRRRRRGGGH!!!
SCREAMING AND SCREAMING AND SCREAMING.
THIS HAS BEEN FUN, BLADE, BUT I'LL BE LEAVING NOW. ONLY QUESTION IS...
GUUGH!
...AM I KILLING YOU BEFORE I GO?
SO MUCH SCREAMING IT FEELS LIKE MY THROAT IS ON FIRE.
STAND DOWN, COLONEL! OR I'LL MAKE YOU WISH TO HELL YOU--
BUT FOR SOME REASON, NO ONE CAN HEAR ME.
UUUGH!

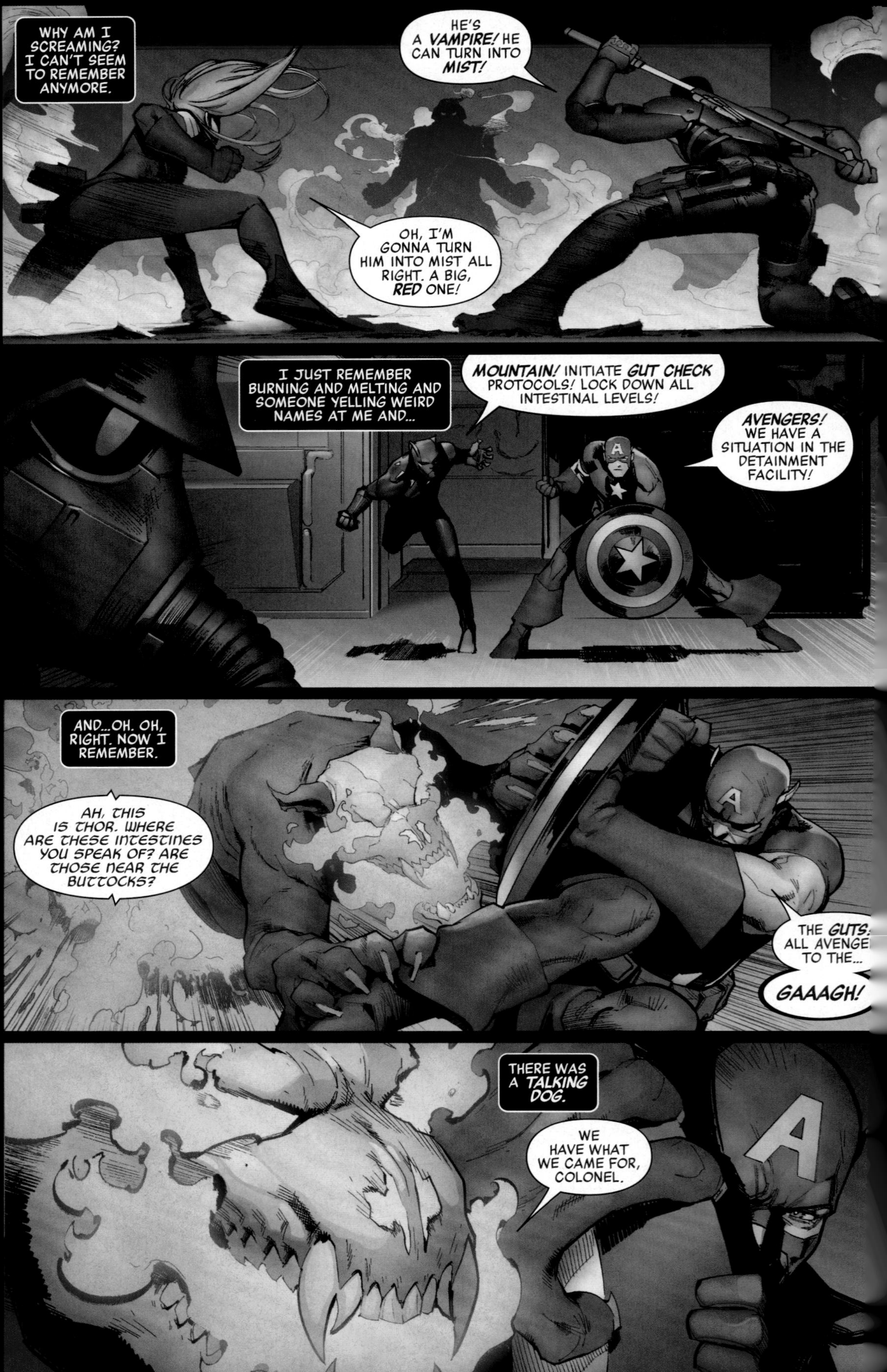
WHY AM I SCREAMING? I CAN'T SEEM TO REMEMBER ANYMORE.
HE'S A VAMPIRE! HE CAN TURN INTO MIST!
OH, I'M GONNA TURN HIM INTO MIST ALL RIGHT. A BIG, RED ONE!
I JUST REMEMBER BURNING AND MELTING AND SOMEONE YELLING WEIRD NAMES AT ME AND...
MOUNTAIN! INITIATE GUT CHECK PROTOCOLS! LOCK DOWN ALL INTESTINAL LEVELS!
AVENGERS! WE HAVE A SITUATION IN THE DETAINMENT FACILITY!
AND...OH. OH, RIGHT. NOW I REMEMBER.
AH, THIS IS THOR. WHERE ARE THESE INTESTINES YOU SPEAK OF? ARE THOSE NEAR THE BUTTOCKS?
THE GUTS! ALL AVENGE TO THE...
GAAAGH!
THERE WAS A TALKING DOG.
WE HAVE WHAT WE CAME FOR, COLONEL.

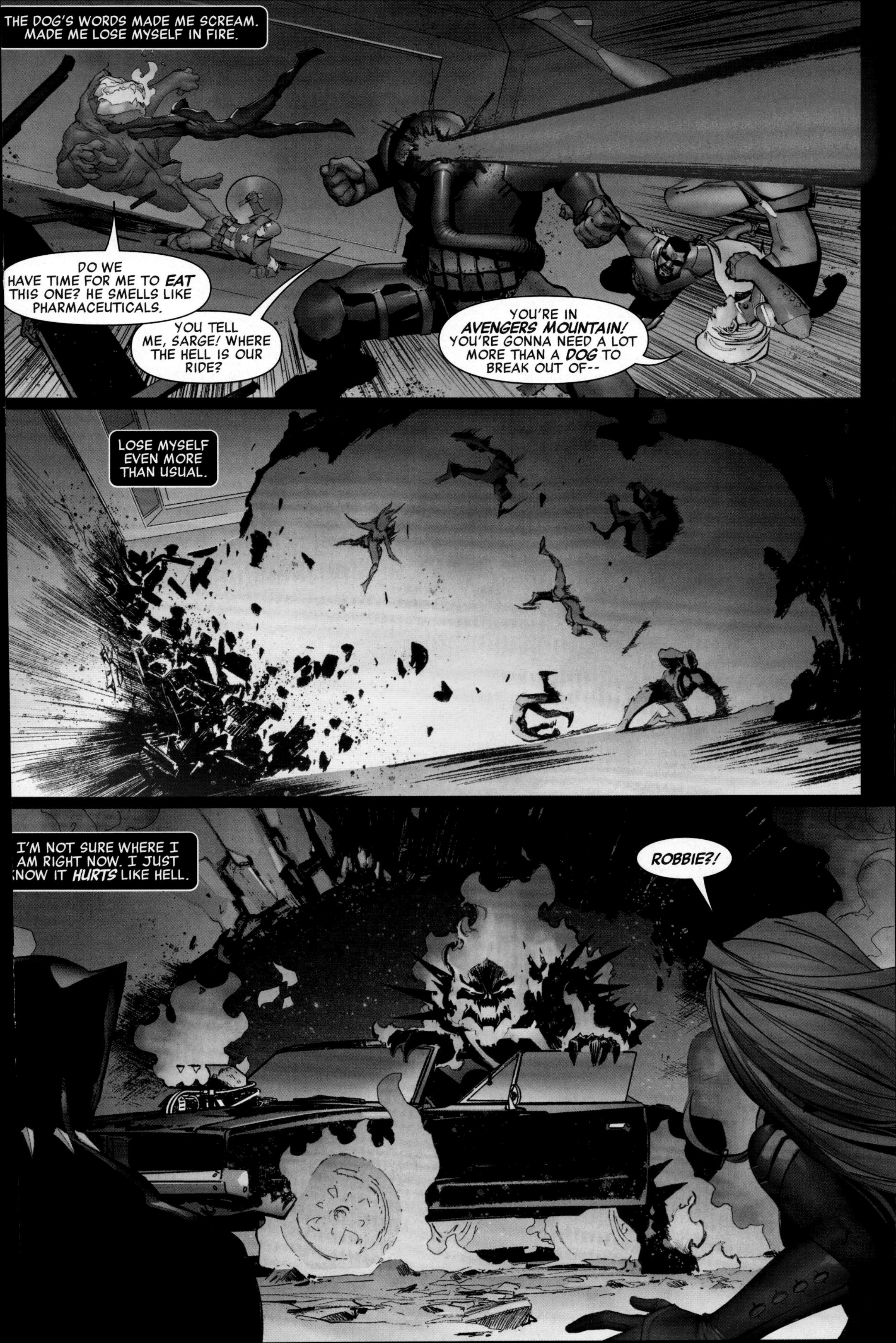
THE DOG'S WORDS MADE ME SCREAM. MADE ME LOSE MYSELF IN FIRE.
DO WE HAVE TIME FOR ME TO EAT THIS ONE? HE SMELLS LIKE PHARMACEUTICALS.
YOU TELL ME, SARGE! WHERE THE HELL IS OUR RIDE?
YOU'RE IN AVENGERS MOUNTAIN! YOU'RE GONNA NEED A LOT MORE THAN A DOG TO BREAK OUT OF--
LOSE MYSELF EVEN MORE THAN USUAL.
I'M NOT SURE WHERE I AM RIGHT NOW. I JUST KNOW IT HURTS LIKE HELL.
ROBBIE?!

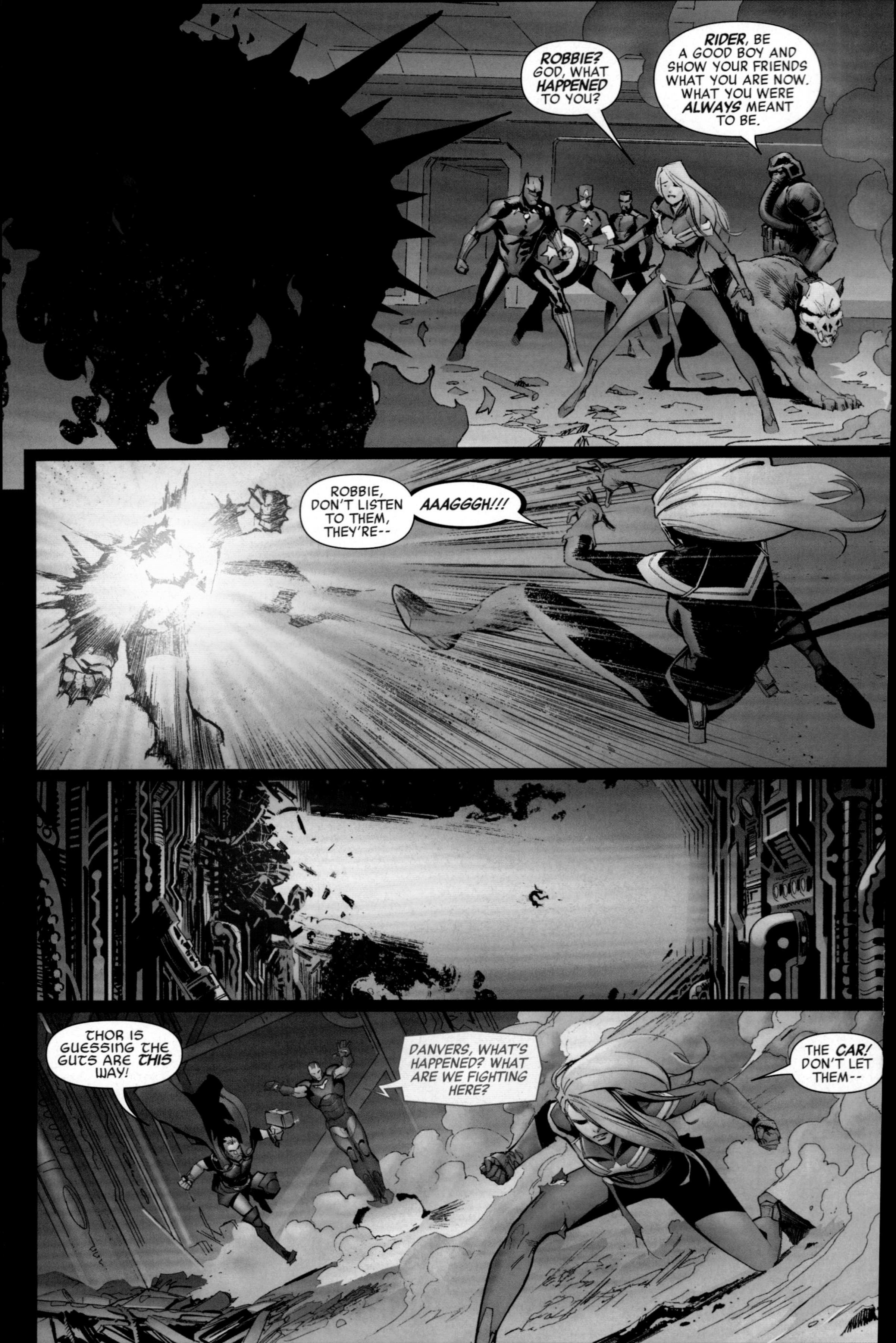
ROBBIE? GOD, WHAT HAPPENED TO YOU?
RIDER, BE A GOOD BOY AND SHOW YOUR FRIENDS WHAT YOU ARE NOW. WHAT YOU WERE ALWAYS MEANT TO BE.
ROBBIE, DON'T LISTEN TO THEM, THEY'RE--
AAAGGGH!!!
THOR IS GUESSING THE GUTS ARE THIS WAY!
DANVERS, WHAT'S HAPPENED? WHAT ARE WE FIGHTING HERE?
THE CAR! DON'T LET THEM--

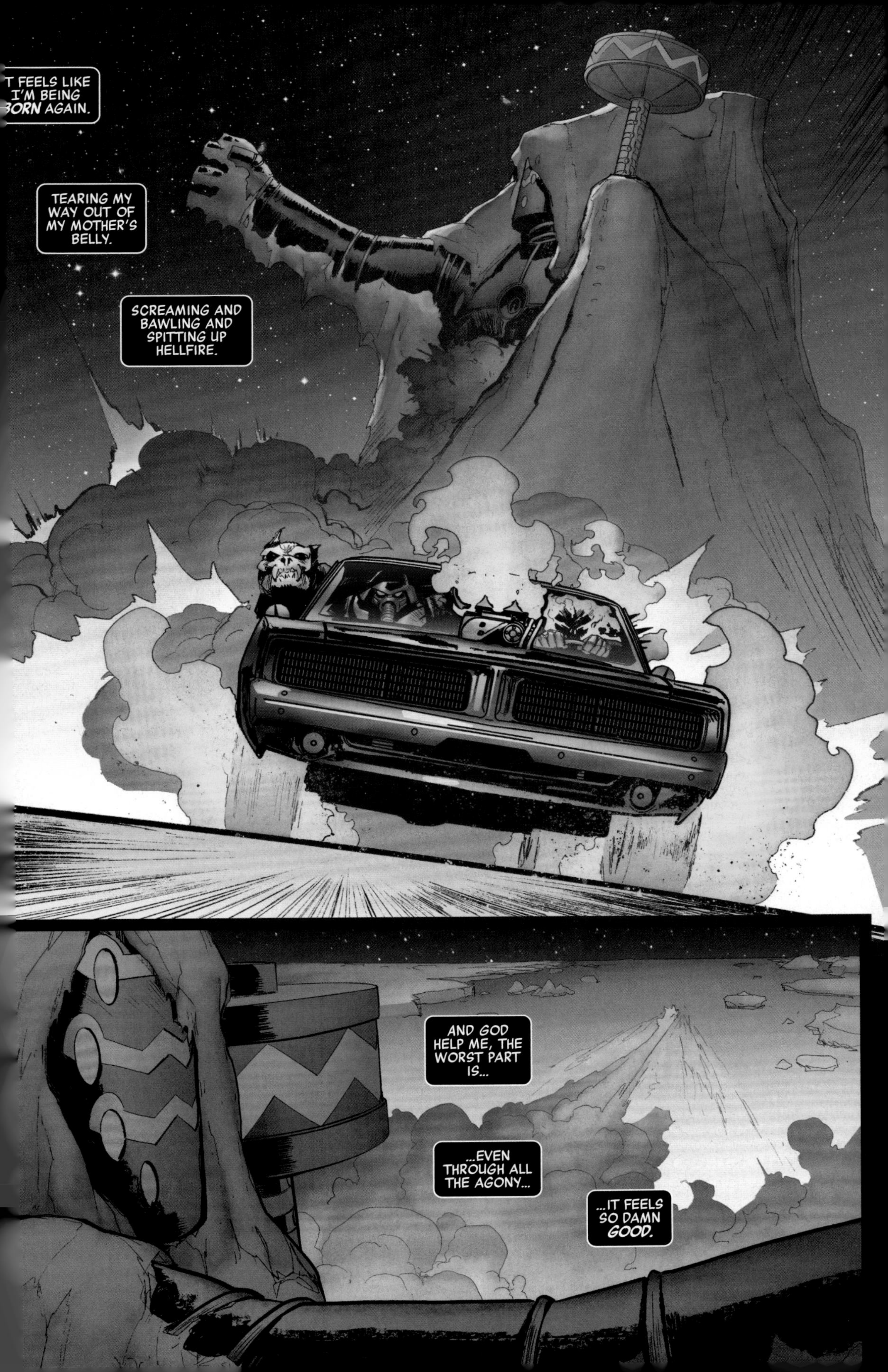
T FEELS LIKE I'M BEING BORN AGAIN.
TEARING MY WAY OUT OF MY MOTHER'S BELLY.
SCREAMING AND BAWLING AND SPITTING UP HELLFIRE.
AND GOD HELP ME, THE WORST PART IS...
...EVEN THROUGH ALL THE AGONY...
...IT FEELS SO DAMN GOOD.

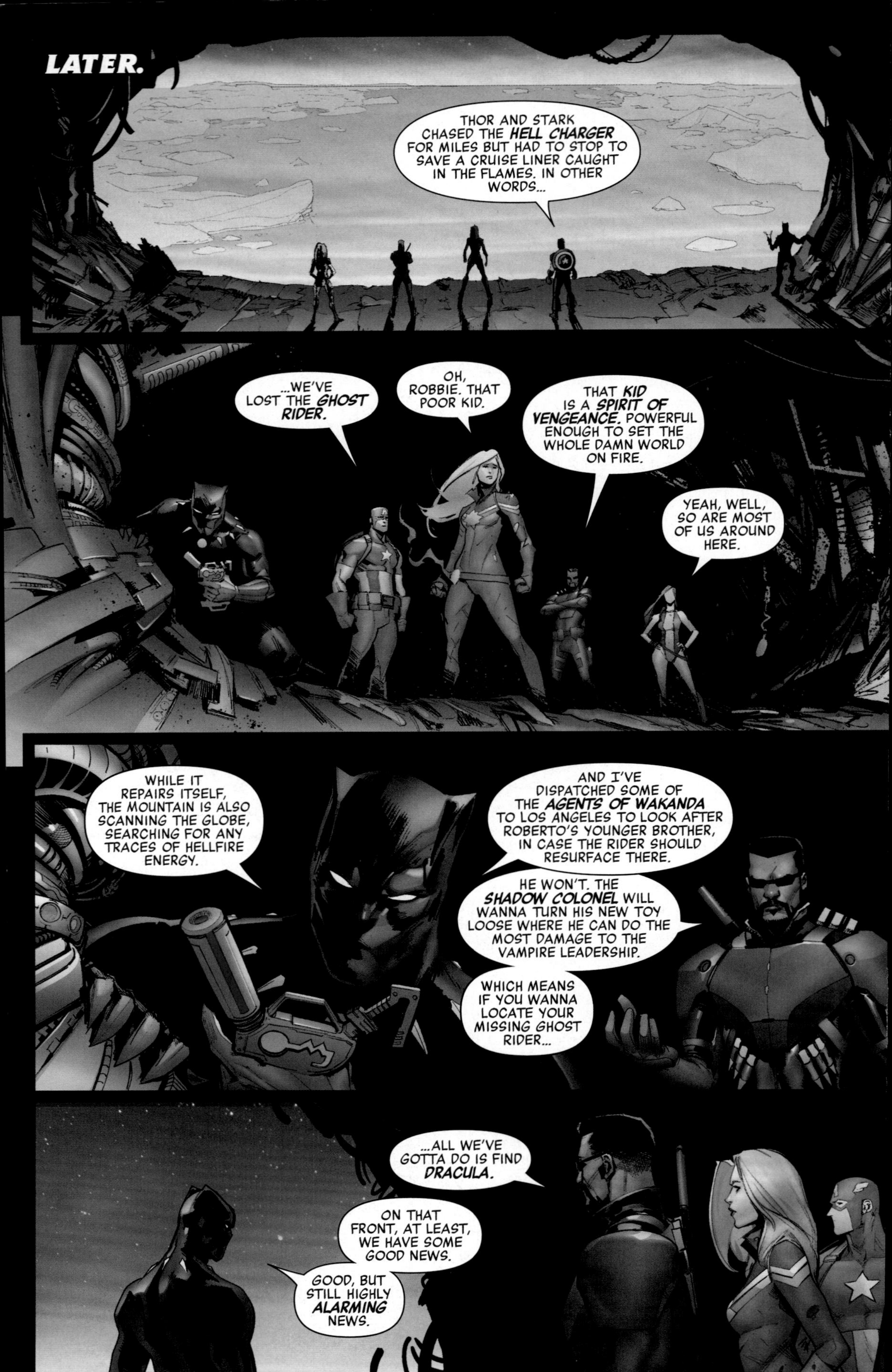
LATER.
THOR AND STARK CHASED THE HELL CHARGER FOR MILES BUT HAD TO STOP TO SAVE A CRUISE LINER CAUGHT IN THE FLAMES. IN OTHER WORDS...
...WE'VE LOST THE GHOST RIDER.
OH, ROBBIE. THAT POOR KID.
THAT KID IS A SPIRIT OF VENGEANCE. POWERFUL ENOUGH TO SET THE WHOLE DAMN WORLD ON FIRE.
YEAH, WELL, SO ARE MOST OF US AROUND HERE.
WHILE IT REPAIRS ITSELF, THE MOUNTAIN IS ALSO SCANNING THE GLOBE, SEARCHING FOR ANY TRACES OF HELLFIRE ENERGY.
AND I'VE DISPATCHED SOME OF THE AGENTS OF WAKANDA TO LOS ANGELES TO LOOK AFTER ROBERTO'S YOUNGER BROTHER, IN CASE THE RIDER SHOULD RESURFACE THERE.
HE WON'T. THE SHADOW COLONEL WILL WANNA TURN HIS NEW TOY LOOSE WHERE HE CAN DO THE MOST DAMAGE TO THE VAMPIRE LEADERSHIP.
WHICH MEANS IF YOU WANNA LOCATE YOUR MISSING GHOST RIDER...
...ALL WE'VE GOTTA DO IS FIND DRACULA.
ON THAT FRONT, AT LEAST, WE HAVE SOME GOOD NEWS.
GOOD, BUT STILL HIGHLY ALARMING NEWS.

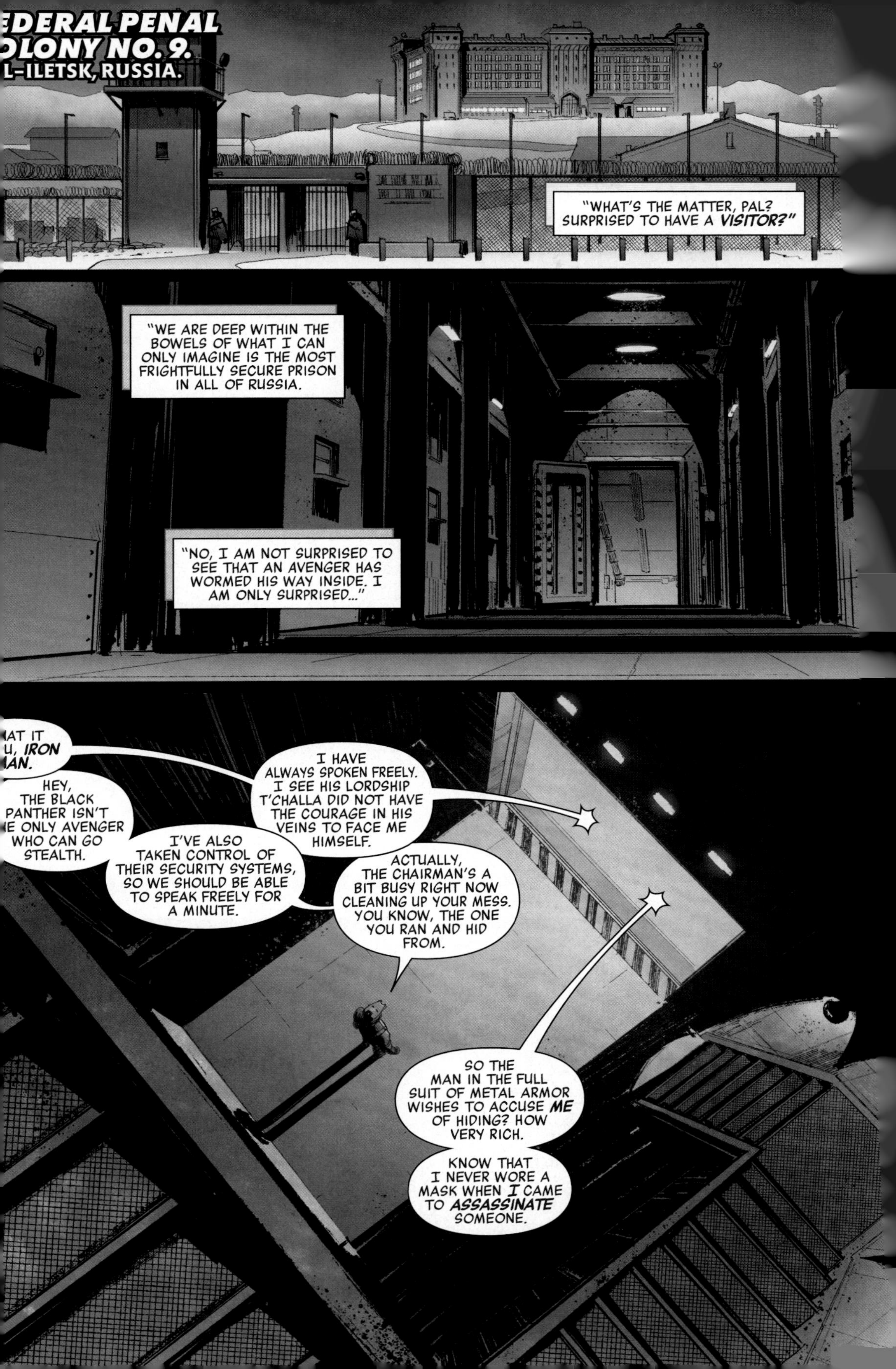
EDERAL PENAL
OLONY NO. 9.
L-ILETSK, RUSSIA.
"WHAT'S THE MATTER, PAL? SURPRISED TO HAVE A *VISITOR?*"
"WE ARE DEEP WITHIN THE BOWELS OF WHAT I CAN ONLY IMAGINE IS THE MOST FRIGHTFULLY SECURE PRISON IN ALL OF RUSSIA.
"NO, I AM NOT SURPRISED TO SEE THAT AN AVENGER HAS WORMED HIS WAY INSIDE. I AM ONLY SURPRISED..."
AT IT U, *IRON AN.*
I HAVE ALWAYS SPOKEN FREELY. I SEE HIS LORDSHIP T'CHALLA DID NOT HAVE THE COURAGE IN HIS VEINS TO FACE ME HIMSELF.
HEY, THE BLACK PANTHER ISN'T E ONLY AVENGER WHO CAN GO STEALTH.
I'VE ALSO TAKEN CONTROL OF THEIR SECURITY SYSTEMS, SO WE SHOULD BE ABLE TO SPEAK FREELY FOR A MINUTE.
ACTUALLY, THE CHAIRMAN'S A BIT BUSY RIGHT NOW CLEANING UP YOUR MESS. YOU KNOW, THE ONE YOU RAN AND HID FROM.
SO THE MAN IN THE FULL SUIT OF METAL ARMOR WISHES TO ACCUSE *ME* OF HIDING? HOW VERY RICH.
KNOW THAT I NEVER WORE A MASK WHEN *I* CAME TO *ASSASSINATE* SOMEONE.

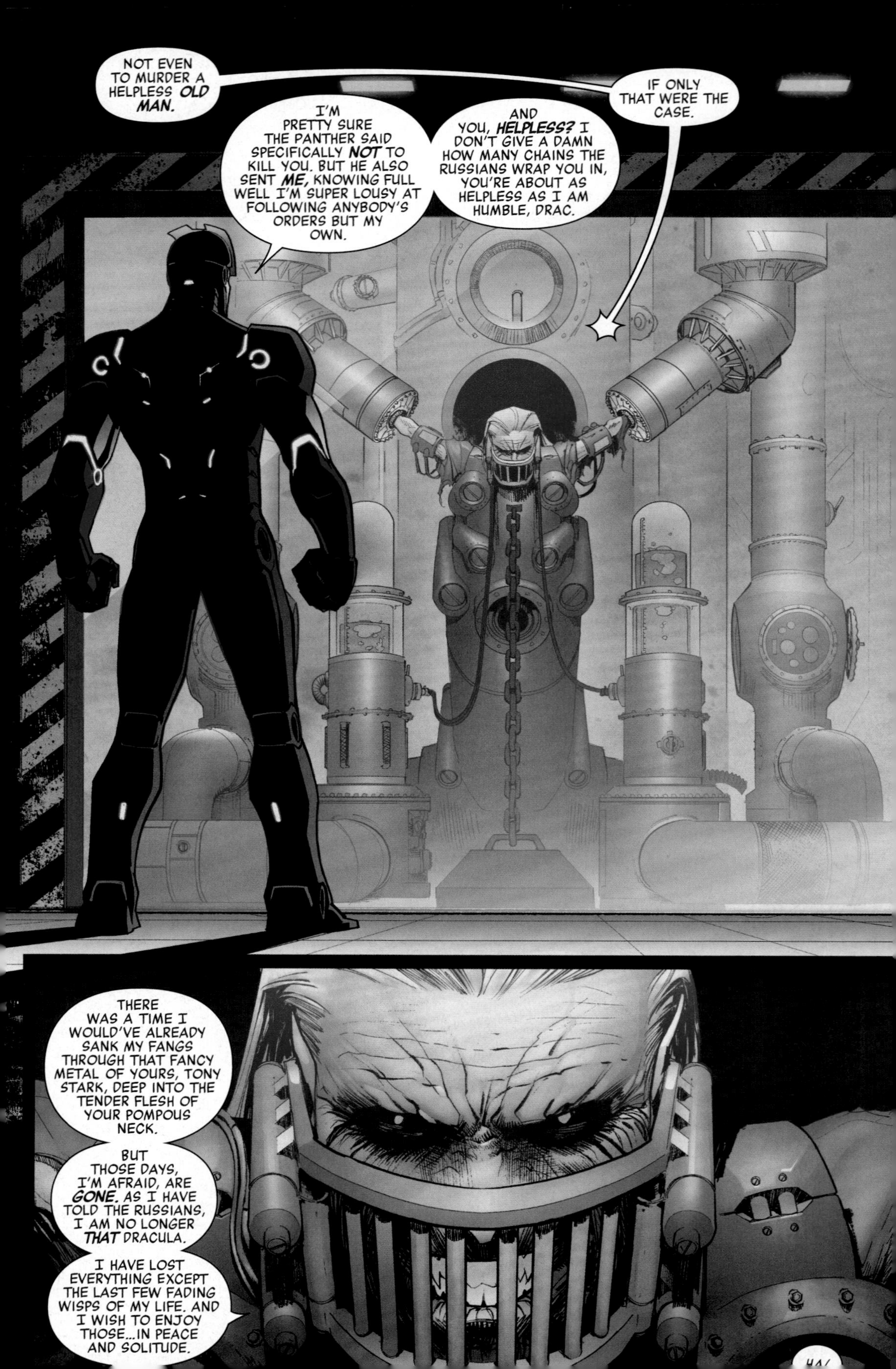
NOT EVEN TO MURDER A HELPLESS OLD MAN.
I'M PRETTY SURE THE PANTHER SAID SPECIFICALLY NOT TO KILL YOU. BUT HE ALSO SENT ME, KNOWING FULL WELL I'M SUPER LOUSY AT FOLLOWING ANYBODY'S ORDERS BUT MY OWN.
AND YOU, HELPLESS? I DON'T GIVE A DAMN HOW MANY CHAINS THE RUSSIANS WRAP YOU IN, YOU'RE ABOUT AS HELPLESS AS I AM HUMBLE, DRAC.
IF ONLY THAT WERE THE CASE.
THERE WAS A TIME I WOULD'VE ALREADY SANK MY FANGS THROUGH THAT FANCY METAL OF YOURS, TONY STARK, DEEP INTO THE TENDER FLESH OF YOUR POMPOUS NECK.
BUT THOSE DAYS, I'M AFRAID, ARE GONE. AS I HAVE TOLD THE RUSSIANS, I AM NO LONGER THAT DRACULA.
I HAVE LOST EVERYTHING EXCEPT THE LAST FEW FADING WISPS OF MY LIFE. AND I WISH TO ENJOY THOSE...IN PEACE AND SOLITUDE.

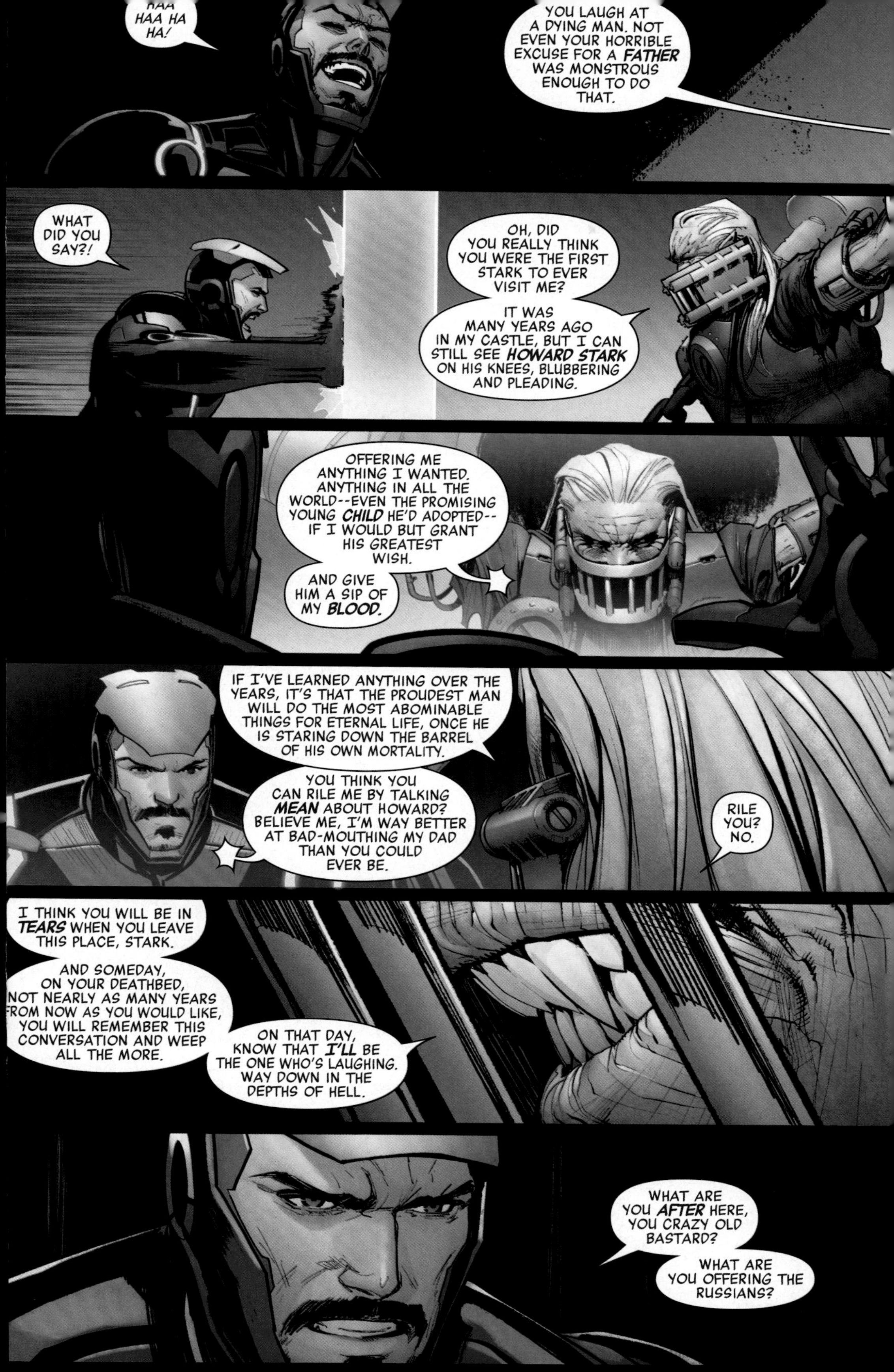
HAA HAA HA HA!
YOU LAUGH AT A DYING MAN. NOT EVEN YOUR HORRIBLE EXCUSE FOR A FATHER WAS MONSTROUS ENOUGH TO DO THAT.
WHAT DID YOU SAY?!
OH, DID YOU REALLY THINK YOU WERE THE FIRST STARK TO EVER VISIT ME?
IT WAS MANY YEARS AGO IN MY CASTLE, BUT I CAN STILL SEE HOWARD STARK ON HIS KNEES, BLUBBERING AND PLEADING.
OFFERING ME ANYTHING I WANTED. ANYTHING IN ALL THE WORLD--EVEN THE PROMISING YOUNG CHILD HE'D ADOPTED--IF I WOULD BUT GRANT HIS GREATEST WISH.
AND GIVE HIM A SIP OF MY BLOOD.
IF I'VE LEARNED ANYTHING OVER THE YEARS, IT'S THAT THE PROUDEST MAN WILL DO THE MOST ABOMINABLE THINGS FOR ETERNAL LIFE, ONCE HE IS STARING DOWN THE BARREL OF HIS OWN MORTALITY.
YOU THINK YOU CAN RILE ME BY TALKING MEAN ABOUT HOWARD? BELIEVE ME, I'M WAY BETTER AT BAD-MOUTHING MY DAD THAN YOU COULD EVER BE.
RILE YOU? NO.
I THINK YOU WILL BE IN TEARS WHEN YOU LEAVE THIS PLACE, STARK.
AND SOMEDAY, ON YOUR DEATHBED, NOT NEARLY AS MANY YEARS FROM NOW AS YOU WOULD LIKE, YOU WILL REMEMBER THIS CONVERSATION AND WEEP ALL THE MORE.
ON THAT DAY, KNOW THAT I'LL BE THE ONE WHO'S LAUGHING. WAY DOWN IN THE DEPTHS OF HELL.
WHAT ARE YOU AFTER HERE, YOU CRAZY OLD BASTARD?
WHAT ARE YOU OFFERING THE RUSSIANS?

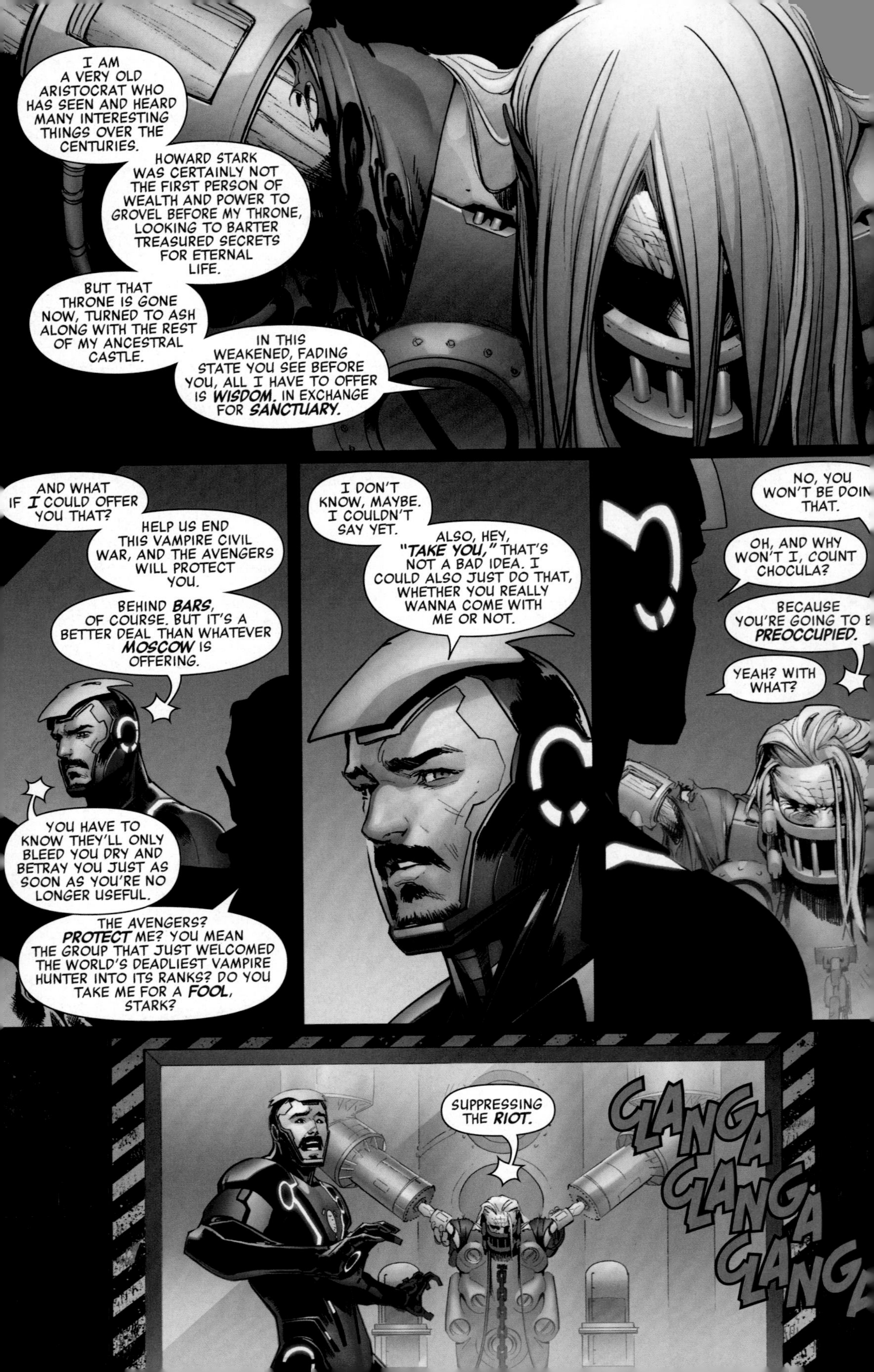

I AM A VERY OLD ARISTOCRAT WHO HAS SEEN AND HEARD MANY INTERESTING THINGS OVER THE CENTURIES.
HOWARD STARK WAS CERTAINLY NOT THE FIRST PERSON OF WEALTH AND POWER TO GROVEL BEFORE MY THRONE, LOOKING TO BARTER TREASURED SECRETS FOR ETERNAL LIFE.
BUT THAT THRONE IS GONE NOW, TURNED TO ASH ALONG WITH THE REST OF MY ANCESTRAL CASTLE.
IN THIS WEAKENED, FADING STATE YOU SEE BEFORE YOU, ALL I HAVE TO OFFER IS **WISDOM.** IN EXCHANGE FOR **SANCTUARY.**
AND WHAT IF ***I*** COULD OFFER YOU THAT?
HELP US END THIS VAMPIRE CIVIL WAR, AND THE AVENGERS WILL PROTECT YOU.
BEHIND **BARS,** OF COURSE. BUT IT'S A BETTER DEAL THAN WHATEVER **MOSCOW** IS OFFERING.
YOU HAVE TO KNOW THEY'LL ONLY BLEED YOU DRY AND BETRAY YOU JUST AS SOON AS YOU'RE NO LONGER USEFUL.
THE AVENGERS? **PROTECT** ME? YOU MEAN THE GROUP THAT JUST WELCOMED THE WORLD'S DEADLIEST VAMPIRE HUNTER INTO ITS RANKS? DO YOU TAKE ME FOR A **FOOL,** STARK?
I DON'T KNOW, MAYBE. I COULDN'T SAY YET.
ALSO, HEY, **"TAKE YOU,"** THAT'S NOT A BAD IDEA. I COULD ALSO JUST DO THAT, WHETHER YOU REALLY WANNA COME WITH ME OR NOT.
NO, YOU WON'T BE DOIN THAT.
OH, AND WHY WON'T I, COUNT CHOCULA?
BECAUSE YOU'RE GOING TO BE **PREOCCUPIED.**
YEAH? WITH WHAT?
SUPPRESSING THE **RIOT.**
CLANGA CLANGA CLANGA

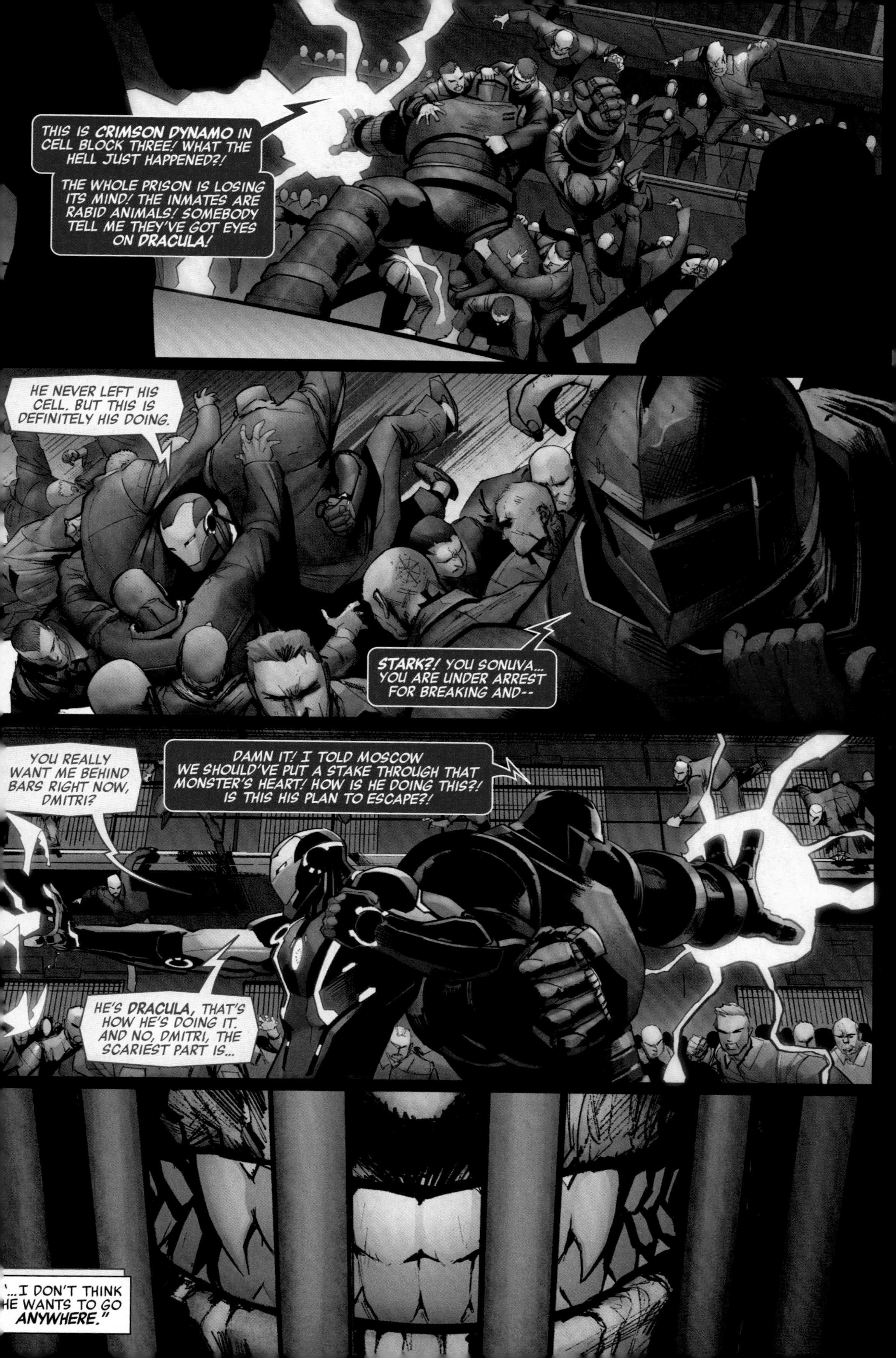
THIS IS CRIMSON DYNAMO IN CELL BLOCK THREE! WHAT THE HELL JUST HAPPENED?!
THE WHOLE PRISON IS LOSING ITS MIND! THE INMATES ARE RABID ANIMALS! SOMEBODY TELL ME THEY'VE GOT EYES ON DRACULA!
HE NEVER LEFT HIS CELL. BUT THIS IS DEFINITELY HIS DOING.
STARK?! YOU SONUVA... YOU ARE UNDER ARREST FOR BREAKING AND--
YOU REALLY WANT ME BEHIND BARS RIGHT NOW, DMITRI?
DAMN IT! I TOLD MOSCOW WE SHOULD'VE PUT A STAKE THROUGH THAT MONSTER'S HEART! HOW IS HE DOING THIS?! IS THIS HIS PLAN TO ESCAPE?!
HE'S DRACULA, THAT'S HOW HE'S DOING IT. AND NO, DMITRI, THE SCARIEST PART IS...
"...I DON'T THINK HE WANTS TO GO ANYWHERE."

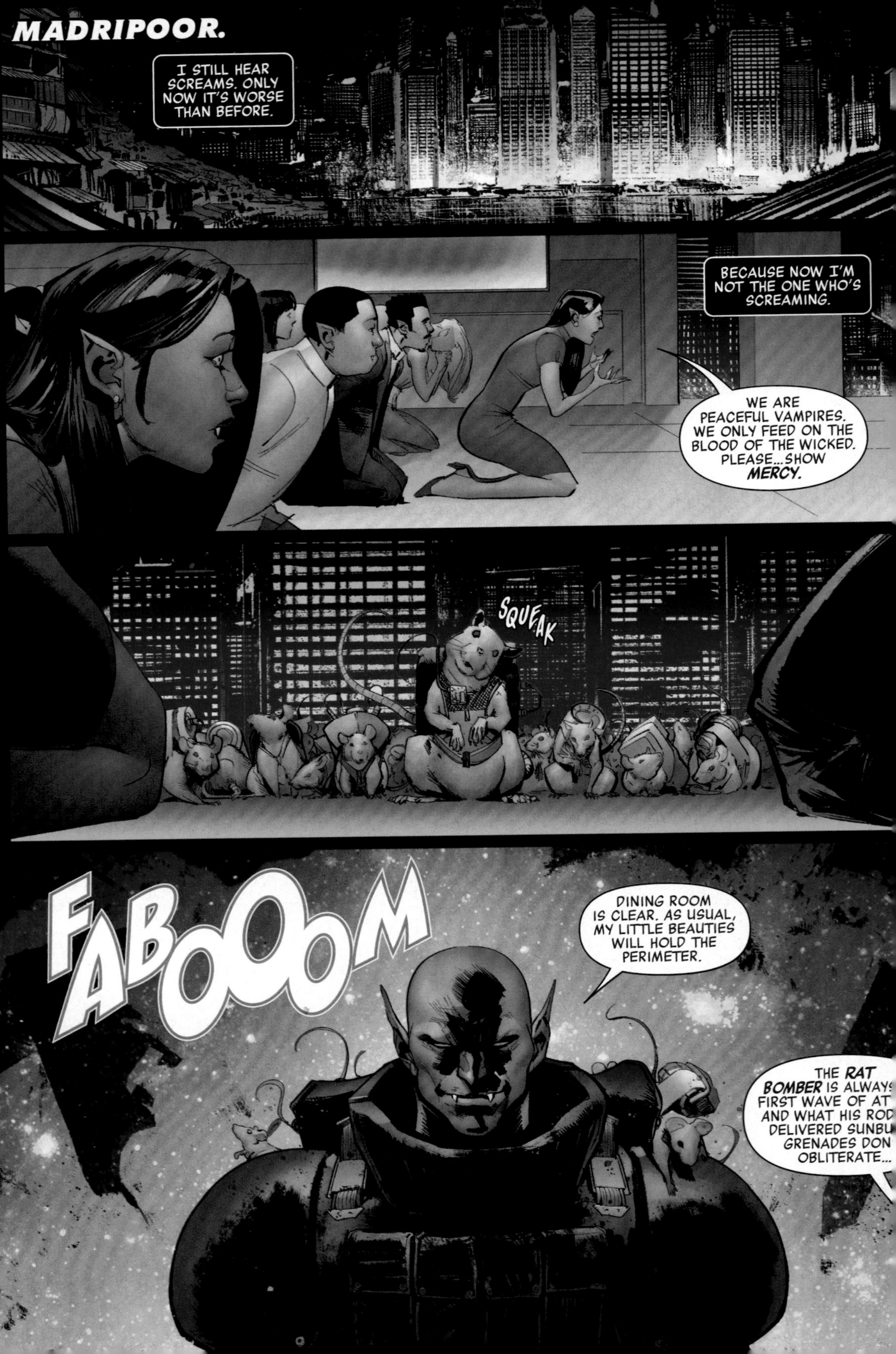
MADRIPOOR.
I STILL HEAR SCREAMS. ONLY NOW IT'S WORSE THAN BEFORE.
BECAUSE NOW I'M NOT THE ONE WHO'S SCREAMING.
WE ARE PEACEFUL VAMPIRES. WE ONLY FEED ON THE BLOOD OF THE WICKED. PLEASE...SHOW MERCY.
SQUEAK
FABOOOOM
DINING ROOM IS CLEAR. AS USUAL, MY LITTLE BEAUTIES WILL HOLD THE PERIMETER.
THE RAT BOMBER IS ALWAYS FIRST WAVE OF AT AND WHAT HIS ROD DELIVERED SUNBU GRENADES DON OBLITERATE...

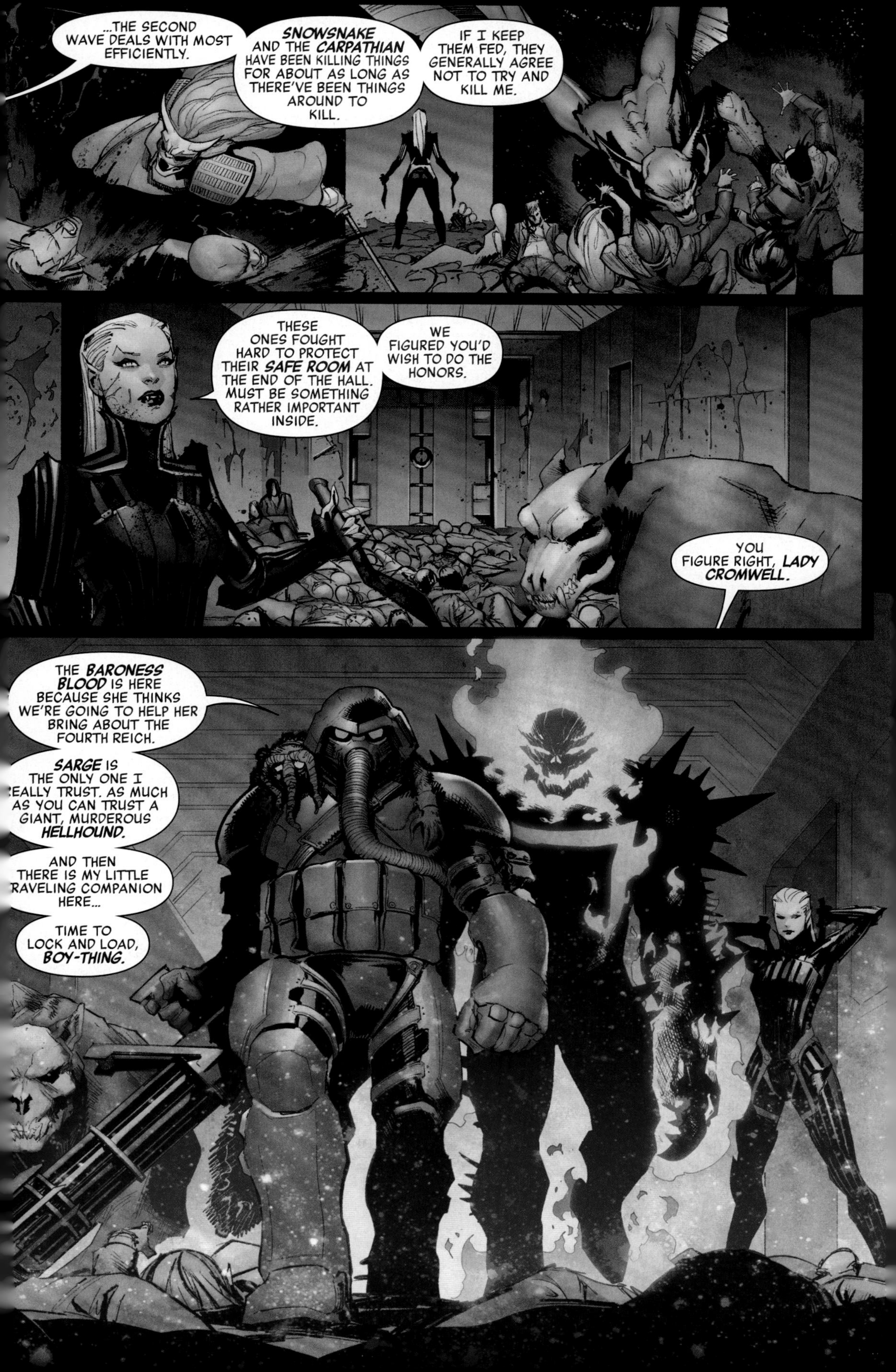
...THE SECOND WAVE DEALS WITH MOST EFFICIENTLY.
SNOWSNAKE AND THE CARPATHIAN HAVE BEEN KILLING THINGS FOR ABOUT AS LONG AS THERE'VE BEEN THINGS AROUND TO KILL.
IF I KEEP THEM FED, THEY GENERALLY AGREE NOT TO TRY AND KILL ME.
THESE ONES FOUGHT HARD TO PROTECT THEIR SAFE ROOM AT THE END OF THE HALL. MUST BE SOMETHING RATHER IMPORTANT INSIDE.
WE FIGURED YOU'D WISH TO DO THE HONORS.
YOU FIGURE RIGHT, LADY CROMWELL.
THE BARONESS BLOOD IS HERE BECAUSE SHE THINKS WE'RE GOING TO HELP HER BRING ABOUT THE FOURTH REICH.
SARGE IS THE ONLY ONE I EALLY TRUST. AS MUCH AS YOU CAN TRUST A GIANT, MURDEROUS HELLHOUND.
AND THEN THERE IS MY LITTLE RAVELING COMPANION HERE...
TIME TO LOCK AND LOAD, BOY-THING.

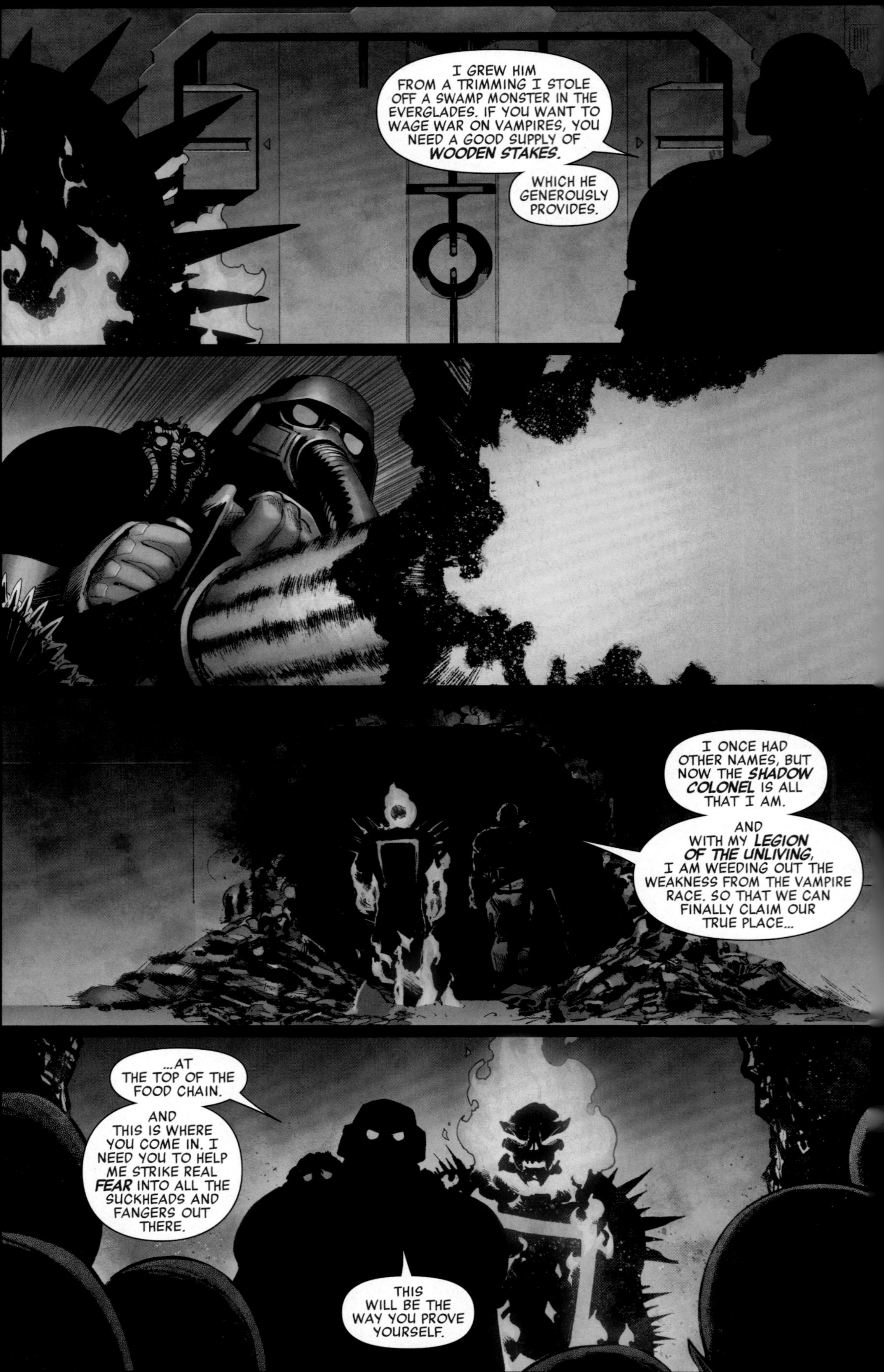
I GREW HIM FROM A TRIMMING I STOLE OFF A SWAMP MONSTER IN THE EVERGLADES. IF YOU WANT TO WAGE WAR ON VAMPIRES, YOU NEED A GOOD SUPPLY OF WOODEN STAKES.
WHICH HE GENEROUSLY PROVIDES.
I ONCE HAD OTHER NAMES, BUT NOW THE SHADOW COLONEL IS ALL THAT I AM.
AND WITH MY LEGION OF THE UNLIVING, I AM WEEDING OUT THE WEAKNESS FROM THE VAMPIRE RACE. SO THAT WE CAN FINALLY CLAIM OUR TRUE PLACE...
...AT THE TOP OF THE FOOD CHAIN.
AND THIS IS WHERE YOU COME IN. I NEED YOU TO HELP ME STRIKE REAL FEAR INTO ALL THE SUCKHEADS AND FANGERS OUT THERE.
THIS WILL BE THE WAY YOU PROVE YOURSELF.

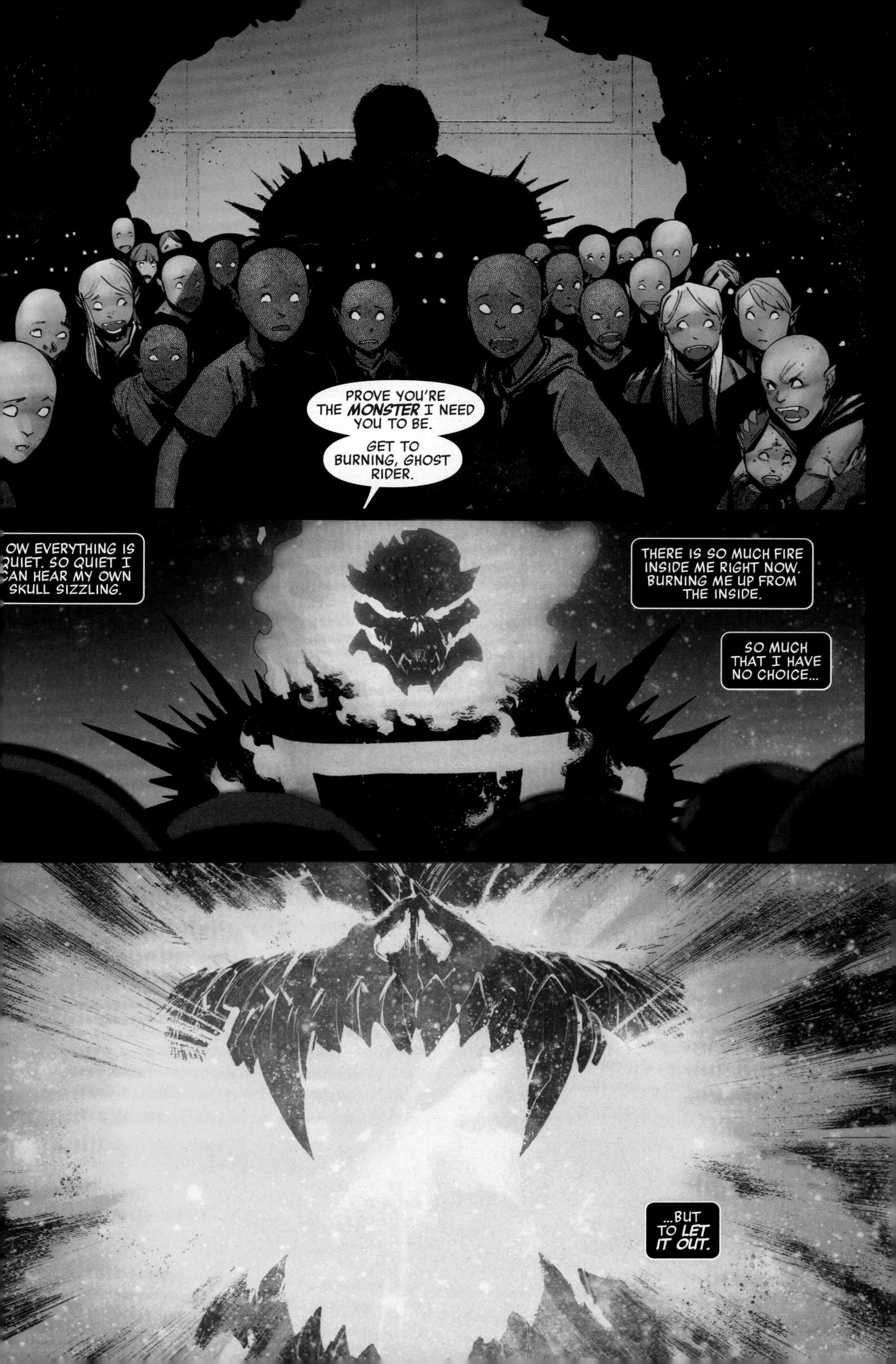
PROVE YOU'RE THE MONSTER I NEED YOU TO BE.
GET TO BURNING, GHOST RIDER.
OW EVERYTHING IS QUIET. SO QUIET I CAN HEAR MY OWN SKULL SIZZLING.
THERE IS SO MUCH FIRE INSIDE ME RIGHT NOW. BURNING ME UP FROM THE INSIDE.
SO MUCH THAT I HAVE NO CHOICE...
...BUT TO LET IT OUT.

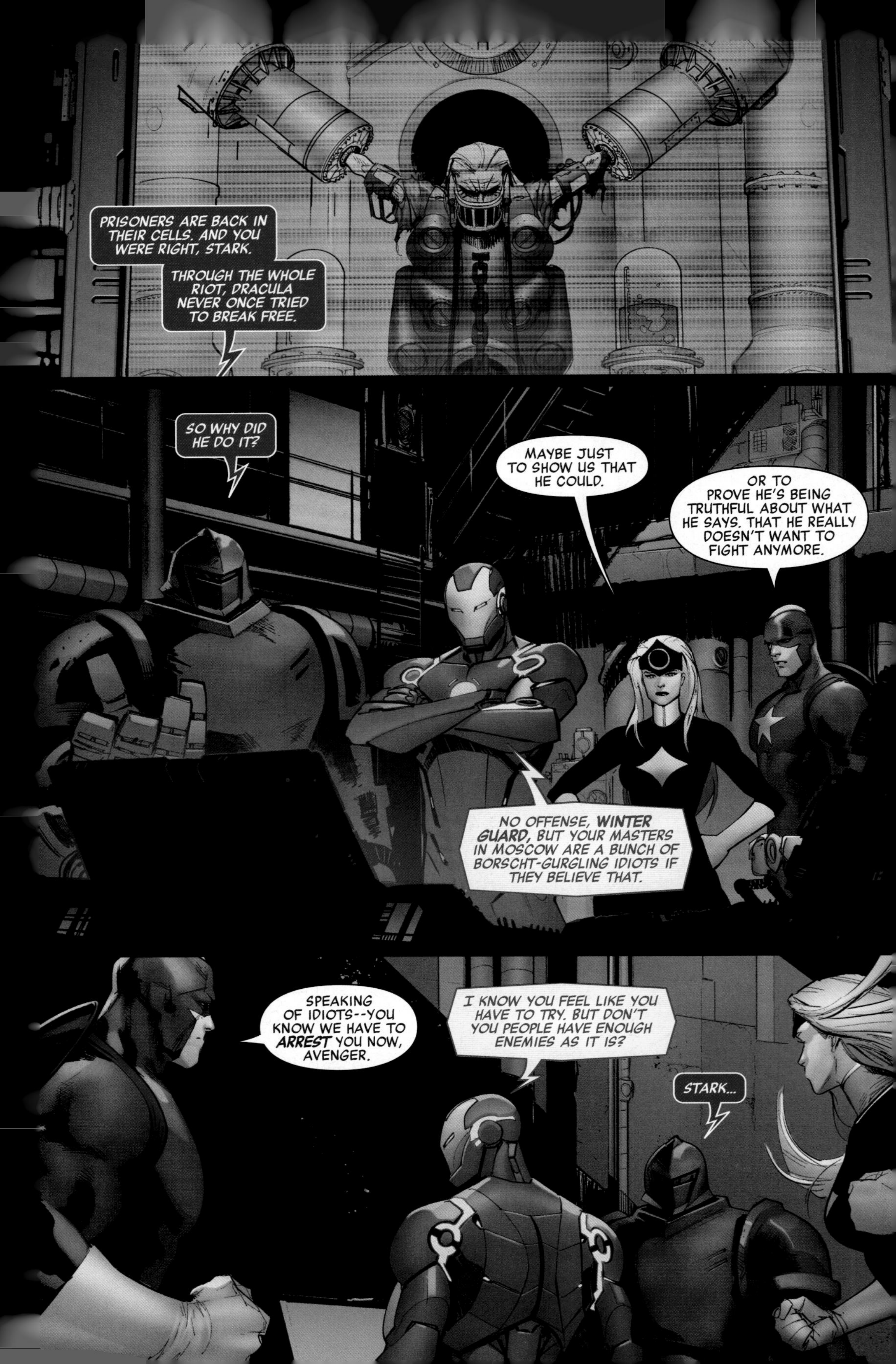
PRISONERS ARE BACK IN THEIR CELLS. AND YOU WERE RIGHT, STARK.
THROUGH THE WHOLE RIOT, DRACULA NEVER ONCE TRIED TO BREAK FREE.
SO WHY DID HE DO IT?
MAYBE JUST TO SHOW US THAT HE COULD.
OR TO PROVE HE'S BEING TRUTHFUL ABOUT WHAT HE SAYS. THAT HE REALLY DOESN'T WANT TO FIGHT ANYMORE.
NO OFFENSE, WINTER GUARD, BUT YOUR MASTERS IN MOSCOW ARE A BUNCH OF BORSCHT-GURGLING IDIOTS IF THEY BELIEVE THAT.
SPEAKING OF IDIOTS--YOU KNOW WE HAVE TO ARREST YOU NOW, AVENGER.
I KNOW YOU FEEL LIKE YOU HAVE TO TRY. BUT DON'T YOU PEOPLE HAVE ENOUGH ENEMIES AS IT IS?
STARK...

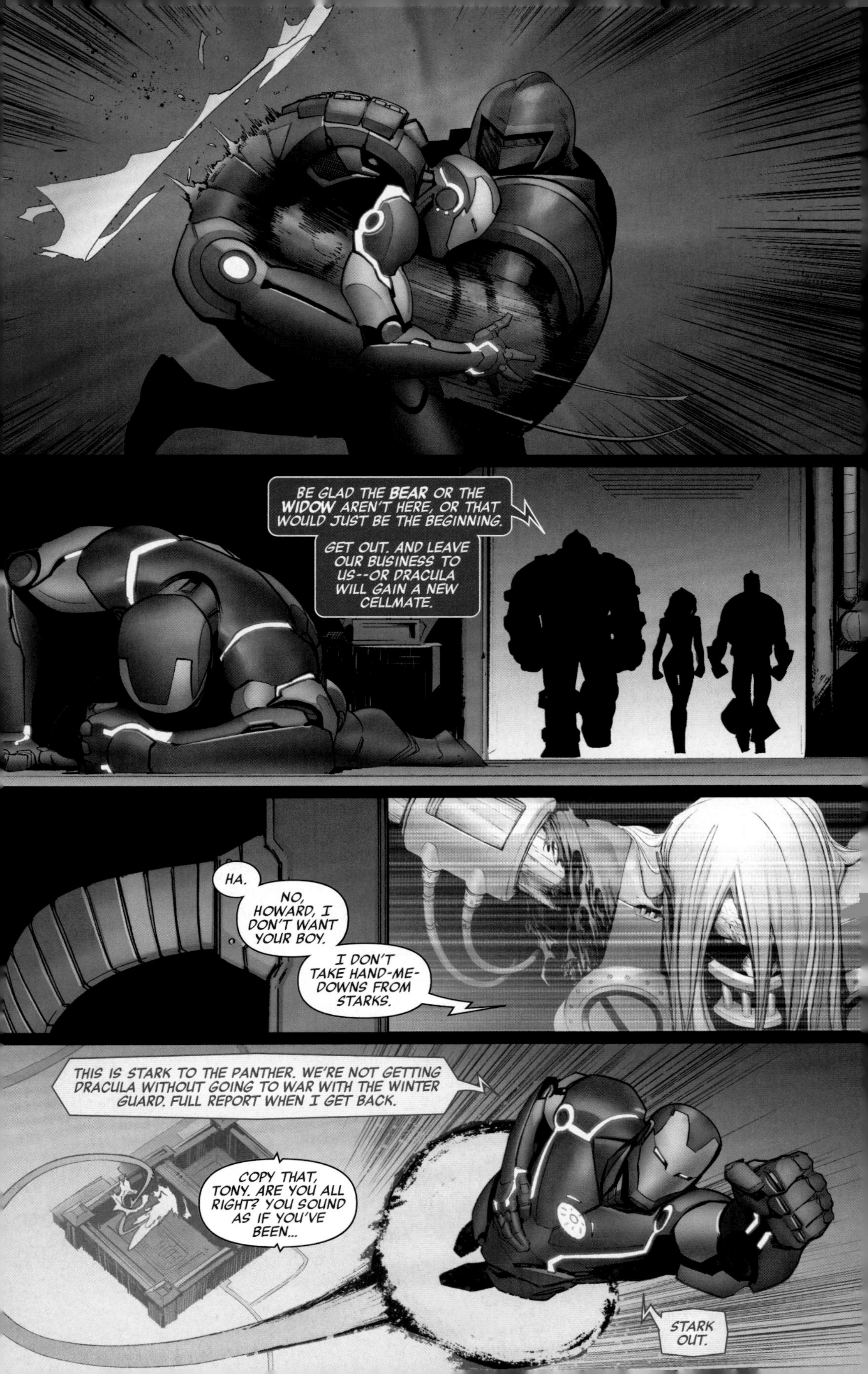
BE GLAD THE BEAR OR THE WIDOW AREN'T HERE, OR THAT WOULD JUST BE THE BEGINNING.
GET OUT. AND LEAVE OUR BUSINESS TO US--OR DRACULA WILL GAIN A NEW CELLMATE.
HA.
NO, HOWARD, I DON'T WANT YOUR BOY.
I DON'T TAKE HAND-ME-DOWNS FROM STARKS.
THIS IS STARK TO THE PANTHER. WE'RE NOT GETTING DRACULA WITHOUT GOING TO WAR WITH THE WINTER GUARD. FULL REPORT WHEN I GET BACK.
COPY THAT, TONY. ARE YOU ALL RIGHT? YOU SOUND AS IF YOU'VE BEEN...
STARK OUT.

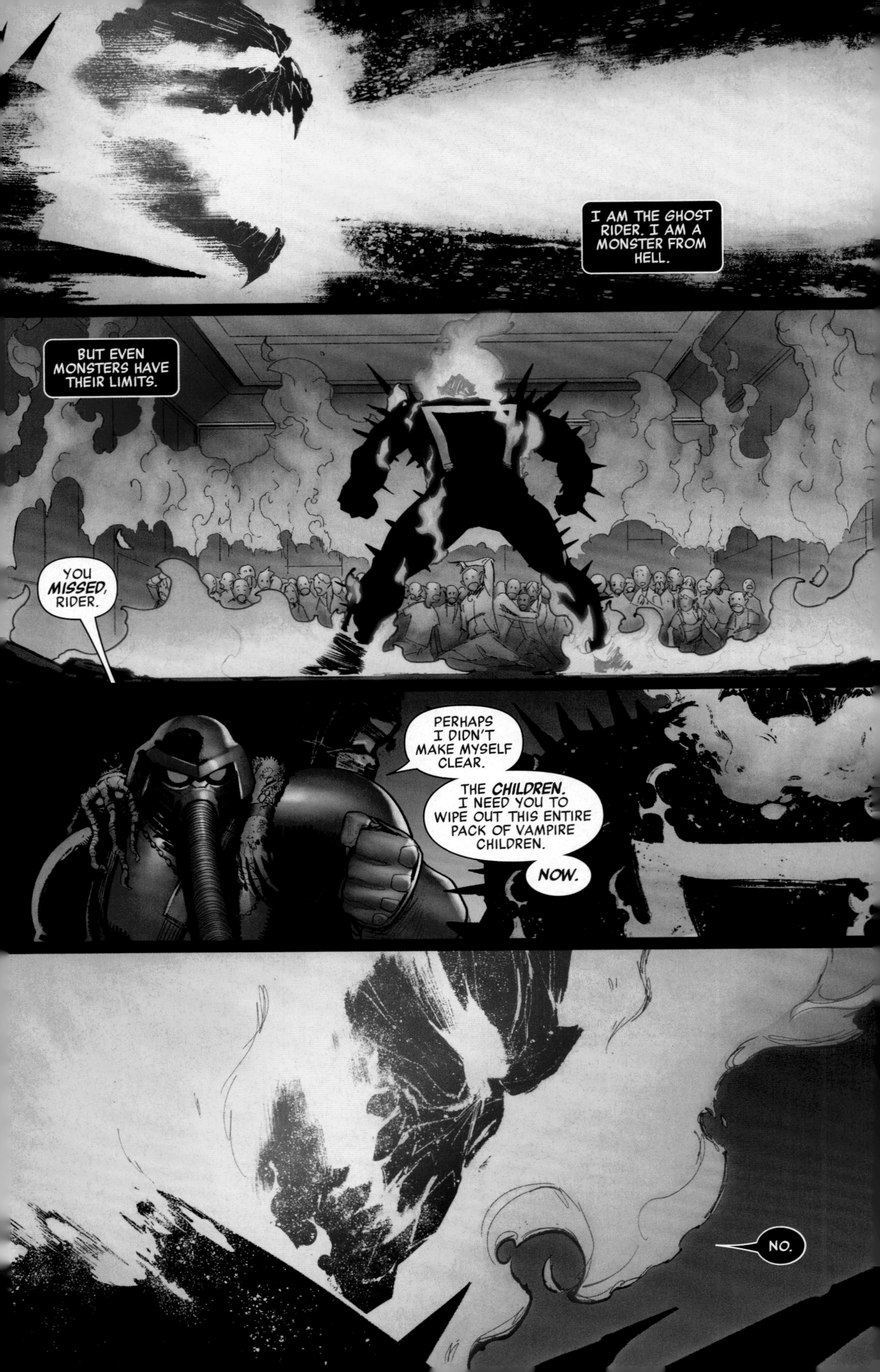
I AM THE GHOST RIDER. I AM A MONSTER FROM HELL.
BUT EVEN MONSTERS HAVE THEIR LIMITS.
YOU MISSED, RIDER.
PERHAPS I DIDN'T MAKE MYSELF CLEAR.
THE CHILDREN. I NEED YOU TO WIPE OUT THIS ENTIRE PACK OF VAMPIRE CHILDREN.
NOW.
NO.

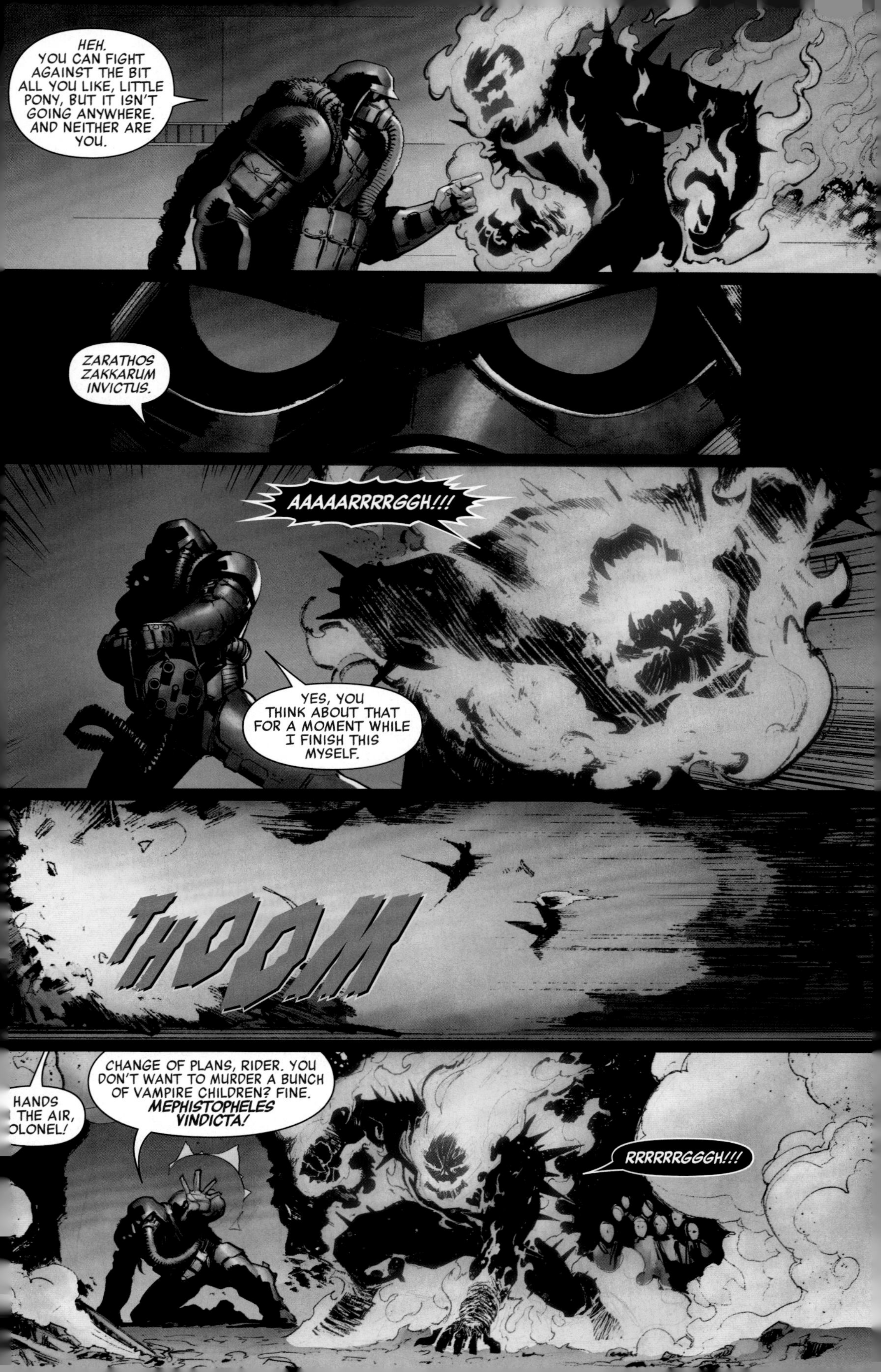
HEH. YOU CAN FIGHT AGAINST THE BIT ALL YOU LIKE, LITTLE PONY, BUT IT ISN'T GOING ANYWHERE. AND NEITHER ARE YOU.
ZARATHOS ZAKKARUM INVICTUS.
AAAAARRRRGGH!!!
YES, YOU THINK ABOUT THAT FOR A MOMENT WHILE I FINISH THIS MYSELF.
THOOM
HANDS THE AIR, OLONEL!
CHANGE OF PLANS, RIDER. YOU DON'T WANT TO MURDER A BUNCH OF VAMPIRE CHILDREN? FINE. MEPHISTOPHELES VINDICTA!
RRRRRRGGGH!!!

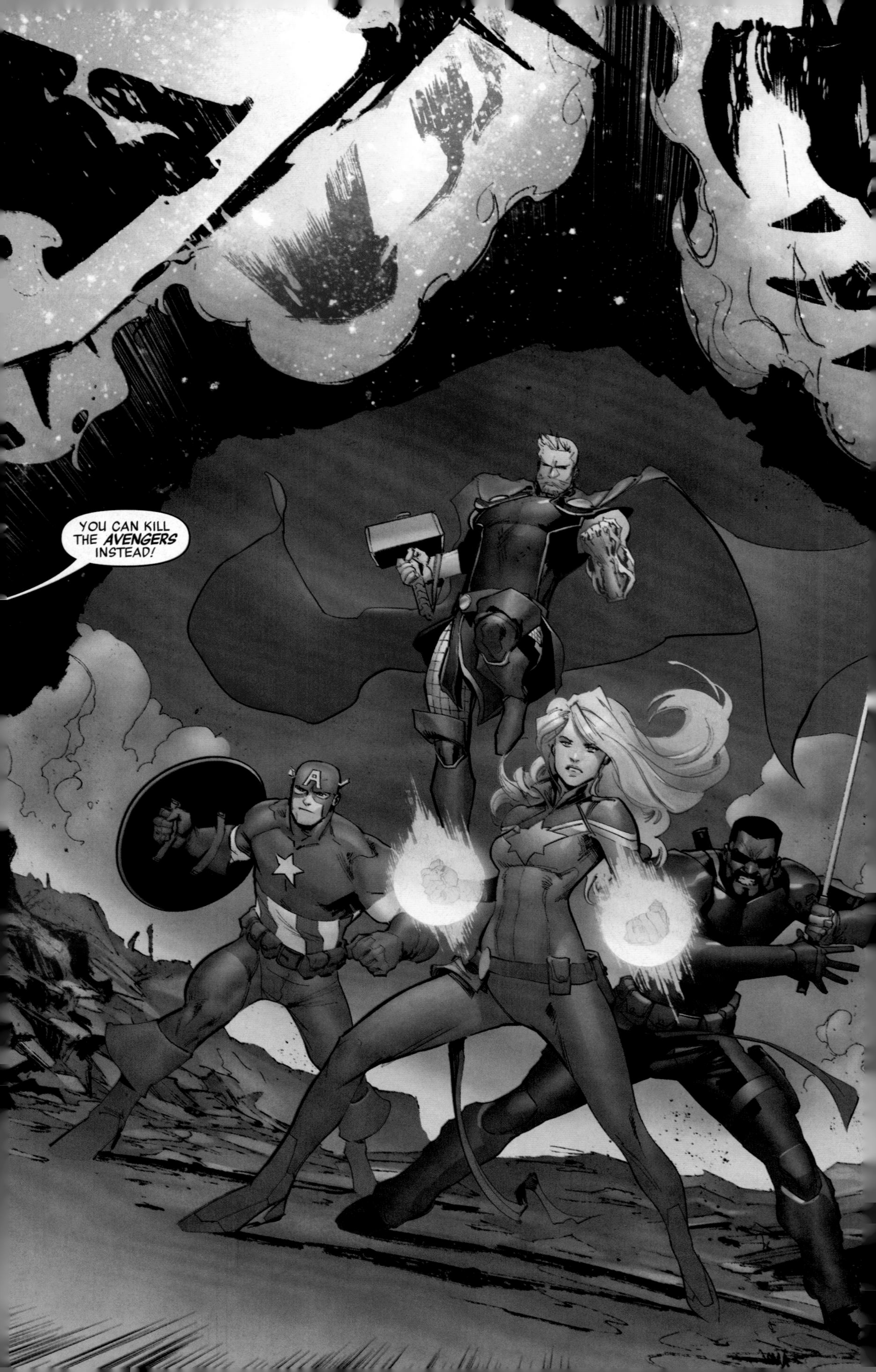
YOU CAN KILL THE AVENGERS INSTEAD!

A FISTFUL OF BLOOD

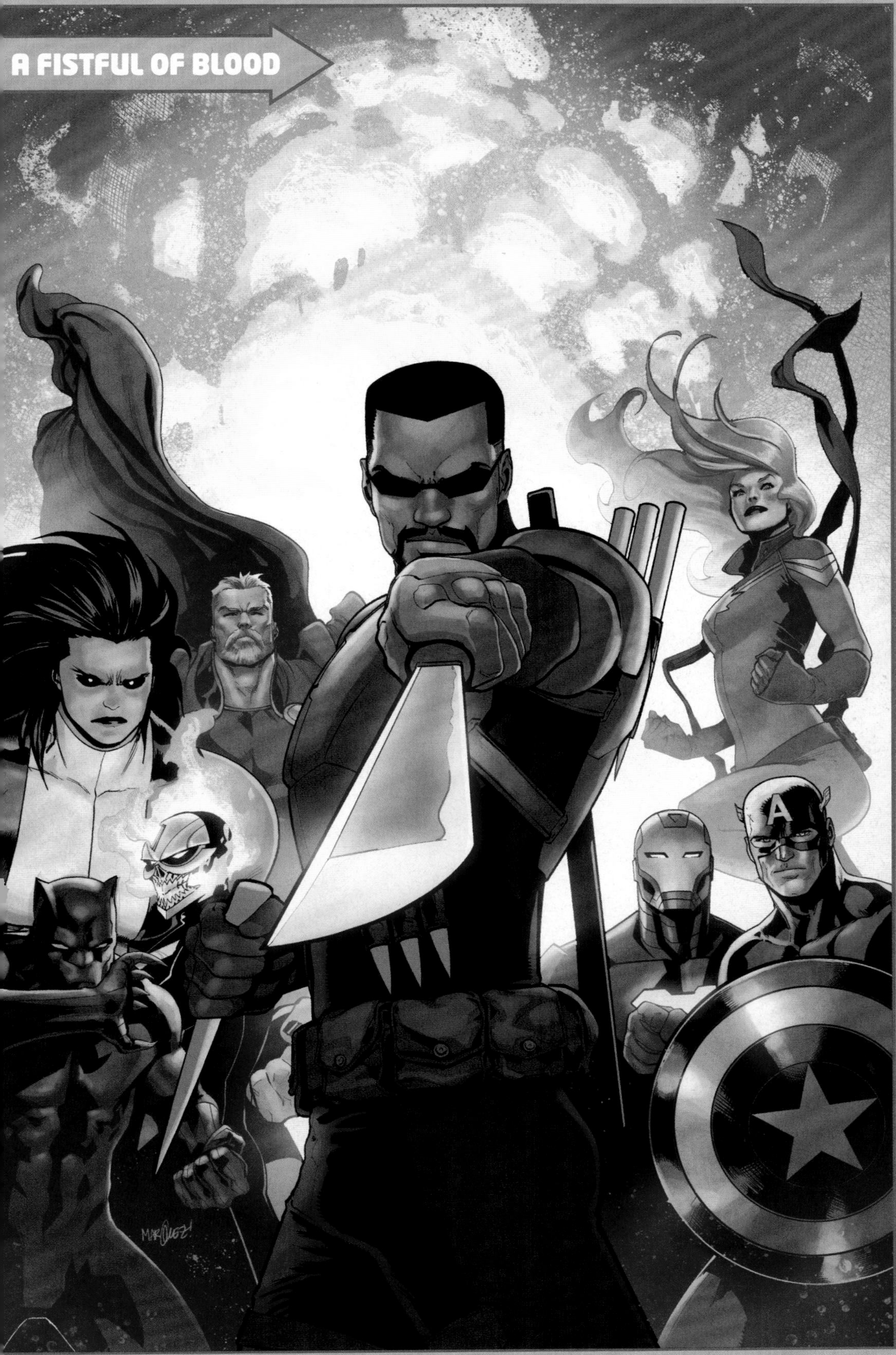
MARQUEZ!

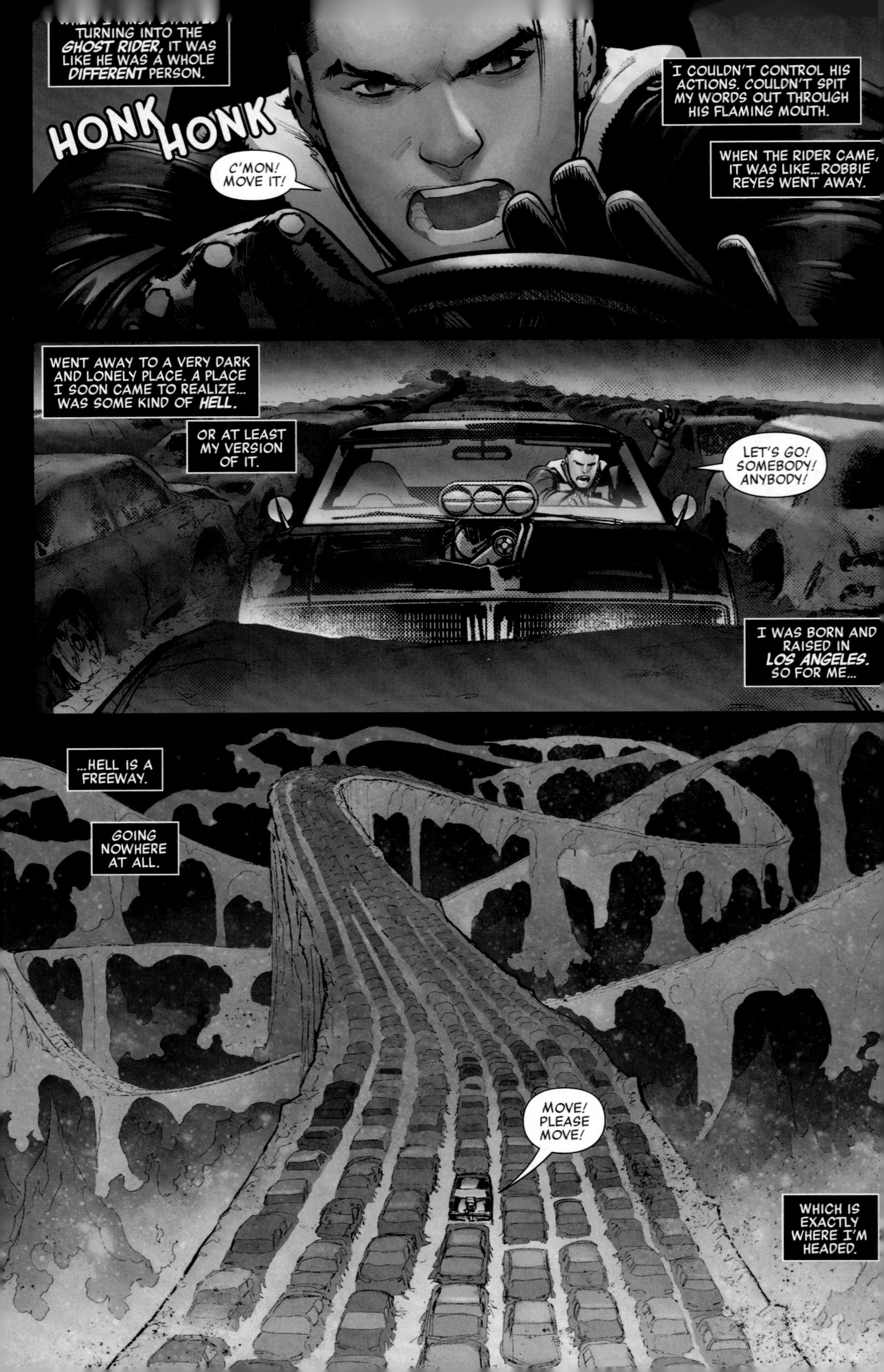
TURNING INTO THE GHOST RIDER, IT WAS LIKE HE WAS A WHOLE DIFFERENT PERSON.
HONK HONK
C'MON! MOVE IT!
I COULDN'T CONTROL HIS ACTIONS. COULDN'T SPIT MY WORDS OUT THROUGH HIS FLAMING MOUTH.
WHEN THE RIDER CAME, IT WAS LIKE...ROBBIE REYES WENT AWAY.
WENT AWAY TO A VERY DARK AND LONELY PLACE. A PLACE I SOON CAME TO REALIZE... WAS SOME KIND OF HELL.
OR AT LEAST MY VERSION OF IT.
LET'S GO! SOMEBODY! ANYBODY!
I WAS BORN AND RAISED IN LOS ANGELES. SO FOR ME...
...HELL IS A FREEWAY.
GOING NOWHERE AT ALL.
MOVE! PLEASE MOVE!
WHICH IS EXACTLY WHERE I'M HEADED.

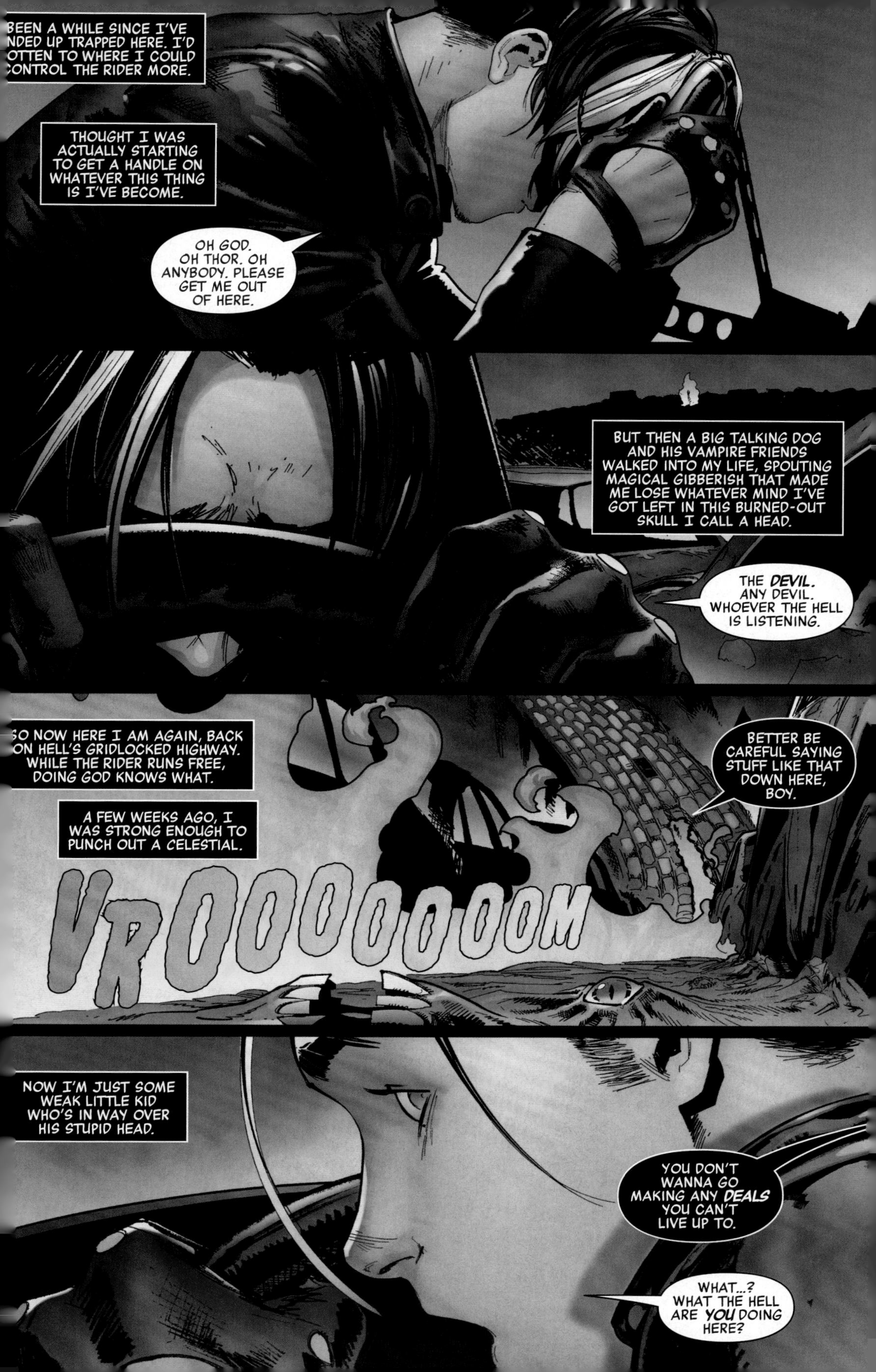
BEEN A WHILE SINCE I'VE ENDED UP TRAPPED HERE. I'D GOTTEN TO WHERE I COULD CONTROL THE RIDER MORE.
THOUGHT I WAS ACTUALLY STARTING TO GET A HANDLE ON WHATEVER THIS THING IS I'VE BECOME.
OH GOD. OH THOR. OH ANYBODY. PLEASE GET ME OUT OF HERE.
BUT THEN A BIG TALKING DOG AND HIS VAMPIRE FRIENDS WALKED INTO MY LIFE, SPOUTING MAGICAL GIBBERISH THAT MADE ME LOSE WHATEVER MIND I'VE GOT LEFT IN THIS BURNED-OUT SKULL I CALL A HEAD.
THE DEVIL. ANY DEVIL. WHOEVER THE HELL IS LISTENING.
SO NOW HERE I AM AGAIN, BACK ON HELL'S GRIDLOCKED HIGHWAY. WHILE THE RIDER RUNS FREE, DOING GOD KNOWS WHAT.
A FEW WEEKS AGO, I WAS STRONG ENOUGH TO PUNCH OUT A CELESTIAL.
BETTER BE CAREFUL SAYING STUFF LIKE THAT DOWN HERE, BOY.
VROOOOOOOM
NOW I'M JUST SOME WEAK LITTLE KID WHO'S IN WAY OVER HIS STUPID HEAD.
YOU DON'T WANNA GO MAKING ANY DEALS YOU CAN'T LIVE UP TO.
WHAT...? WHAT THE HELL ARE YOU DOING HERE?

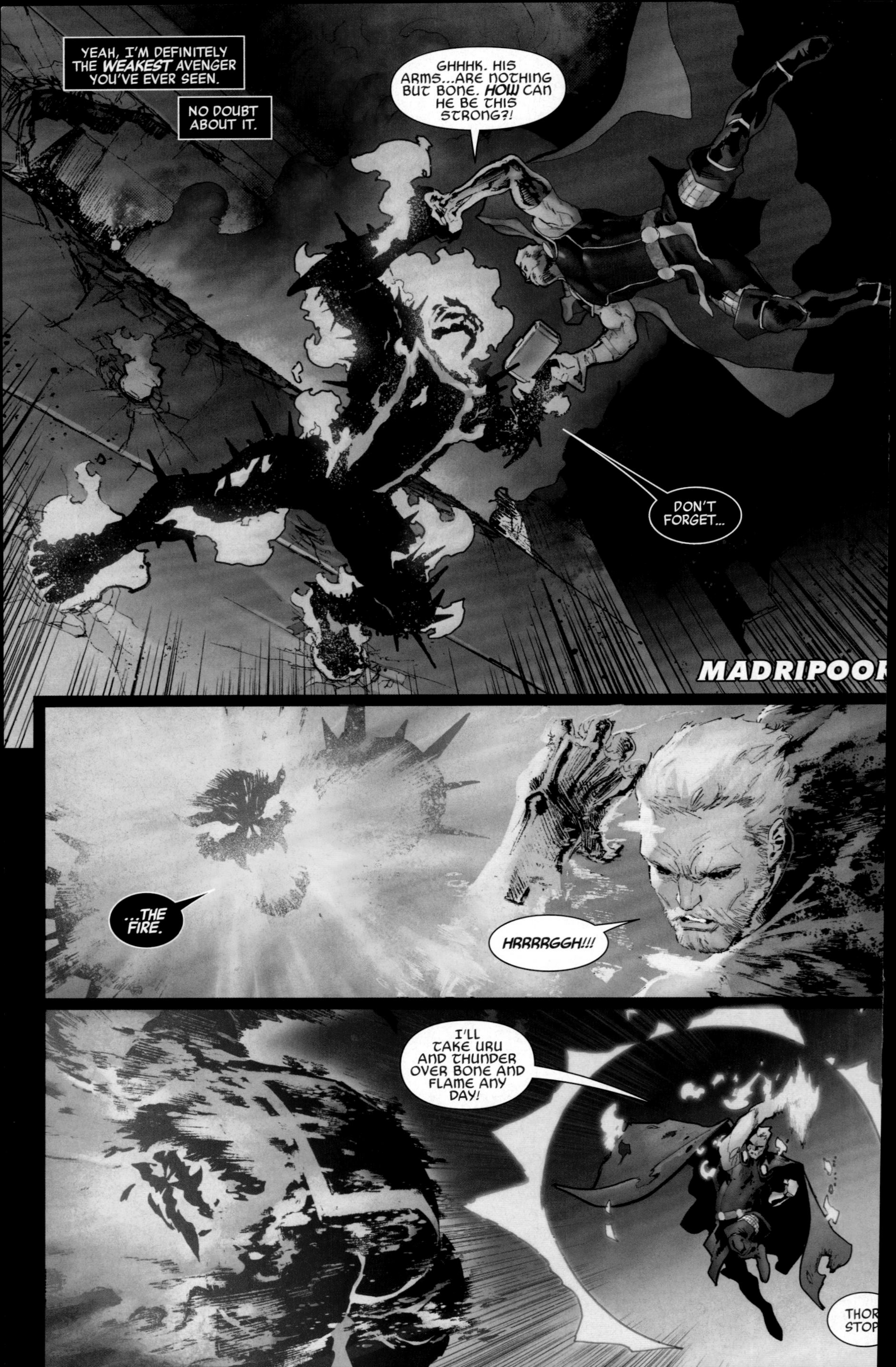

YEAH, I'M DEFINITELY THE WEAKEST AVENGER YOU'VE EVER SEEN.
NO DOUBT ABOUT IT.
GHHHK. HIS ARMS...ARE NOTHING BUT BONE. HOW CAN HE BE THIS STRONG?!
DON'T FORGET...
MADRIPOOR
...THE FIRE.
HRRRRGGH!!!
I'LL TAKE URU AND THUNDER OVER BONE AND FLAME ANY DAY!
THOR STOP

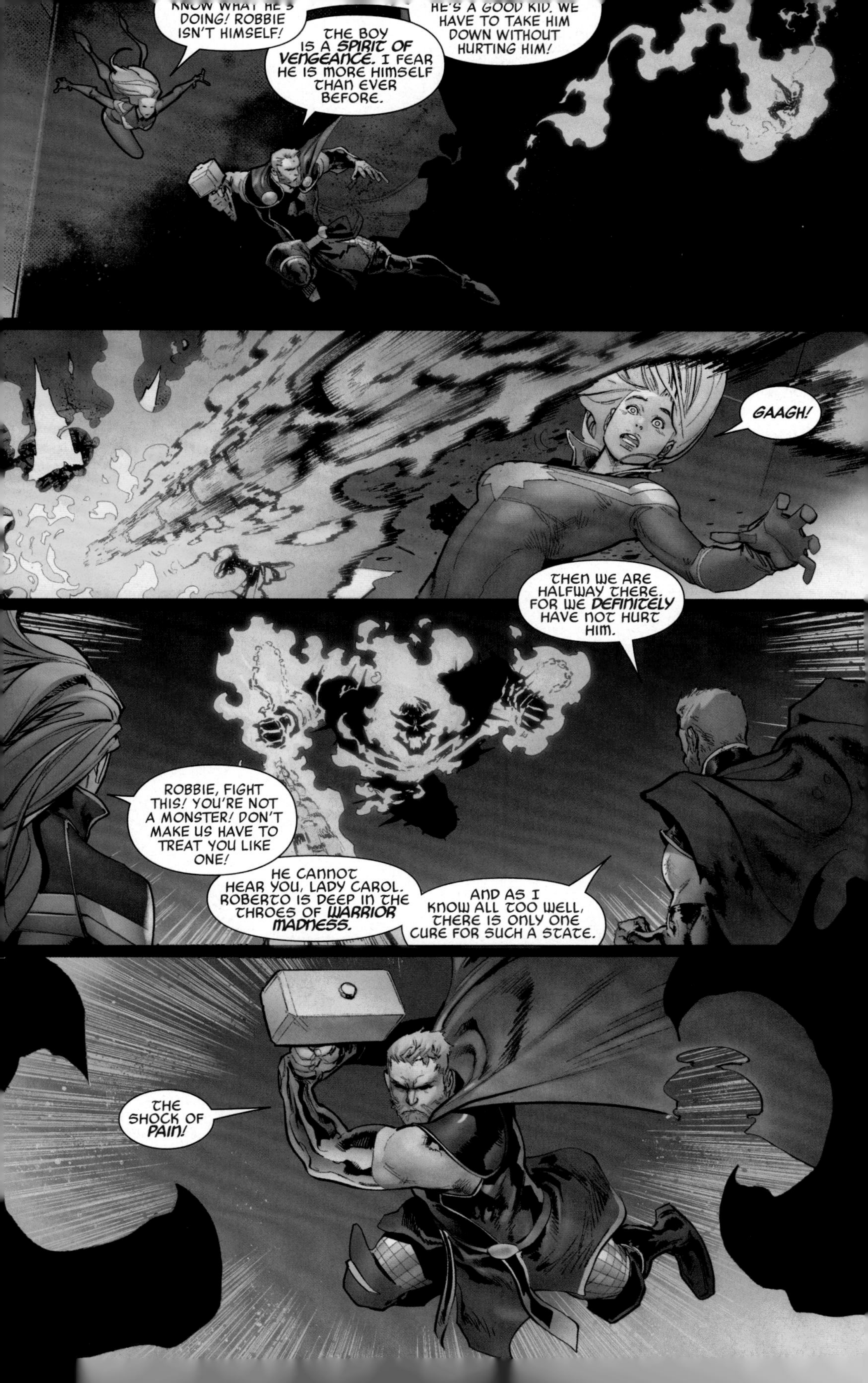
KNOW WHAT HE'S DOING! ROBBIE ISN'T HIMSELF!
THE BOY IS A SPIRIT OF VENGEANCE. I FEAR HE IS MORE HIMSELF THAN EVER BEFORE.
HE'S A GOOD KID. WE HAVE TO TAKE HIM DOWN WITHOUT HURTING HIM!
GAAGH!
THEN WE ARE HALFWAY THERE, FOR WE DEFINITELY HAVE NOT HURT HIM.
ROBBIE, FIGHT THIS! YOU'RE NOT A MONSTER! DON'T MAKE US HAVE TO TREAT YOU LIKE ONE!
HE CANNOT HEAR YOU, LADY CAROL. ROBERTO IS DEEP IN THE THROES OF WARRIOR MADNESS.
AND AS I KNOW ALL TOO WELL, THERE IS ONLY ONE CURE FOR SUCH A STATE.
THE SHOCK OF PAIN!

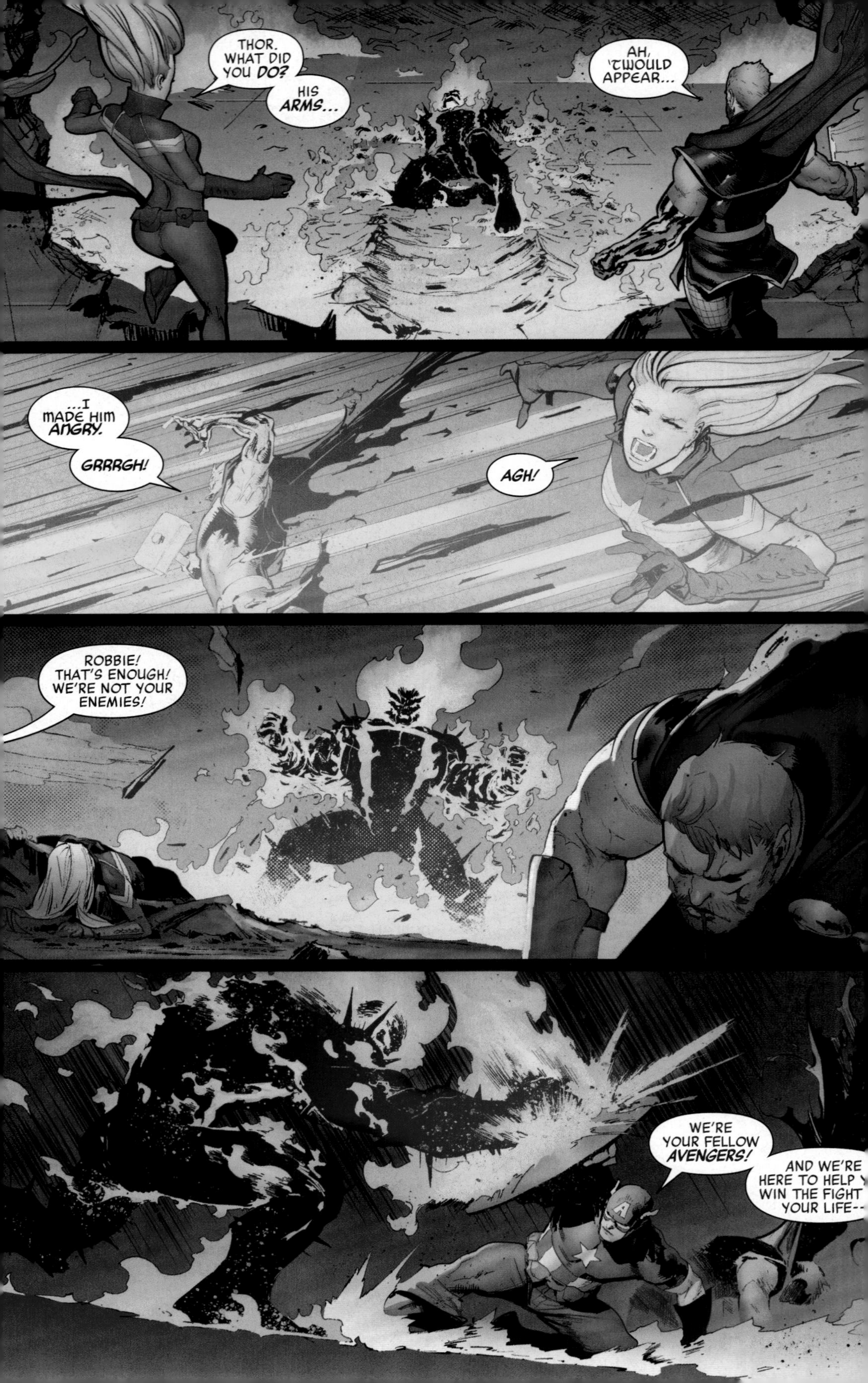
THOR. WHAT DID YOU DO?
HIS ARMS...
AH, 'TWOULD APPEAR...
...I MADE HIM ANGRY.
GRRRGH!
AGH!
ROBBIE! THAT'S ENOUGH! WE'RE NOT YOUR ENEMIES!
WE'RE YOUR FELLOW AVENGERS!
AND WE'RE HERE TO HELP WIN THE FIGHT YOUR LIFE--

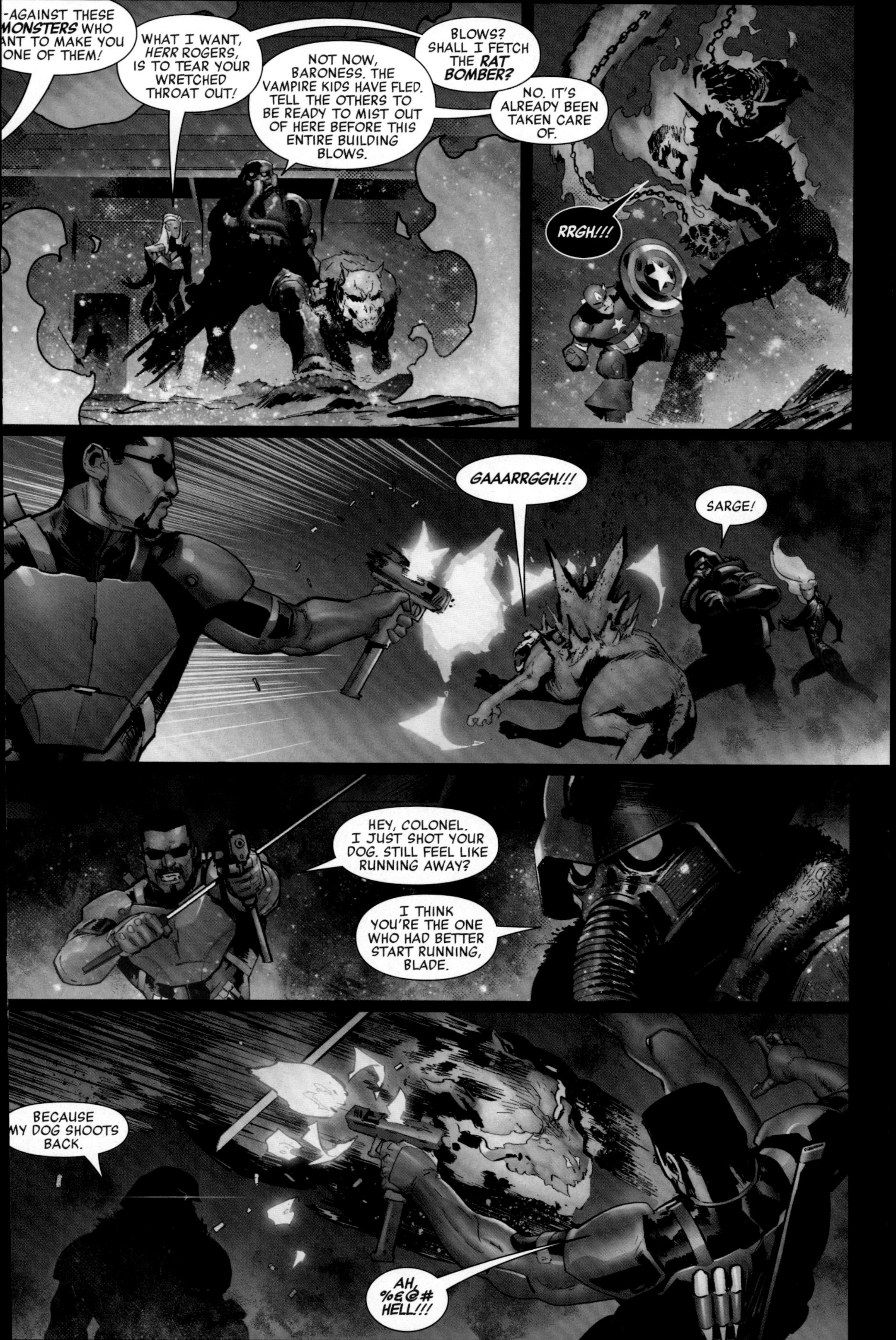
-AGAINST THESE MONSTERS WHO ANT TO MAKE YOU ONE OF THEM!
WHAT I WANT, HERR ROGERS, IS TO TEAR YOUR WRETCHED THROAT OUT!
BLOWS? SHALL I FETCH THE RAT BOMBER?
NOT NOW, BARONESS. THE VAMPIRE KIDS HAVE FLED. TELL THE OTHERS TO BE READY TO MIST OUT OF HERE BEFORE THIS ENTIRE BUILDING BLOWS.
NO. IT'S ALREADY BEEN TAKEN CARE OF.
RRGH!!!
GAAARRGGH!!!
SARGE!
HEY, COLONEL. I JUST SHOT YOUR DOG. STILL FEEL LIKE RUNNING AWAY?
I THINK YOU'RE THE ONE WHO HAD BETTER START RUNNING, BLADE.
BECAUSE MY DOG SHOOTS BACK.
AH, %&@# HELL!!!

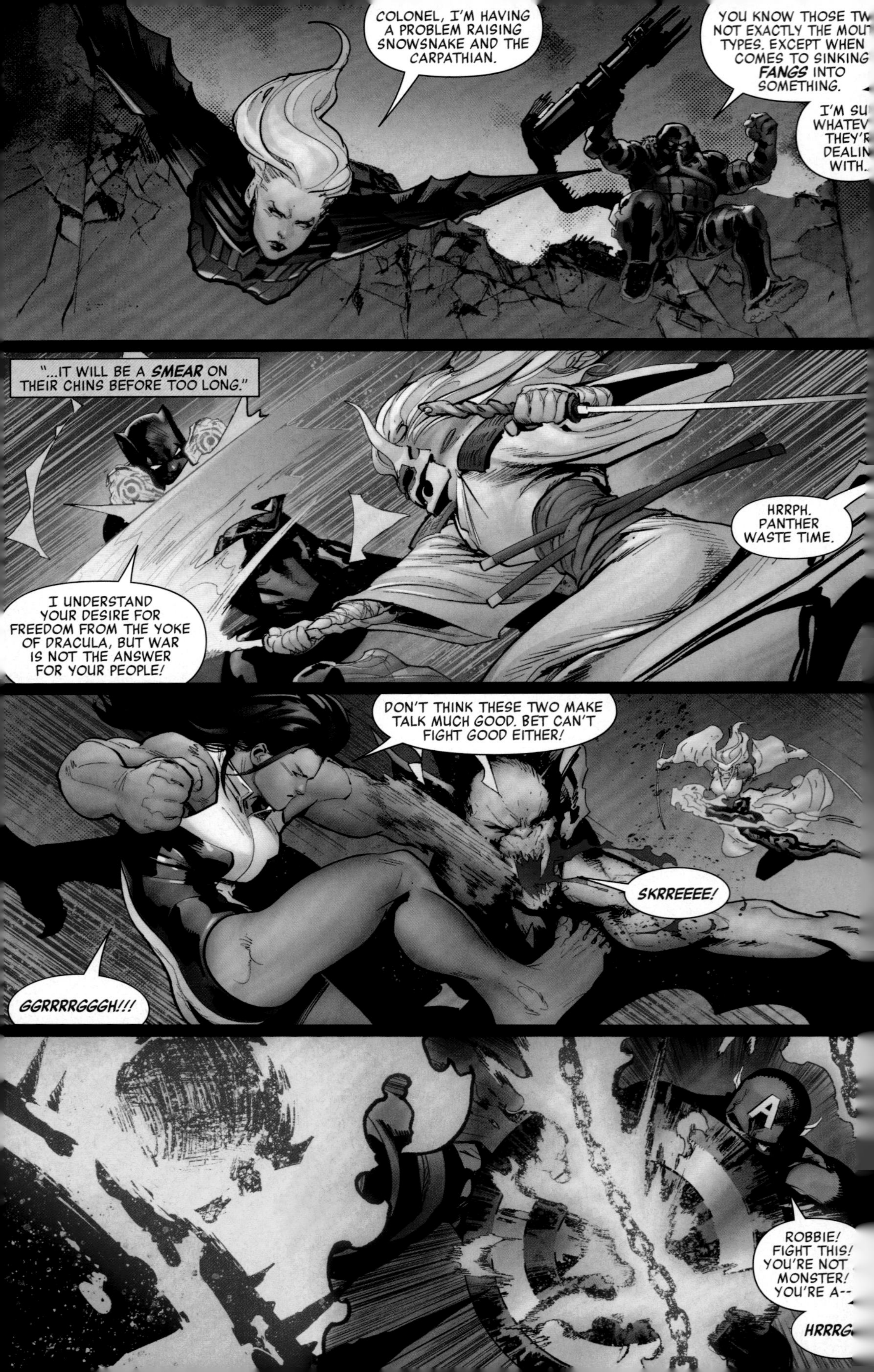
COLONEL, I'M HAVING A PROBLEM RAISING SNOWSNAKE AND THE CARPATHIAN.
YOU KNOW THOSE TW NOT EXACTLY THE MOUT TYPES. EXCEPT WHEN COMES TO SINKING FANGS INTO SOMETHING.
I'M SU WHATEV THEY'R DEALIN WITH...
"...IT WILL BE A SMEAR ON THEIR CHINS BEFORE TOO LONG."
HRRPH. PANTHER WASTE TIME.
I UNDERSTAND YOUR DESIRE FOR FREEDOM FROM THE YOKE OF DRACULA, BUT WAR IS NOT THE ANSWER FOR YOUR PEOPLE!
DON'T THINK THESE TWO MAKE TALK MUCH GOOD. BET CAN'T FIGHT GOOD EITHER!
SKRREEEE!
GGRRRRGGGH!!!
ROBBIE! FIGHT THIS! YOU'RE NOT MONSTER! YOU'RE A--
HRRRG

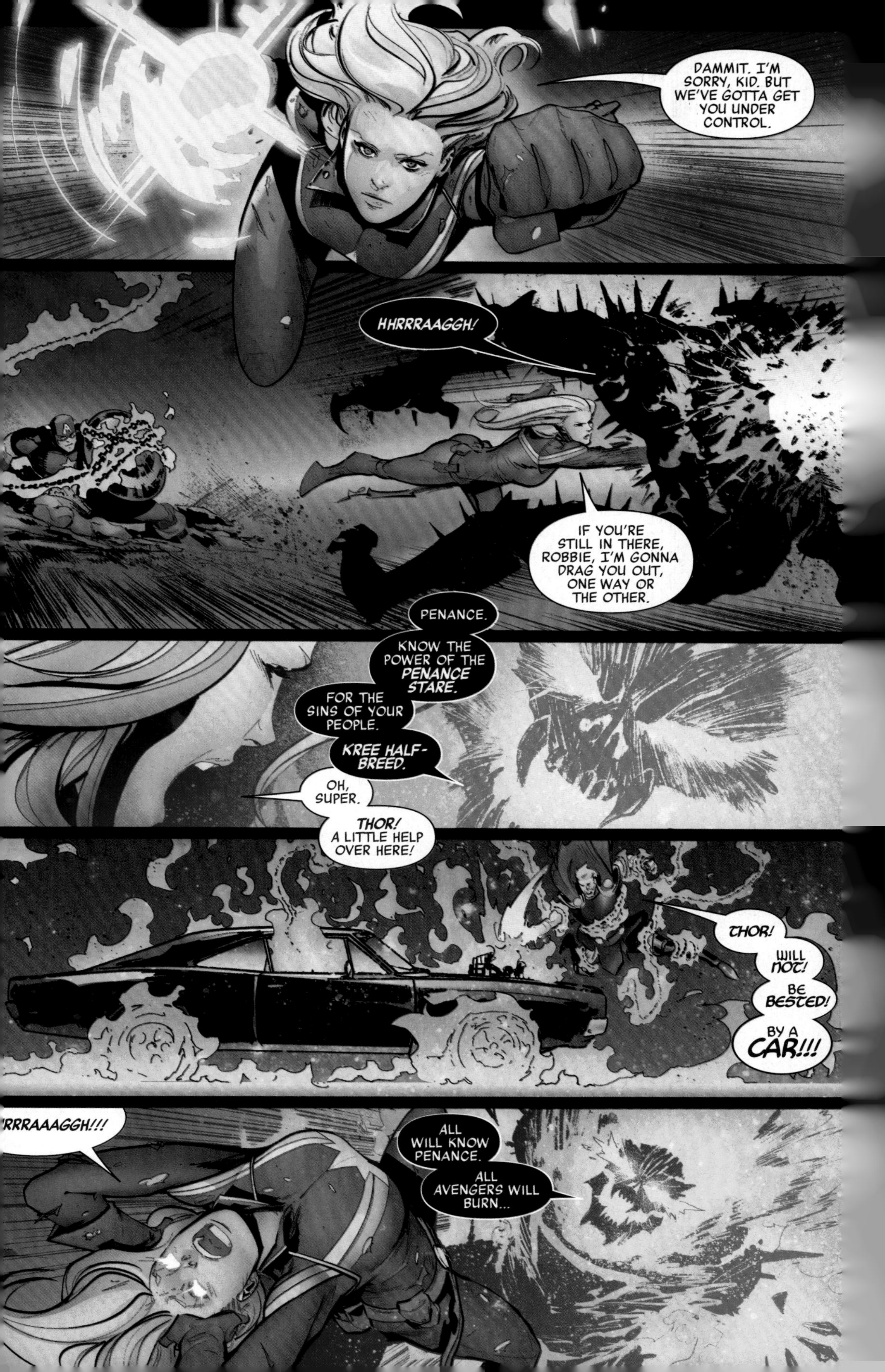

DAMMIT. I'M SORRY, KID. BUT WE'VE GOTTA GET YOU UNDER CONTROL.
HHRRRAAGGH!
IF YOU'RE STILL IN THERE, ROBBIE, I'M GONNA DRAG YOU OUT, ONE WAY OR THE OTHER.
PENANCE.
KNOW THE POWER OF THE PENANCE STARE.
FOR THE SINS OF YOUR PEOPLE.
KREE HALF-BREED.
OH, SUPER.
THOR! A LITTLE HELP OVER HERE!
THOR!
WILL NOT!
BE BESTED!
BY A CAR!!!
RRRAAAGGH!!!
ALL WILL KNOW PENANCE.
ALL AVENGERS WILL BURN...

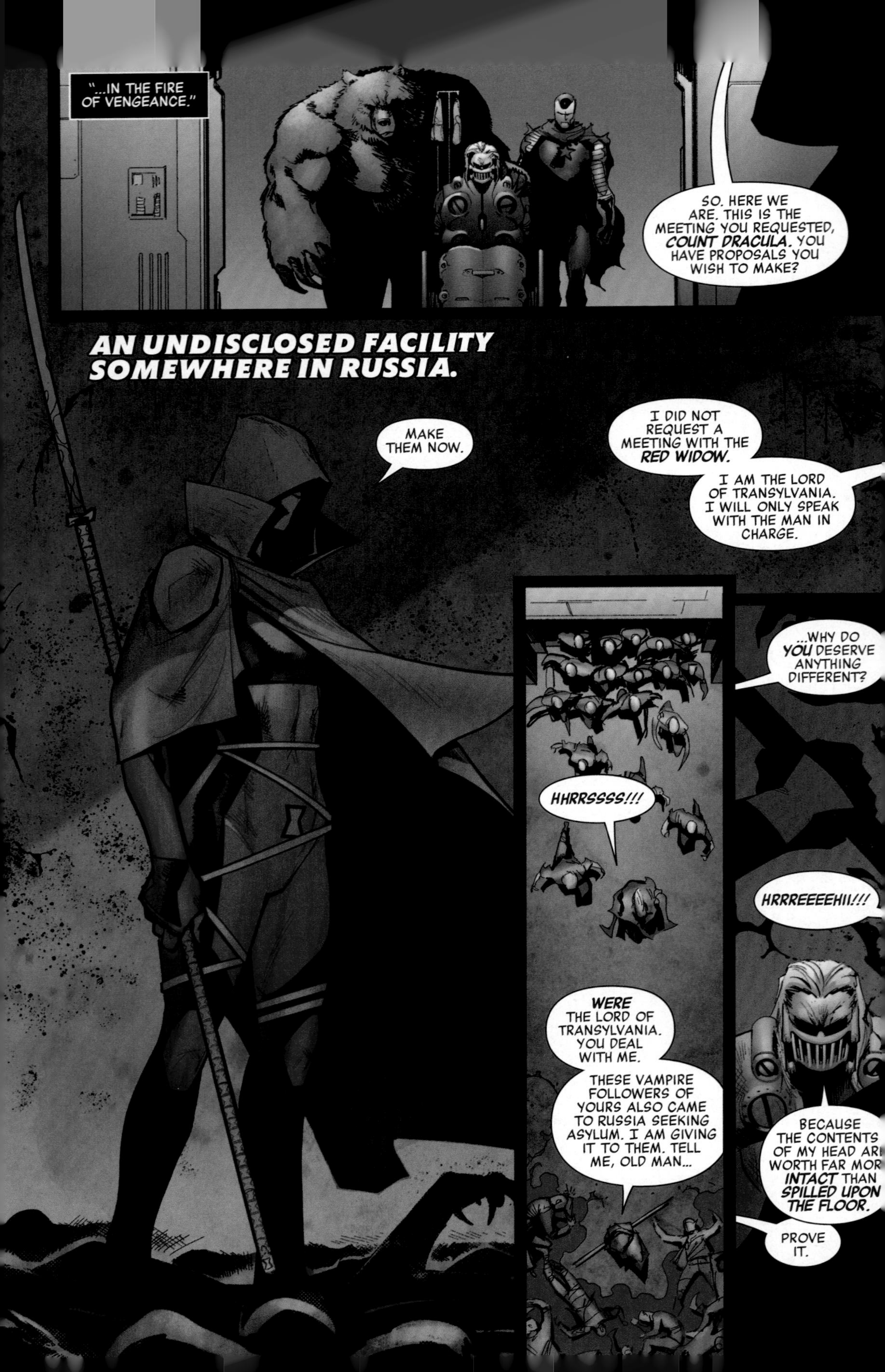
"...IN THE FIRE OF VENGEANCE."
SO. HERE WE ARE. THIS IS THE MEETING YOU REQUESTED, COUNT DRACULA. YOU HAVE PROPOSALS YOU WISH TO MAKE?
AN UNDISCLOSED FACILITY SOMEWHERE IN RUSSIA.
MAKE THEM NOW.
I DID NOT REQUEST A MEETING WITH THE RED WIDOW.
I AM THE LORD OF TRANSYLVANIA. I WILL ONLY SPEAK WITH THE MAN IN CHARGE.
...WHY DO YOU DESERVE ANYTHING DIFFERENT?
HHRRSSSS!!!
HRRREEEEHII!!!
WERE THE LORD OF TRANSYLVANIA. YOU DEAL WITH ME.
THESE VAMPIRE FOLLOWERS OF YOURS ALSO CAME TO RUSSIA SEEKING ASYLUM. I AM GIVING IT TO THEM. TELL ME, OLD MAN...
BECAUSE THE CONTENTS OF MY HEAD AR WORTH FAR MOR INTACT THAN SPILLED UPON THE FLOOR.
PROVE IT.

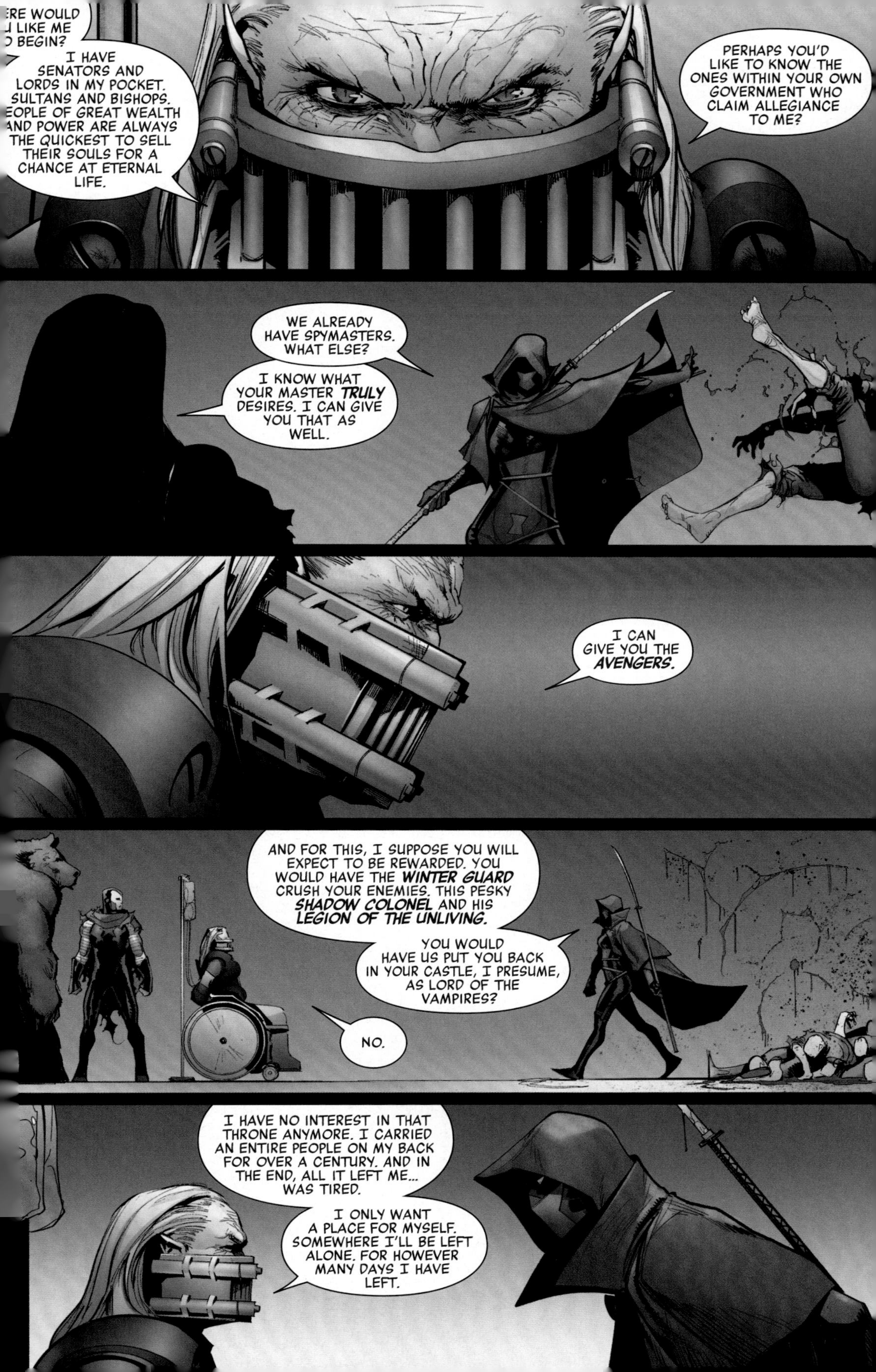

ERE WOULD U LIKE ME O BEGIN?
I HAVE SENATORS AND LORDS IN MY POCKET. SULTANS AND BISHOPS. EOPLE OF GREAT WEALTH AND POWER ARE ALWAYS THE QUICKEST TO SELL THEIR SOULS FOR A CHANCE AT ETERNAL LIFE.
PERHAPS YOU'D LIKE TO KNOW THE ONES WITHIN YOUR OWN GOVERNMENT WHO CLAIM ALLEGIANCE TO ME?
WE ALREADY HAVE SPYMASTERS. WHAT ELSE?
I KNOW WHAT YOUR MASTER *TRULY* DESIRES. I CAN GIVE YOU THAT AS WELL.
I CAN GIVE YOU THE *AVENGERS.*
AND FOR THIS, I SUPPOSE YOU WILL EXPECT TO BE REWARDED. YOU WOULD HAVE THE *WINTER GUARD* CRUSH YOUR ENEMIES. THIS PESKY *SHADOW COLONEL* AND HIS *LEGION OF THE UNLIVING.*
YOU WOULD HAVE US PUT YOU BACK IN YOUR CASTLE, I PRESUME, AS LORD OF THE VAMPIRES?
NO.
I HAVE NO INTEREST IN THAT THRONE ANYMORE. I CARRIED AN ENTIRE PEOPLE ON MY BACK FOR OVER A CENTURY. AND IN THE END, ALL IT LEFT ME... WAS TIRED.
I ONLY WANT A PLACE FOR MYSELF. SOMEWHERE I'LL BE LEFT ALONE. FOR HOWEVER MANY DAYS I HAVE LEFT.

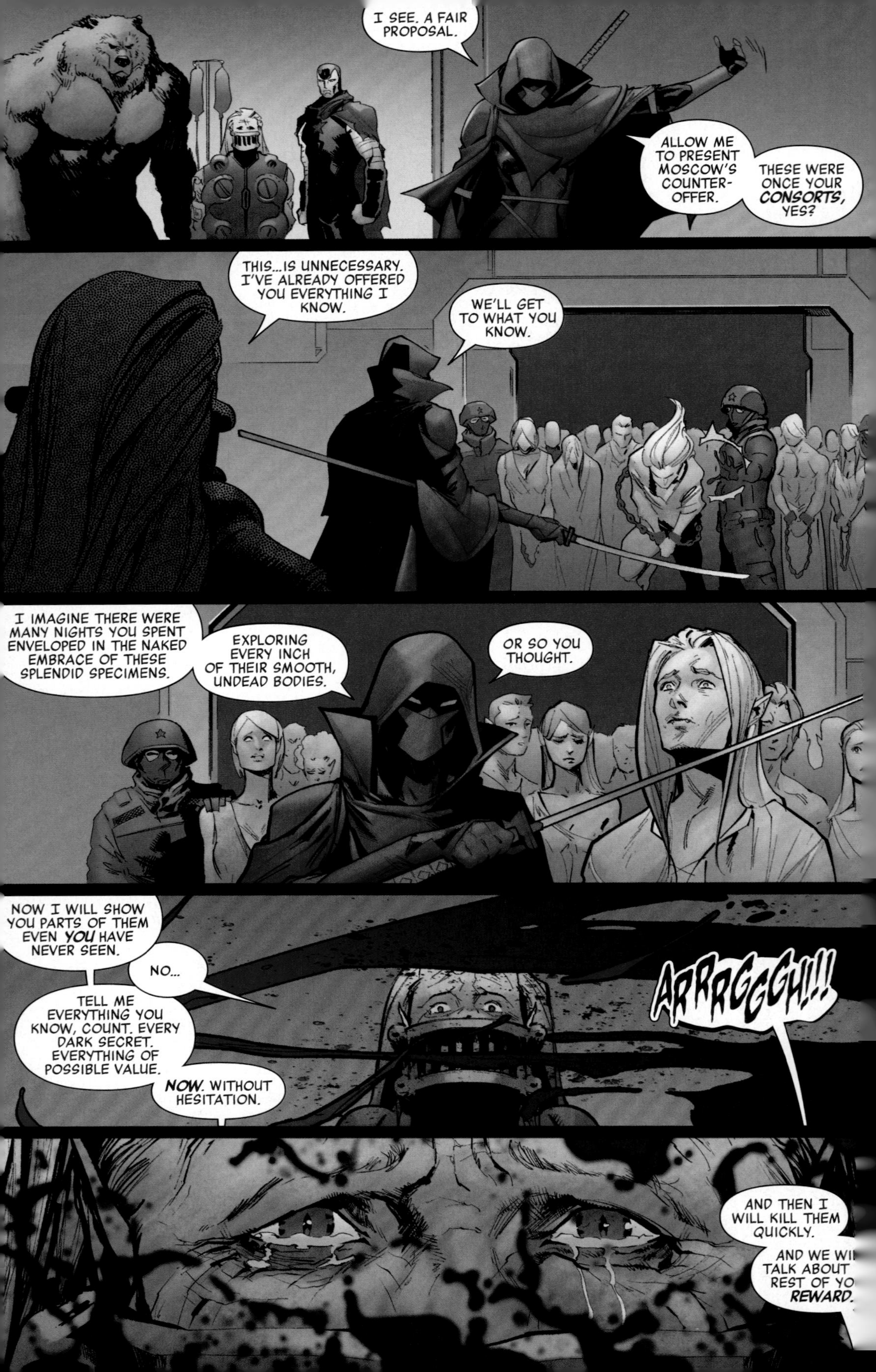

I SEE. A FAIR PROPOSAL.
ALLOW ME TO PRESENT MOSCOW'S COUNTER-OFFER.
THESE WERE ONCE YOUR CONSORTS, YES?
THIS...IS UNNECESSARY. I'VE ALREADY OFFERED YOU EVERYTHING I KNOW.
WE'LL GET TO WHAT YOU KNOW.
I IMAGINE THERE WERE MANY NIGHTS YOU SPENT ENVELOPED IN THE NAKED EMBRACE OF THESE SPLENDID SPECIMENS.
EXPLORING EVERY INCH OF THEIR SMOOTH, UNDEAD BODIES.
OR SO YOU THOUGHT.
NOW I WILL SHOW YOU PARTS OF THEM EVEN YOU HAVE NEVER SEEN.
NO...
TELL ME EVERYTHING YOU KNOW, COUNT. EVERY DARK SECRET. EVERYTHING OF POSSIBLE VALUE.
NOW. WITHOUT HESITATION.
ARRRGGGH!!!
AND THEN I WILL KILL THEM QUICKLY.
AND WE WI TALK ABOUT REST OF YO REWARD.

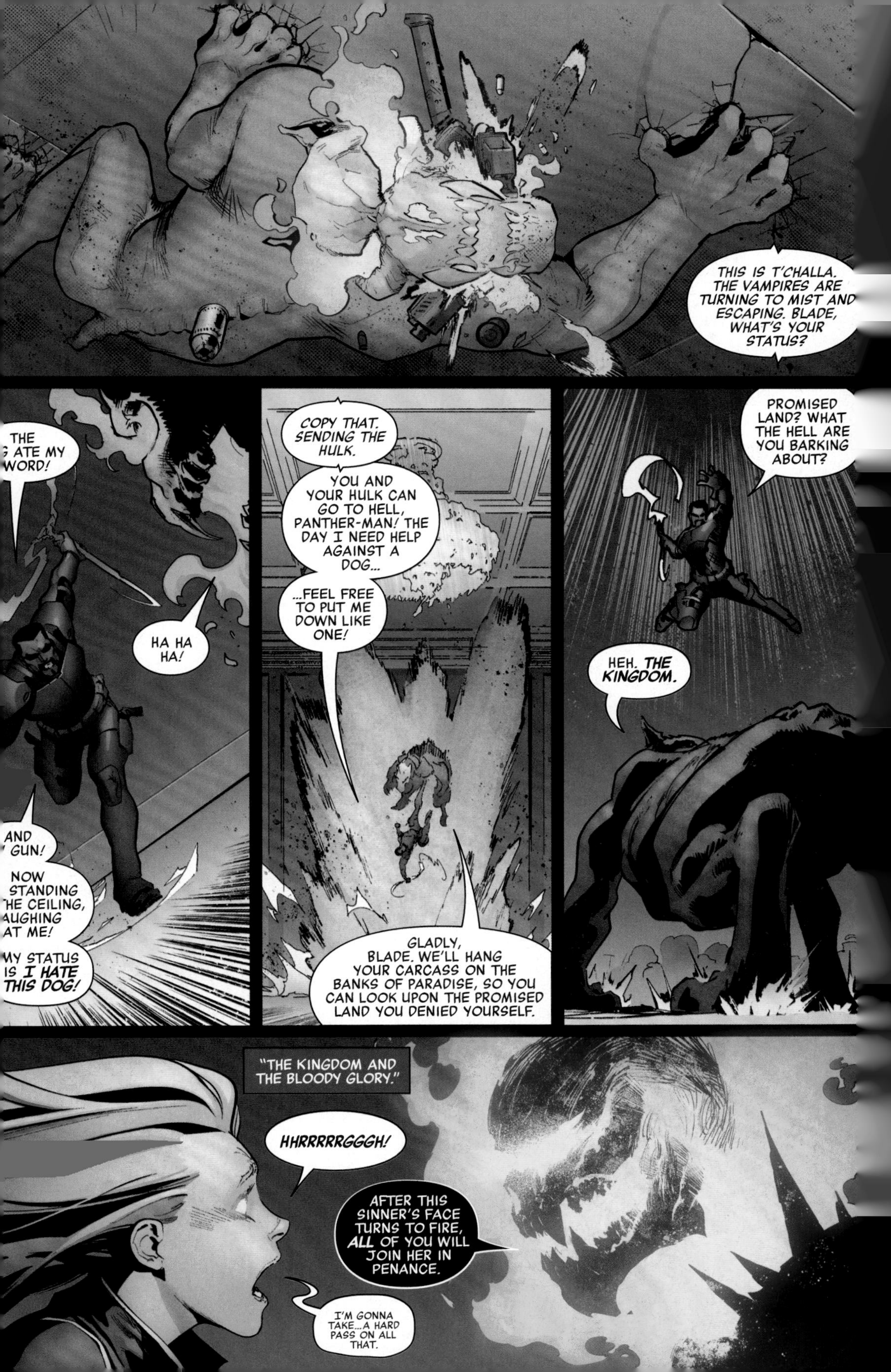

THIS IS T'CHALLA. THE VAMPIRES ARE TURNING TO MIST AND ESCAPING. BLADE, WHAT'S YOUR STATUS?
THE ATE MY WORD!
HA HA HA!
AND GUN!
NOW STANDING THE CEILING, AUGHING AT ME!
MY STATUS IS I HATE THIS DOG!
COPY THAT. SENDING THE HULK.
YOU AND YOUR HULK CAN GO TO HELL, PANTHER-MAN! THE DAY I NEED HELP AGAINST A DOG...
...FEEL FREE TO PUT ME DOWN LIKE ONE!
GLADLY, BLADE. WE'LL HANG YOUR CARCASS ON THE BANKS OF PARADISE, SO YOU CAN LOOK UPON THE PROMISED LAND YOU DENIED YOURSELF.
PROMISED LAND? WHAT THE HELL ARE YOU BARKING ABOUT?
HEH. THE KINGDOM.
"THE KINGDOM AND THE BLOODY GLORY."
HHRRRRRGGGH!
AFTER THIS SINNER'S FACE TURNS TO FIRE, ALL OF YOU WILL JOIN HER IN PENANCE.
I'M GONNA TAKE...A HARD PASS ON ALL THAT.

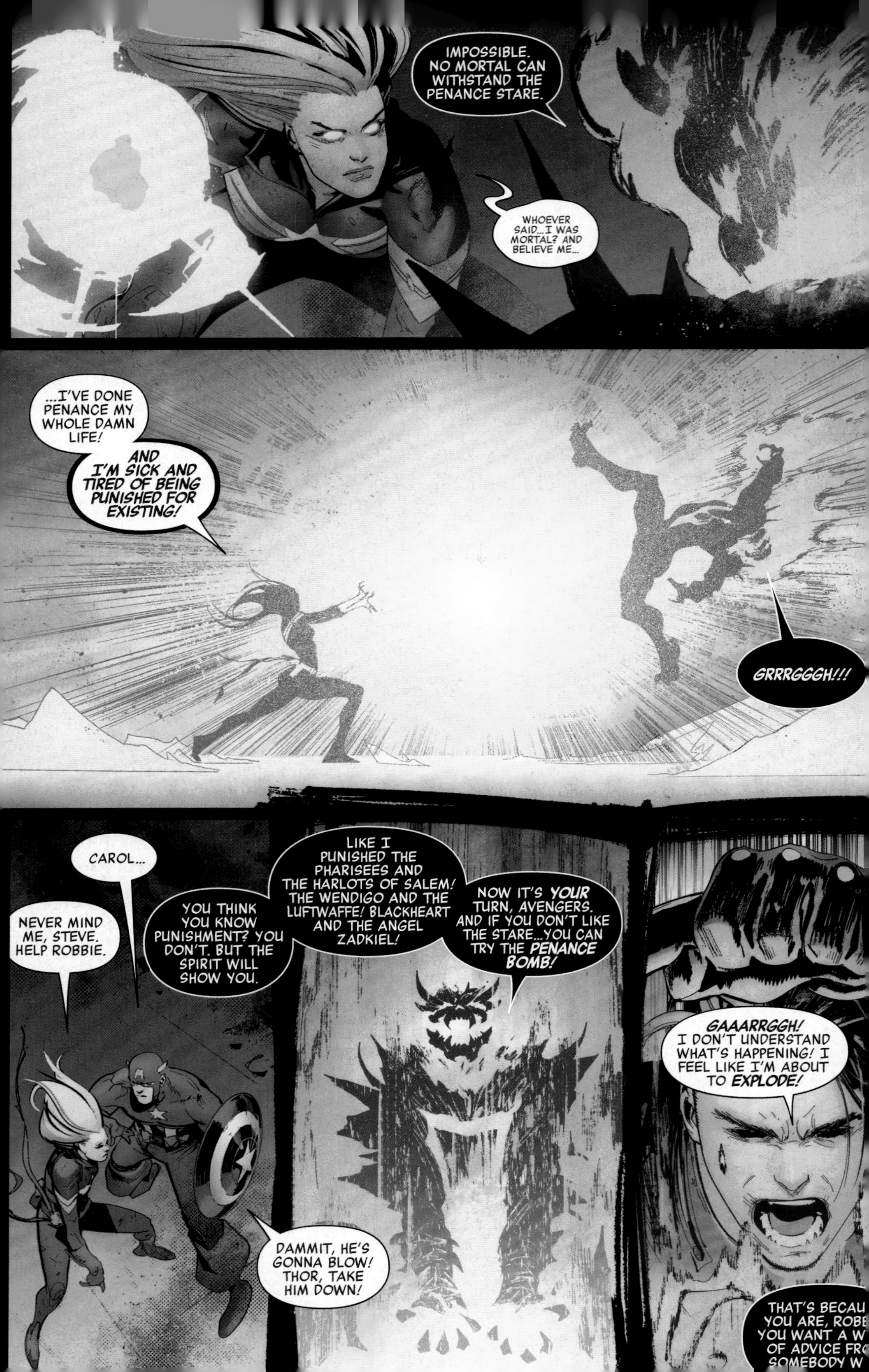
IMPOSSIBLE. NO MORTAL CAN WITHSTAND THE PENANCE STARE.
WHOEVER SAID...I WAS MORTAL? AND BELIEVE ME...
...I'VE DONE PENANCE MY WHOLE DAMN LIFE!
AND I'M SICK AND TIRED OF BEING PUNISHED FOR EXISTING!
GRRRGGGH!!!
CAROL...
NEVER MIND ME, STEVE. HELP ROBBIE.
YOU THINK YOU KNOW PUNISHMENT? YOU DON'T. BUT THE SPIRIT WILL SHOW YOU.
LIKE I PUNISHED THE PHARISEES AND THE HARLOTS OF SALEM! THE WENDIGO AND THE LUFTWAFFE! BLACKHEART AND THE ANGEL ZADKIEL!
NOW IT'S YOUR TURN, AVENGERS. AND IF YOU DON'T LIKE THE STARE...YOU CAN TRY THE PENANCE BOMB!
DAMMIT, HE'S GONNA BLOW! THOR, TAKE HIM DOWN!
GAAARRGGH! I DON'T UNDERSTAND WHAT'S HAPPENING! I FEEL LIKE I'M ABOUT TO EXPLODE!
THAT'S BECAU
YOU ARE, ROBE
YOU WANT A W
OF ADVICE FRO
SOMEBODY W

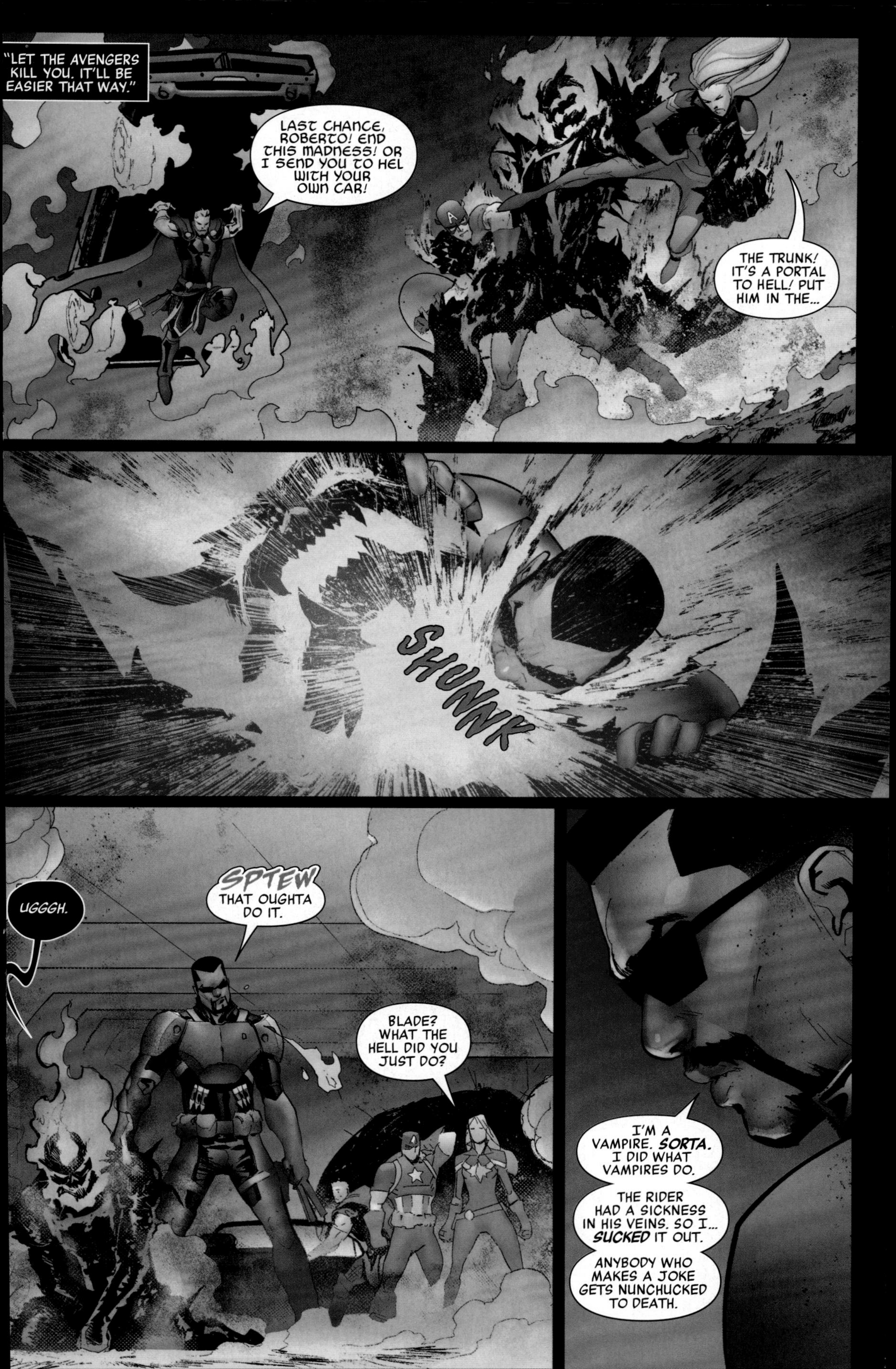
"LET THE AVENGERS KILL YOU. IT'LL BE EASIER THAT WAY."
LAST CHANCE, ROBERTO! END THIS MADNESS! OR I SEND YOU TO HEL WITH YOUR OWN CAR!
THE TRUNK! IT'S A PORTAL TO HELL! PUT HIM IN THE...
SHUNNK
UGGGH.
SPTEW
THAT OUGHTA DO IT.
BLADE? WHAT THE HELL DID YOU JUST DO?
I'M A VAMPIRE. SORTA. I DID WHAT VAMPIRES DO.
THE RIDER HAD A SICKNESS IN HIS VEINS. SO I... SUCKED IT OUT.
ANYBODY WHO MAKES A JOKE GETS NUNCHUCKED TO DEATH.

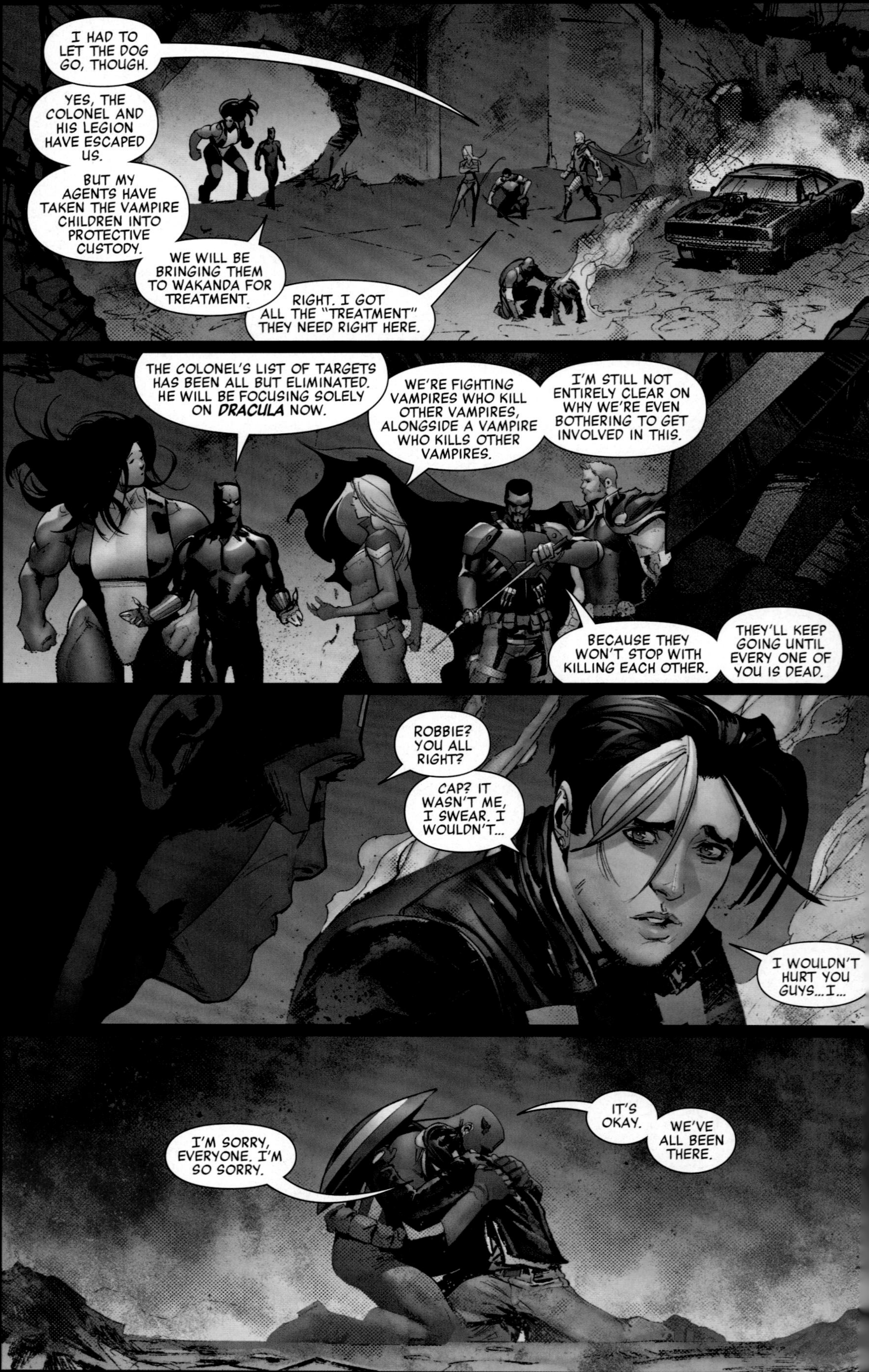
I HAD TO LET THE DOG GO, THOUGH.
YES, THE COLONEL AND HIS LEGION HAVE ESCAPED US.
BUT MY AGENTS HAVE TAKEN THE VAMPIRE CHILDREN INTO PROTECTIVE CUSTODY.
WE WILL BE BRINGING THEM TO WAKANDA FOR TREATMENT.
RIGHT. I GOT ALL THE "TREATMENT" THEY NEED RIGHT HERE.
THE COLONEL'S LIST OF TARGETS HAS BEEN ALL BUT ELIMINATED. HE WILL BE FOCUSING SOLELY ON DRACULA NOW.
WE'RE FIGHTING VAMPIRES WHO KILL OTHER VAMPIRES, ALONGSIDE A VAMPIRE WHO KILLS OTHER VAMPIRES.
I'M STILL NOT ENTIRELY CLEAR ON WHY WE'RE EVEN BOTHERING TO GET INVOLVED IN THIS.
BECAUSE THEY WON'T STOP WITH KILLING EACH OTHER.
THEY'LL KEEP GOING UNTIL EVERY ONE OF YOU IS DEAD.
ROBBIE? YOU ALL RIGHT?
CAP? IT WASN'T ME, I SWEAR. I WOULDN'T...
I WOULDN'T HURT YOU GUYS...I...
I'M SORRY, EVERYONE. I'M SO SORRY.
IT'S OKAY.
WE'VE ALL BEEN THERE.

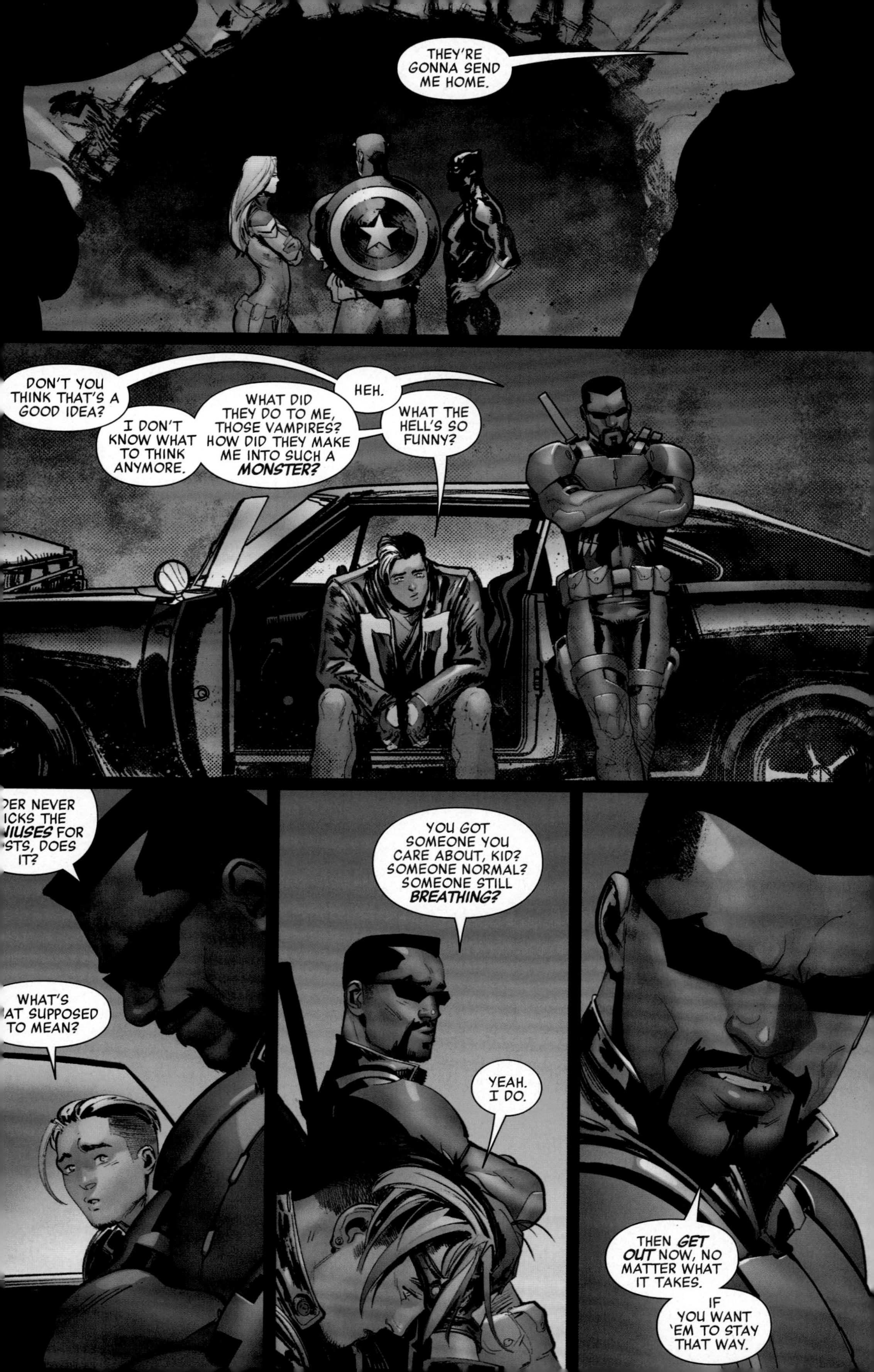
THEY'RE GONNA SEND ME HOME.
DON'T YOU THINK THAT'S A GOOD IDEA?
I DON'T KNOW WHAT TO THINK ANYMORE.
WHAT DID THEY DO TO ME, THOSE VAMPIRES? HOW DID THEY MAKE ME INTO SUCH A MONSTER?
HEH.
WHAT THE HELL'S SO FUNNY?
YOU GOT SOMEONE YOU CARE ABOUT, KID? SOMEONE NORMAL? SOMEONE STILL BREATHING?
YEAH. I DO.
THEN GET OUT NOW, NO MATTER WHAT IT TAKES.
IF YOU WANT 'EM TO STAY THAT WAY.
WHAT'S
TO MEAN?

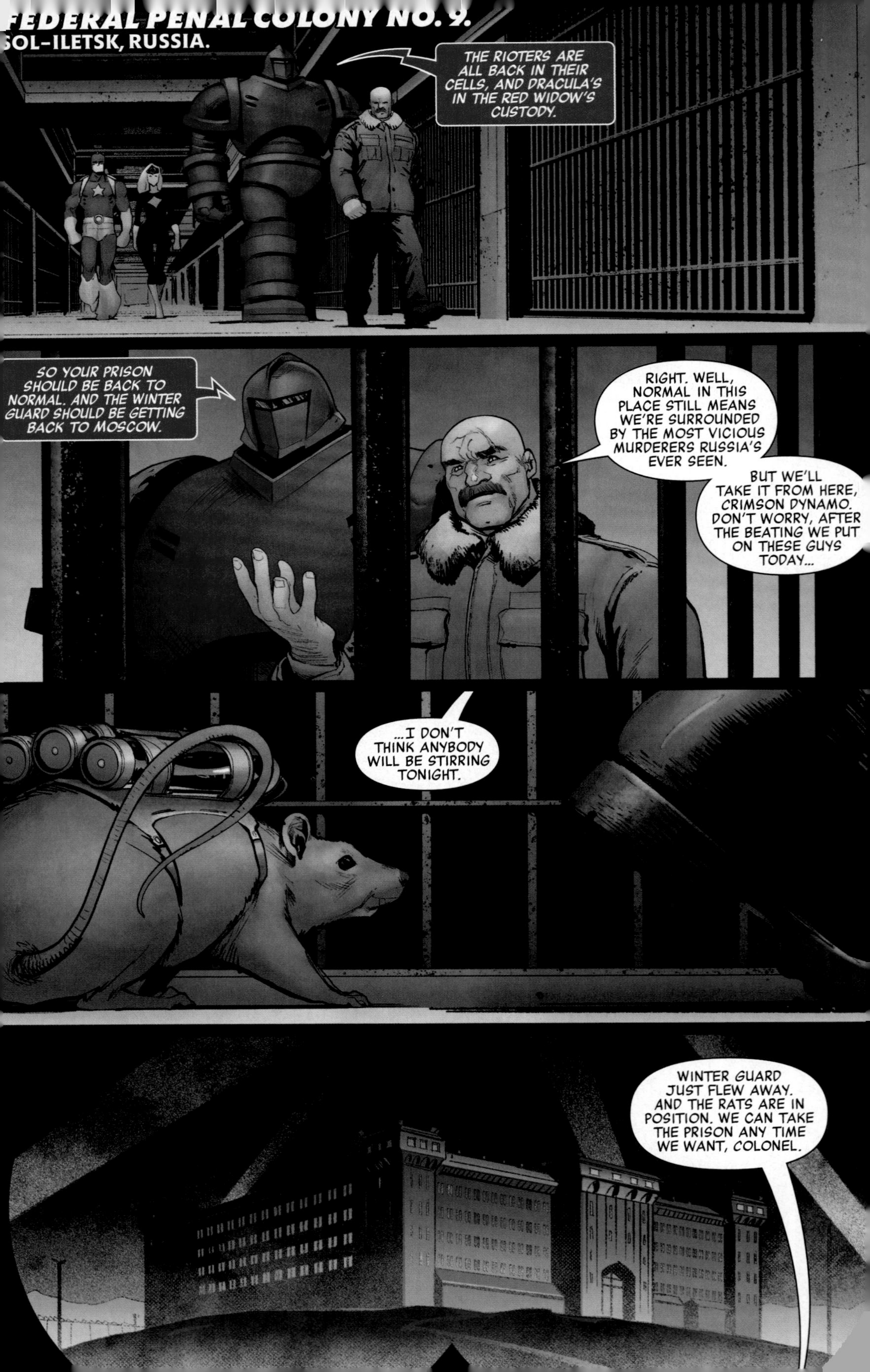
FEDERAL PENAL COLONY NO. 9.
SOL-ILETSK, RUSSIA.
THE RIOTERS ARE ALL BACK IN THEIR CELLS, AND DRACULA'S IN THE RED WIDOW'S CUSTODY.
SO YOUR PRISON SHOULD BE BACK TO NORMAL. AND THE WINTER GUARD SHOULD BE GETTING BACK TO MOSCOW.
RIGHT. WELL, NORMAL IN THIS PLACE STILL MEANS WE'RE SURROUNDED BY THE MOST VICIOUS MURDERERS RUSSIA'S EVER SEEN.
BUT WE'LL TAKE IT FROM HERE, CRIMSON DYNAMO. DON'T WORRY, AFTER THE BEATING WE PUT ON THESE GUYS TODAY...
...I DON'T THINK ANYBODY WILL BE STIRRING TONIGHT.
WINTER GUARD JUST FLEW AWAY. AND THE RATS ARE IN POSITION. WE CAN TAKE THE PRISON ANY TIME WE WANT, COLONEL.

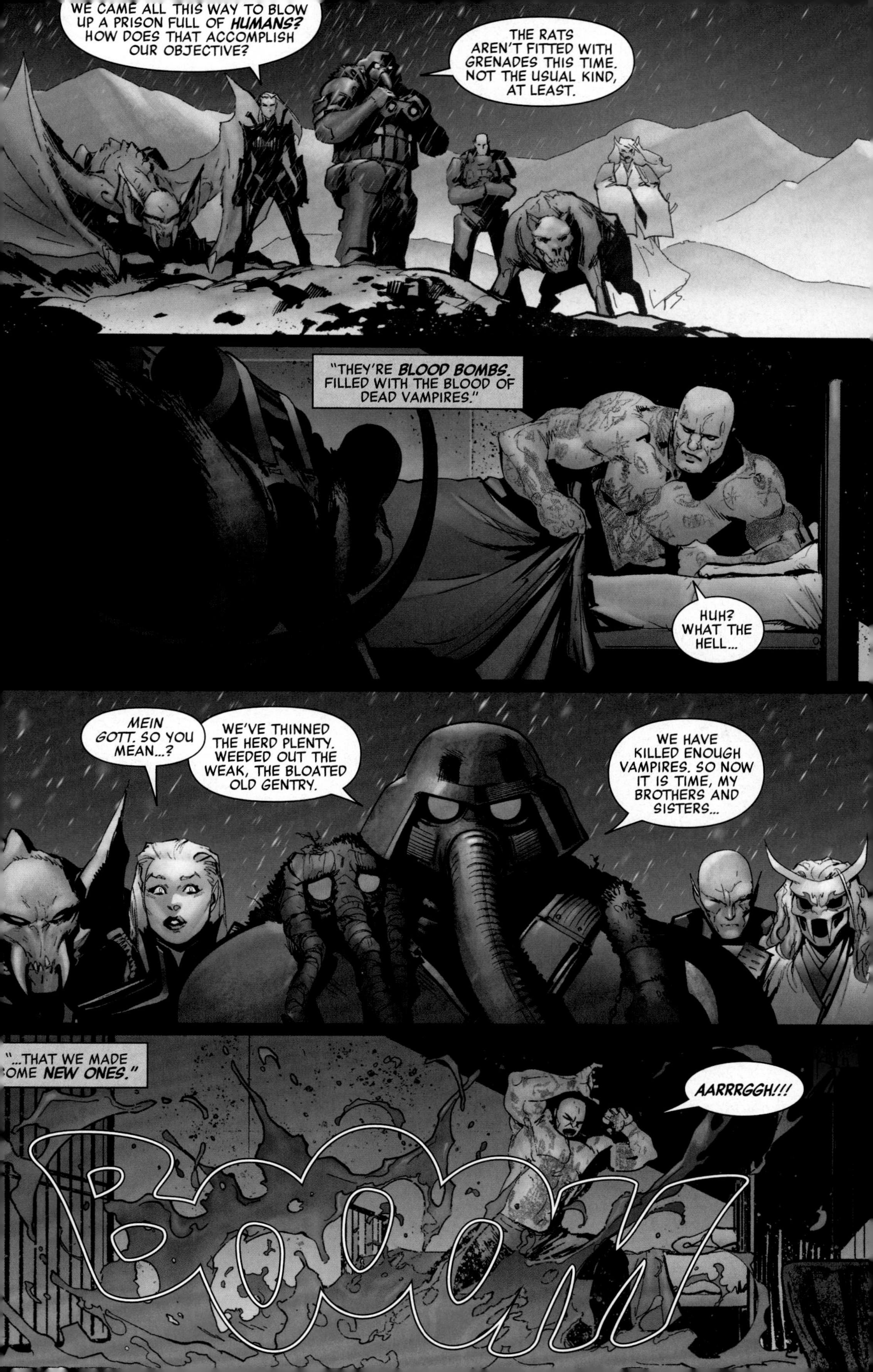
WE CAME ALL THIS WAY TO BLOW UP A PRISON FULL OF ***HUMANS?*** HOW DOES THAT ACCOMPLISH OUR OBJECTIVE?
THE RATS AREN'T FITTED WITH GRENADES THIS TIME. NOT THE USUAL KIND, AT LEAST.
"THEY'RE ***BLOOD BOMBS.*** FILLED WITH THE BLOOD OF DEAD VAMPIRES."
HUH? WHAT THE HELL...
MEIN GOTT. SO YOU MEAN...?
WE'VE THINNED THE HERD PLENTY. WEEDED OUT THE WEAK, THE BLOATED OLD GENTRY.
WE HAVE KILLED ENOUGH VAMPIRES. SO NOW IT IS TIME, MY BROTHERS AND SISTERS...
"...THAT WE MADE SOME ***NEW ONES.***"
AARRRGGH!!!
BOOOM!

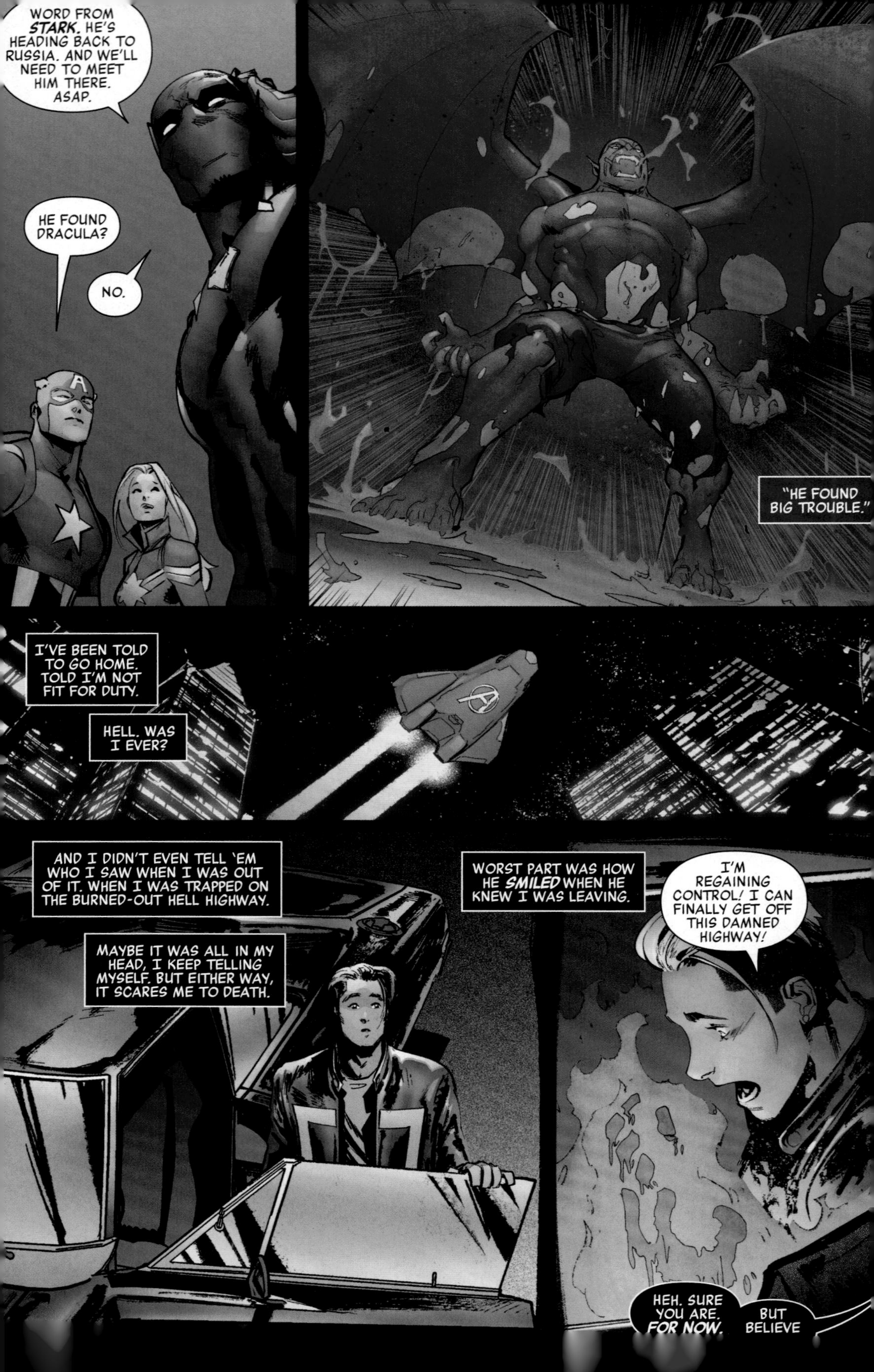
WORD FROM STARK. HE'S HEADING BACK TO RUSSIA. AND WE'LL NEED TO MEET HIM THERE. ASAP.
HE FOUND DRACULA?
NO.
"HE FOUND BIG TROUBLE."
I'VE BEEN TOLD TO GO HOME. TOLD I'M NOT FIT FOR DUTY.
HELL. WAS I EVER?
AND I DIDN'T EVEN TELL 'EM WHO I SAW WHEN I WAS OUT OF IT. WHEN I WAS TRAPPED ON THE BURNED-OUT HELL HIGHWAY.
MAYBE IT WAS ALL IN MY HEAD, I KEEP TELLING MYSELF. BUT EITHER WAY, IT SCARES ME TO DEATH.
WORST PART WAS HOW HE SMILED WHEN HE KNEW I WAS LEAVING.
I'M REGAINING CONTROL! I CAN FINALLY GET OFF THIS DAMNED HIGHWAY!
HEH. SURE YOU ARE. FOR NOW.
BUT BELIEVE

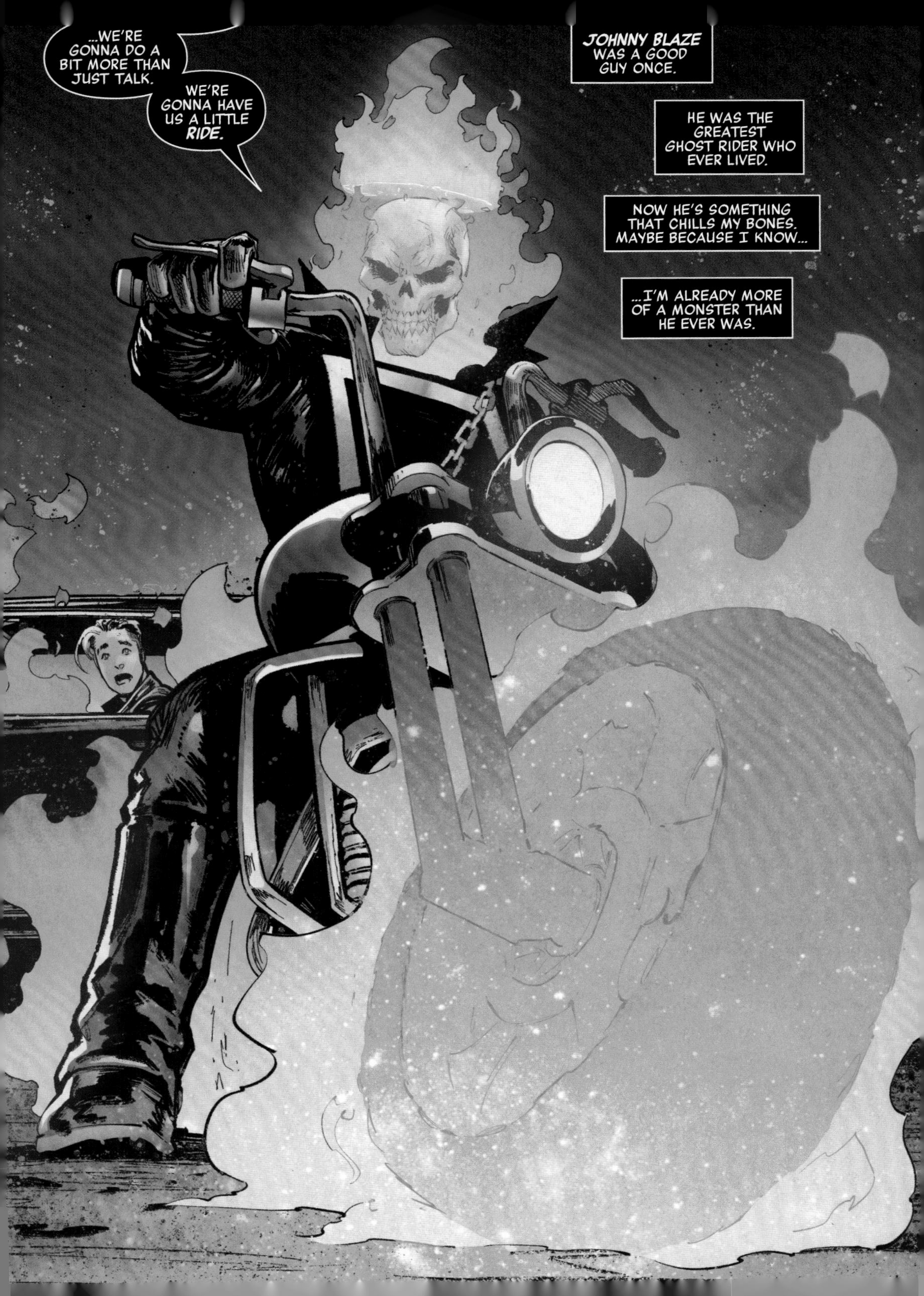

...WE'RE GONNA DO A BIT MORE THAN JUST TALK.
WE'RE GONNA HAVE US A LITTLE *RIDE*.
JOHNNY BLAZE WAS A GOOD GUY ONCE.
HE WAS THE GREATEST GHOST RIDER WHO EVER LIVED.
NOW HE'S SOMETHING THAT CHILLS MY BONES. MAYBE BECAUSE I KNOW...
...I'M ALREADY MORE OF A MONSTER THAN HE EVER WAS.

17 THE KINGDOM OF THE VAMPIRES

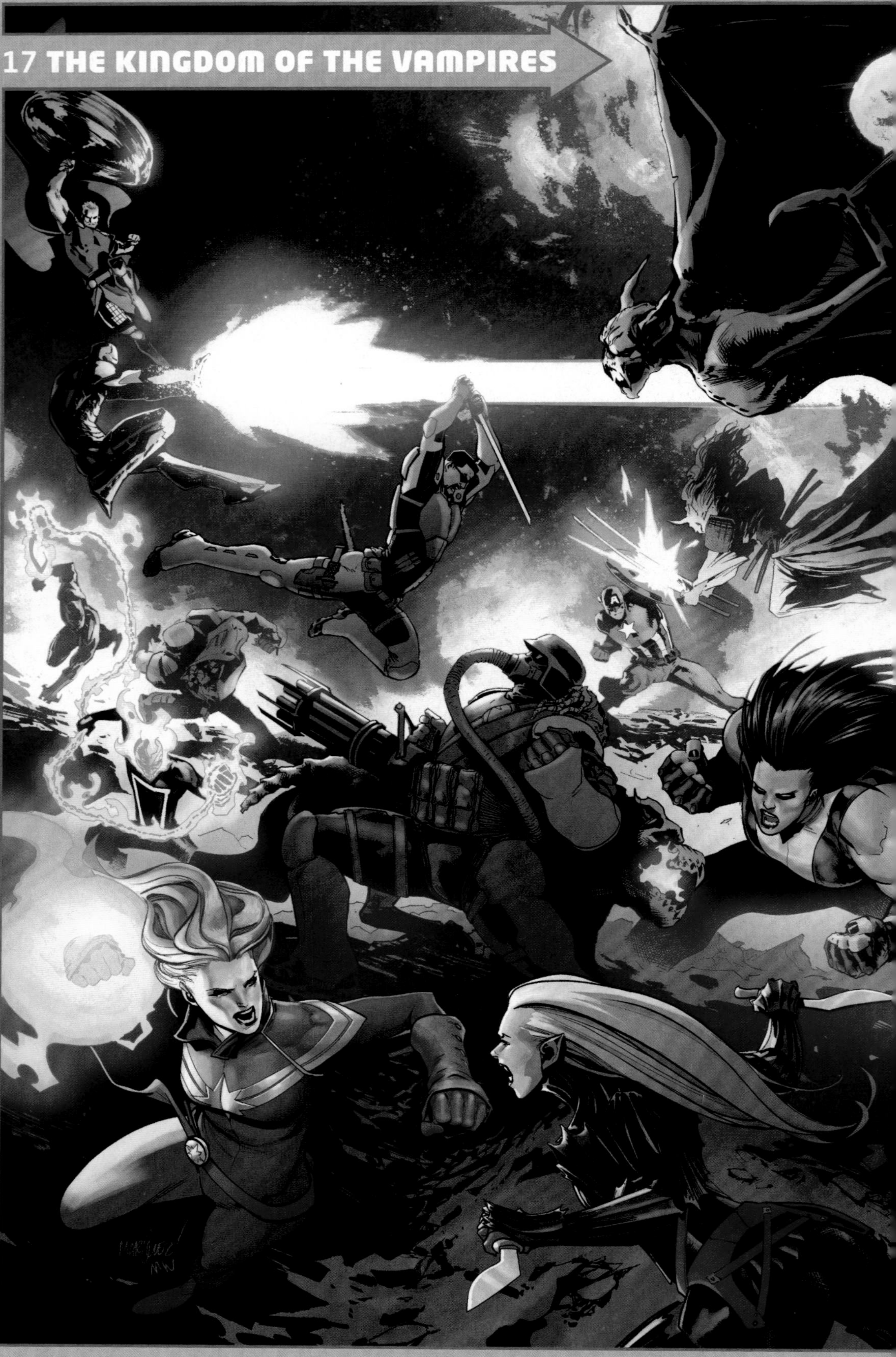

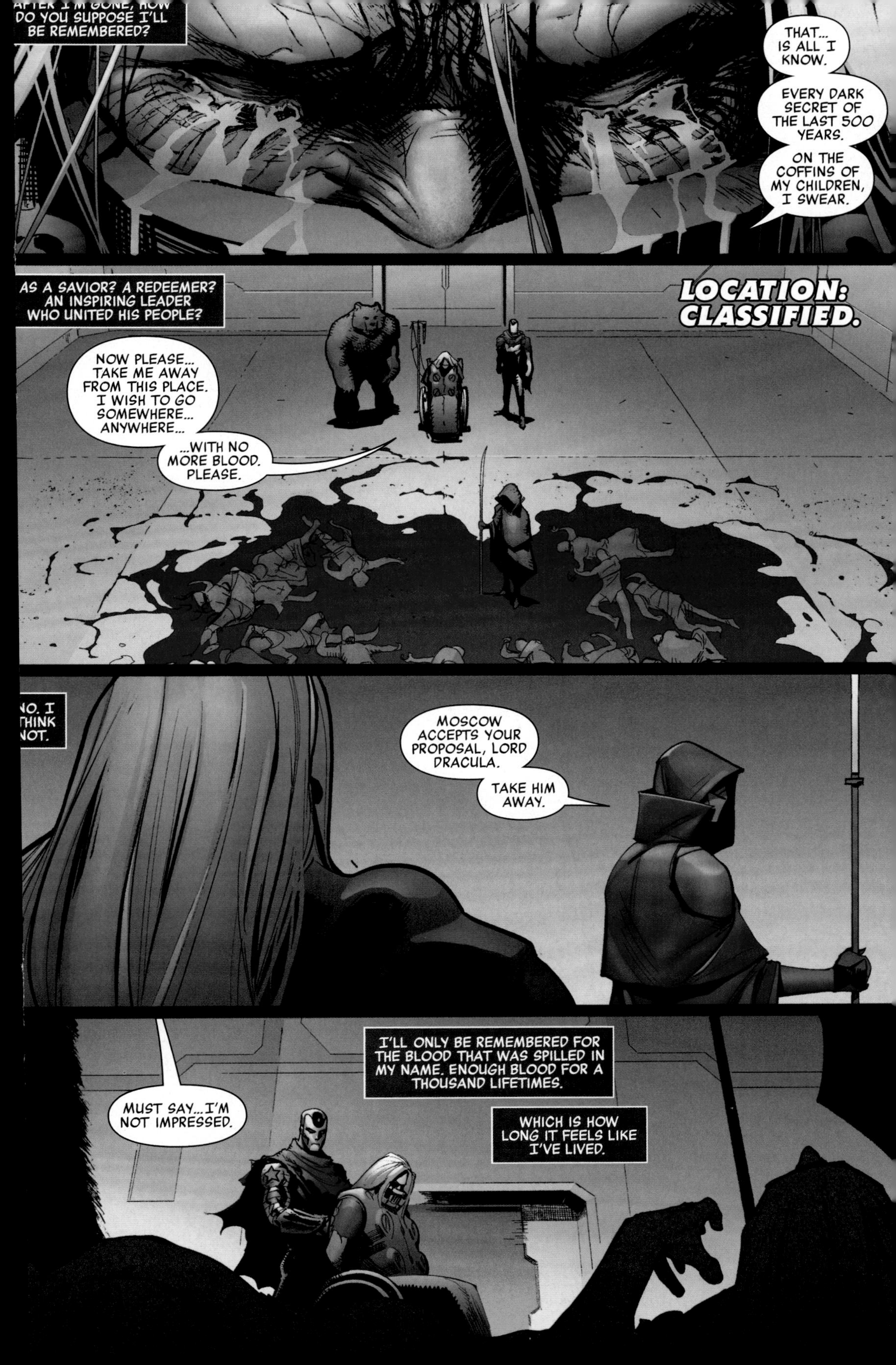
AFTER I'M GONE, HOW DO YOU SUPPOSE I'LL BE REMEMBERED?
THAT... IS ALL I KNOW.
EVERY DARK SECRET OF THE LAST 500 YEARS.
ON THE COFFINS OF MY CHILDREN, I SWEAR.
AS A SAVIOR? A REDEEMER? AN INSPIRING LEADER WHO UNITED HIS PEOPLE?
LOCATION: CLASSIFIED.
NOW PLEASE... TAKE ME AWAY FROM THIS PLACE. I WISH TO GO SOMEWHERE... ANYWHERE...
...WITH NO MORE BLOOD. PLEASE.
NO. I THINK NOT.
MOSCOW ACCEPTS YOUR PROPOSAL, LORD DRACULA.
TAKE HIM AWAY.
I'LL ONLY BE REMEMBERED FOR THE BLOOD THAT WAS SPILLED IN MY NAME. ENOUGH BLOOD FOR A THOUSAND LIFETIMES.
MUST SAY...I'M NOT IMPRESSED.
WHICH IS HOW LONG IT FEELS LIKE I'VE LIVED.

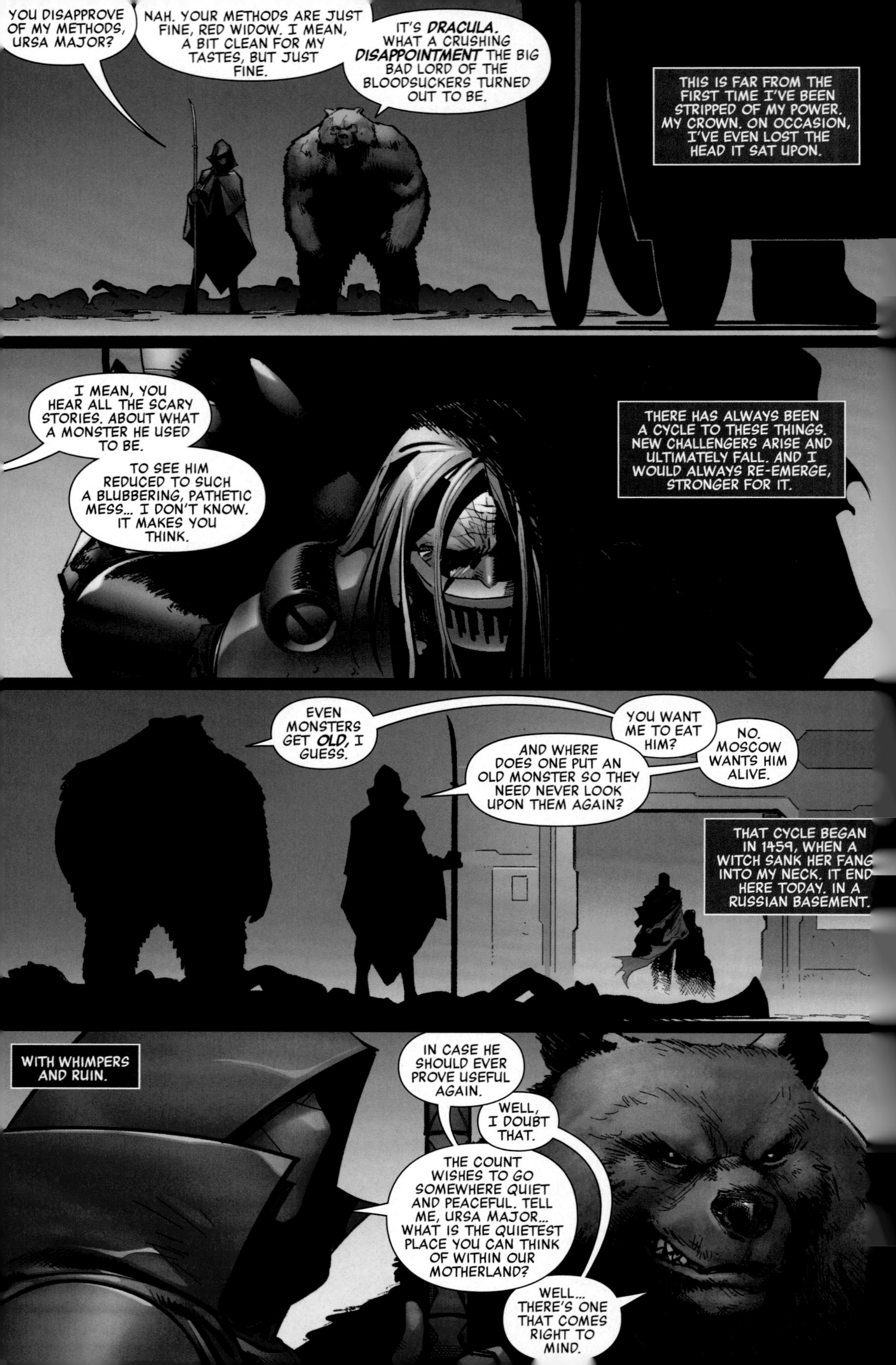
YOU DISAPPROVE OF MY METHODS, URSA MAJOR?
NAH. YOUR METHODS ARE JUST FINE, RED WIDOW. I MEAN, A BIT CLEAN FOR MY TASTES, BUT JUST FINE.
IT'S DRACULA. WHAT A CRUSHING DISAPPOINTMENT THE BIG BAD LORD OF THE BLOODSUCKERS TURNED OUT TO BE.
THIS IS FAR FROM THE FIRST TIME I'VE BEEN STRIPPED OF MY POWER. MY CROWN. ON OCCASION, I'VE EVEN LOST THE HEAD IT SAT UPON.
I MEAN, YOU HEAR ALL THE SCARY STORIES. ABOUT WHAT A MONSTER HE USED TO BE.
TO SEE HIM REDUCED TO SUCH A BLUBBERING, PATHETIC MESS... I DON'T KNOW. IT MAKES YOU THINK.
THERE HAS ALWAYS BEEN A CYCLE TO THESE THINGS. NEW CHALLENGERS ARISE AND ULTIMATELY FALL. AND I WOULD ALWAYS RE-EMERGE, STRONGER FOR IT.
EVEN MONSTERS GET OLD, I GUESS.
AND WHERE DOES ONE PUT AN OLD MONSTER SO THEY NEED NEVER LOOK UPON THEM AGAIN?
YOU WANT ME TO EAT HIM?
NO. MOSCOW WANTS HIM ALIVE.
THAT CYCLE BEGAN IN 1459, WHEN A WITCH SANK HER FANG INTO MY NECK. IT END HERE TODAY. IN A RUSSIAN BASEMENT.
WITH WHIMPERS AND RUIN.
IN CASE HE SHOULD EVER PROVE USEFUL AGAIN.
WELL, I DOUBT THAT.
THE COUNT WISHES TO GO SOMEWHERE QUIET AND PEACEFUL. TELL ME, URSA MAJOR... WHAT IS THE QUIETEST PLACE YOU CAN THINK OF WITHIN OUR MOTHERLAND?
WELL... THERE'S ONE THAT COMES RIGHT TO MIND.

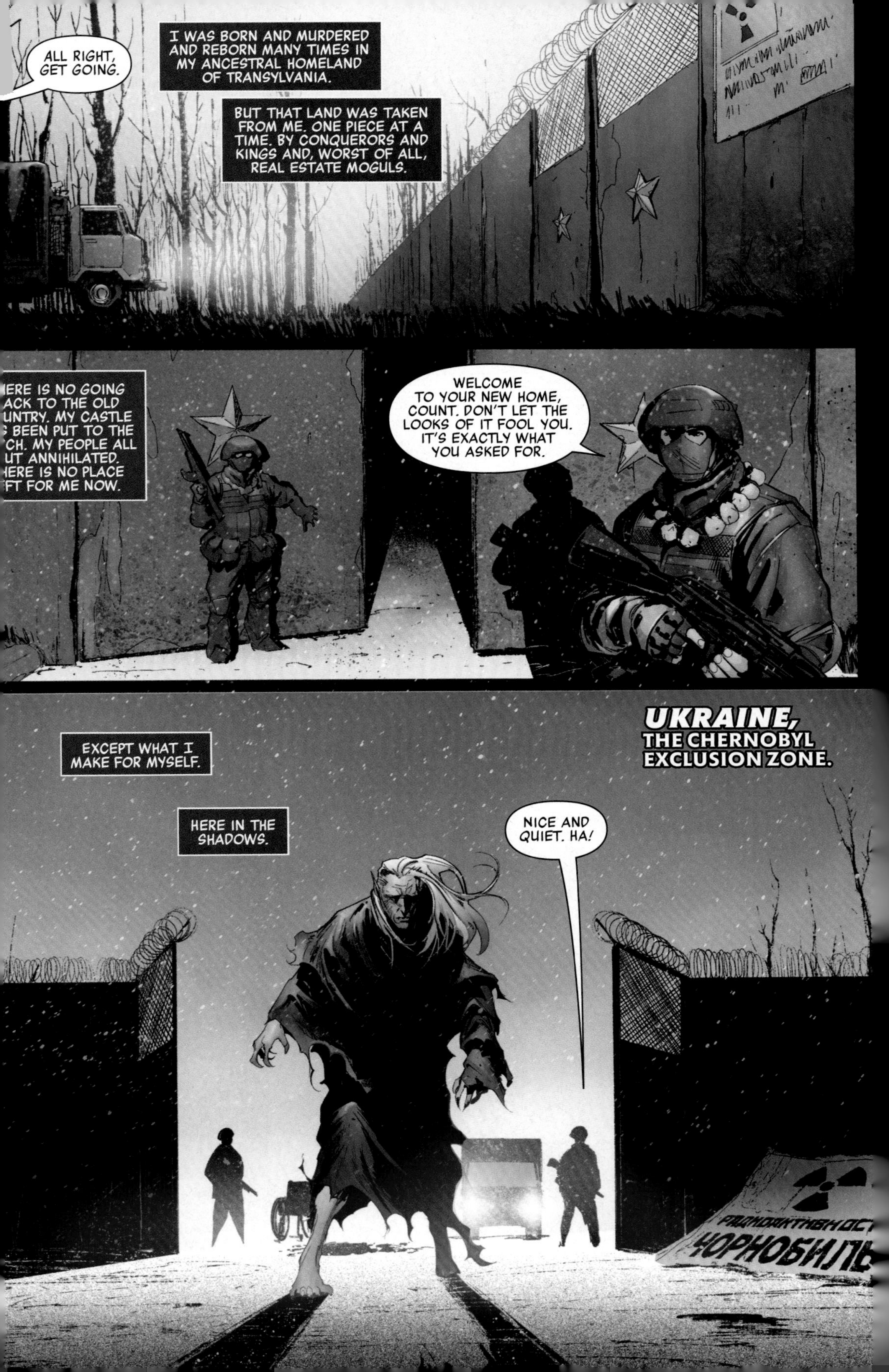

ALL RIGHT, GET GOING.
I WAS BORN AND MURDERED AND REBORN MANY TIMES IN MY ANCESTRAL HOMELAND OF TRANSYLVANIA.
BUT THAT LAND WAS TAKEN FROM ME. ONE PIECE AT A TIME. BY CONQUERORS AND KINGS AND, WORST OF ALL, REAL ESTATE MOGULS.
HERE IS NO GOING ACK TO THE OLD UNTRY. MY CASTLE S BEEN PUT TO THE CH. MY PEOPLE ALL UT ANNIHILATED. HERE IS NO PLACE FT FOR ME NOW.
WELCOME TO YOUR NEW HOME, COUNT. DON'T LET THE LOOKS OF IT FOOL YOU. IT'S EXACTLY WHAT YOU ASKED FOR.
UKRAINE, THE CHERNOBYL EXCLUSION ZONE.
EXCEPT WHAT I MAKE FOR MYSELF.
HERE IN THE SHADOWS.
NICE AND QUIET. HA!
ЧОРНОБИЛЬ

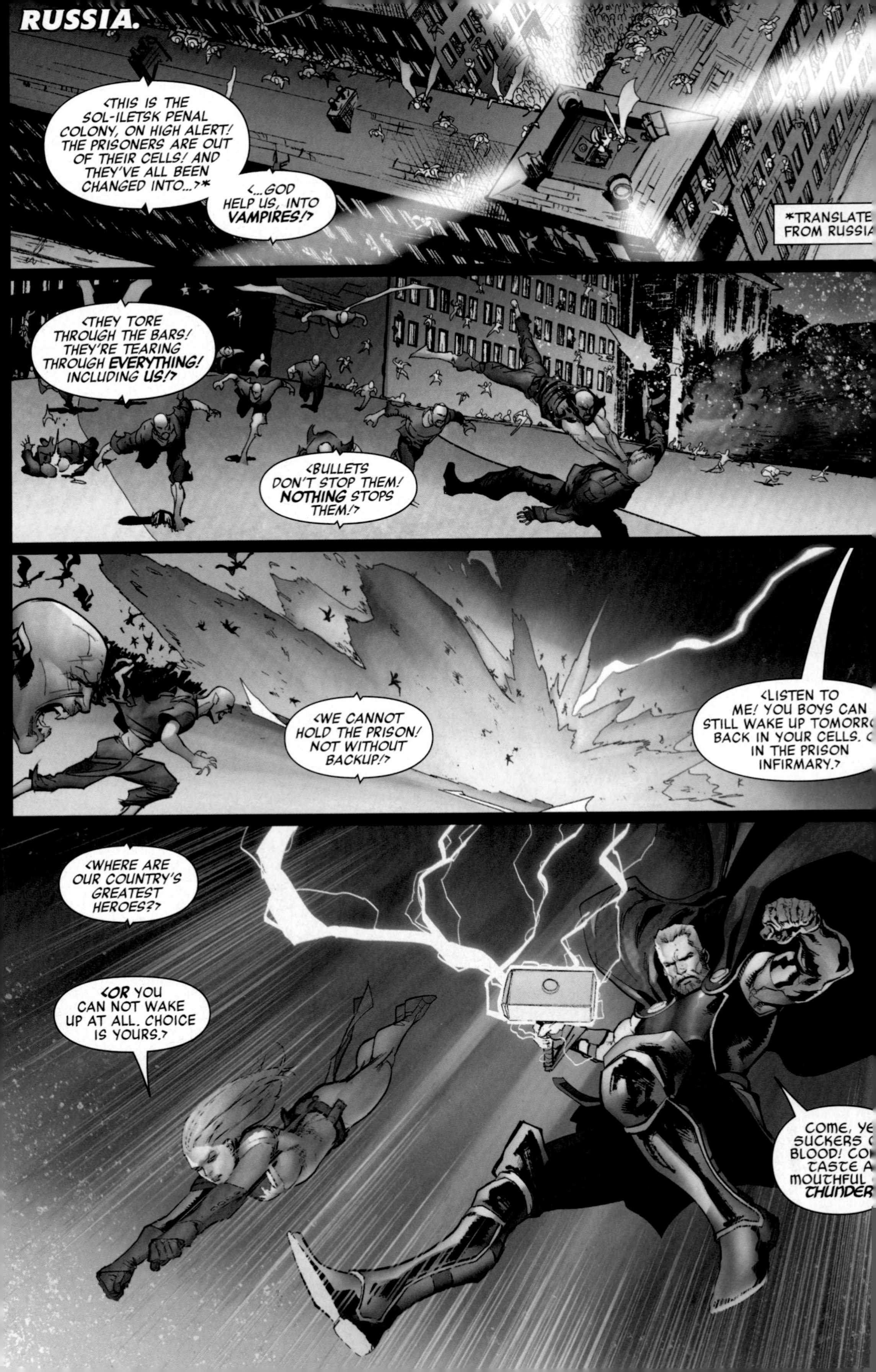
RUSSIA.
<THIS IS THE SOL-ILETSK PENAL COLONY, ON HIGH ALERT! THE PRISONERS ARE OUT OF THEIR CELLS! AND THEY'VE ALL BEEN CHANGED INTO...?*
<...GOD HELP US, INTO VAMPIRES!?
*TRANSLATE FROM RUSSIA
<THEY TORE THROUGH THE BARS! THEY'RE TEARING THROUGH EVERYTHING! INCLUDING US!?
<BULLETS DON'T STOP THEM! NOTHING STOPS THEM!?
<WE CANNOT HOLD THE PRISON! NOT WITHOUT BACKUP!?
<LISTEN TO ME! YOU BOYS CAN STILL WAKE UP TOMORRO BACK IN YOUR CELLS. O IN THE PRISON INFIRMARY.?
<WHERE ARE OUR COUNTRY'S GREATEST HEROES??
<OR YOU CAN NOT WAKE UP AT ALL. CHOICE IS YOURS.?
COME, YE SUCKERS O BLOOD! CO TASTE A MOUTHFUL THUNDER

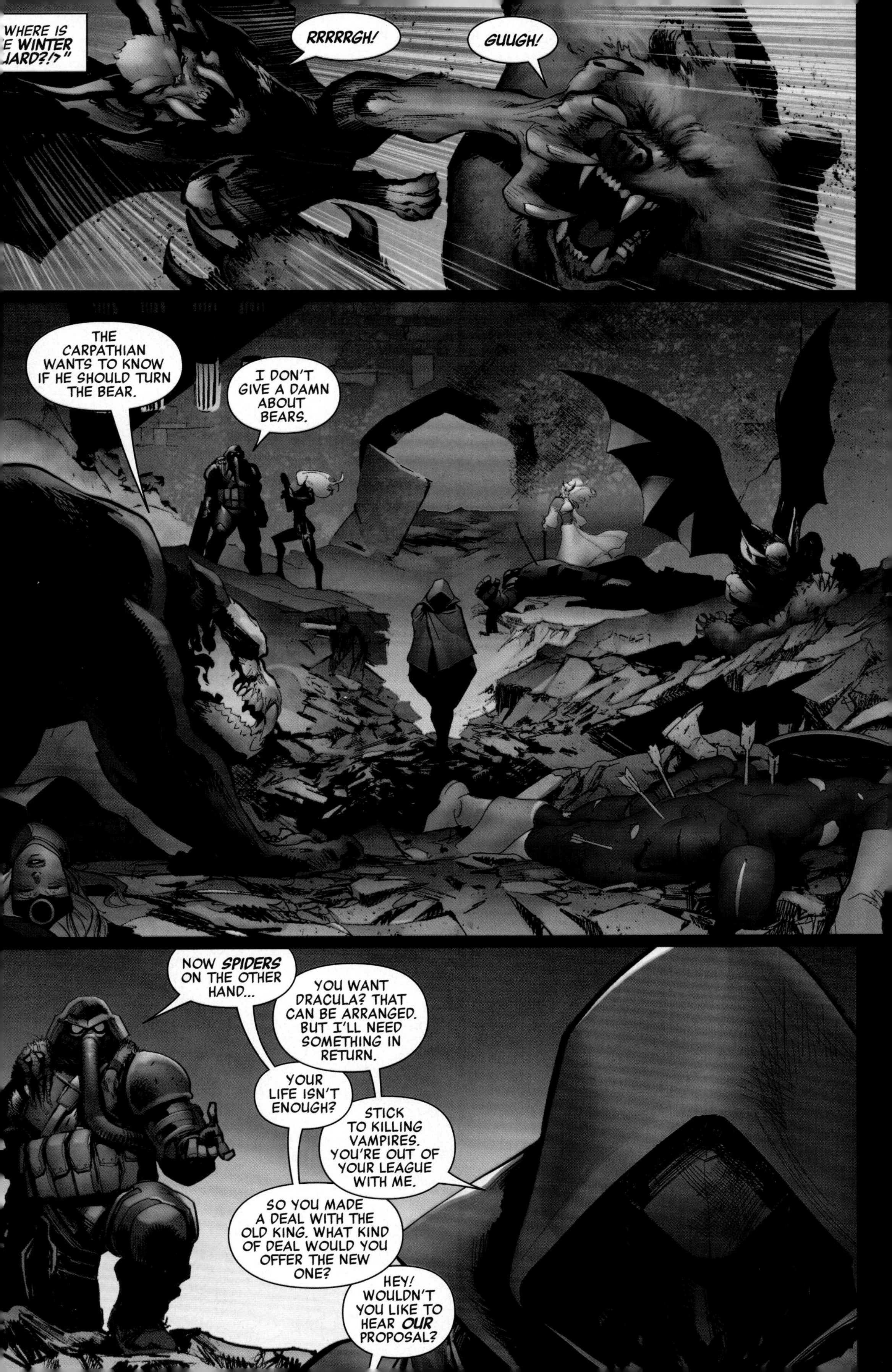
WHERE IS
E WINTER
UARD?!?"
RRRRRGH!
GUUGH!
THE CARPATHIAN WANTS TO KNOW IF HE SHOULD TURN THE BEAR.
I DON'T GIVE A DAMN ABOUT BEARS.
NOW SPIDERS ON THE OTHER HAND...
YOU WANT DRACULA? THAT CAN BE ARRANGED. BUT I'LL NEED SOMETHING IN RETURN.
YOUR LIFE ISN'T ENOUGH?
STICK TO KILLING VAMPIRES. YOU'RE OUT OF YOUR LEAGUE WITH ME.
SO YOU MADE A DEAL WITH THE OLD KING. WHAT KIND OF DEAL WOULD YOU OFFER THE NEW ONE?
HEY! WOULDN'T YOU LIKE TO HEAR OUR PROPOSAL?

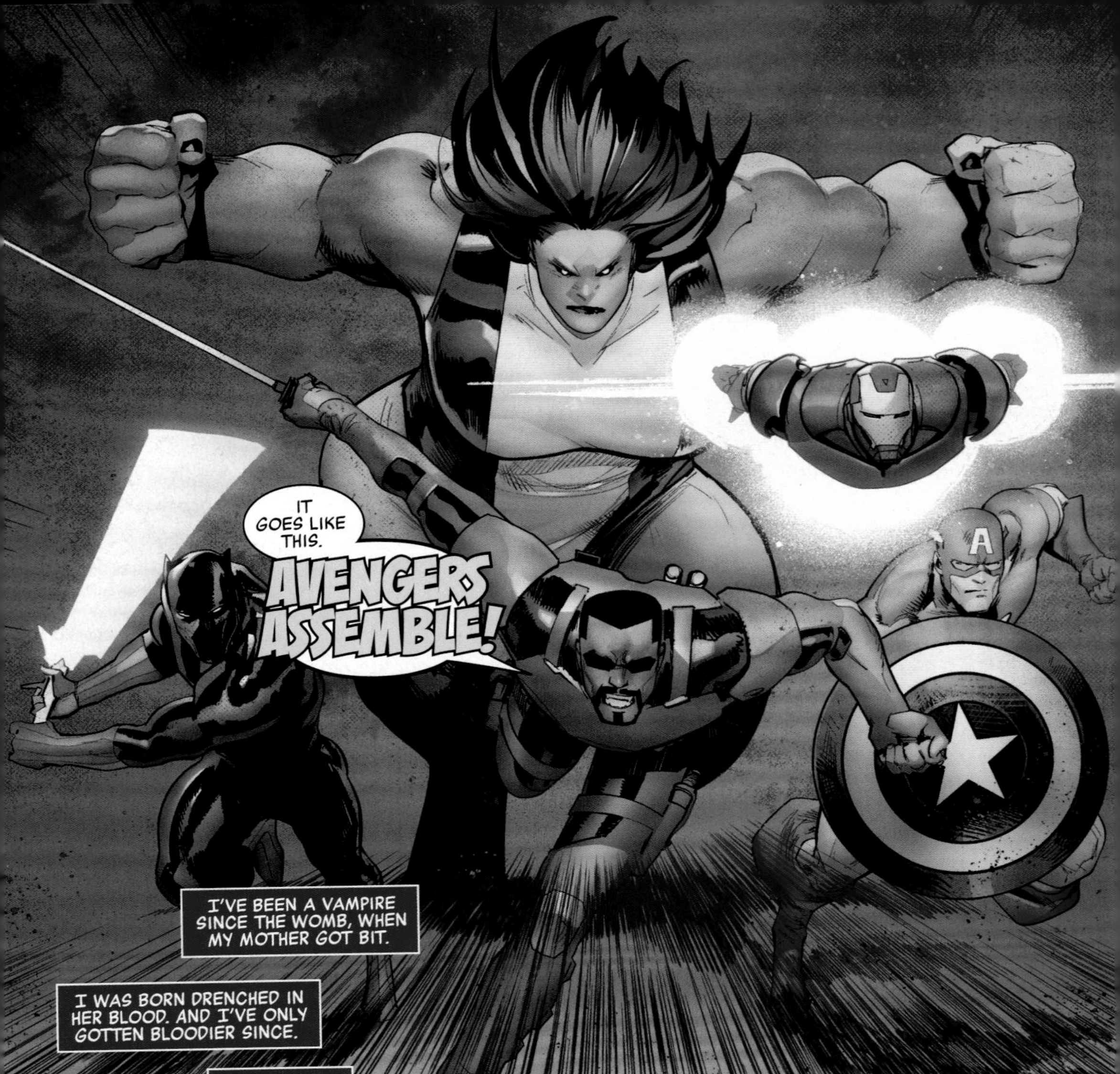
IT GOES LIKE THIS.
AVENGERS ASSEMBLE!
I'VE BEEN A VAMPIRE SINCE THE WOMB, WHEN MY MOTHER GOT BIT.
I WAS BORN DRENCHED IN HER BLOOD. AND I'VE ONLY GOTTEN BLOODIER SINCE.
MUST BE WHY THEY CALL ME *BLADE.*
BUT I'M AN AVENGER NOW. FIGHTING ALONGSIDE GODS AND HULKS AND THE BLACK POPE AND A LIVING HISTORY MUSEUM.
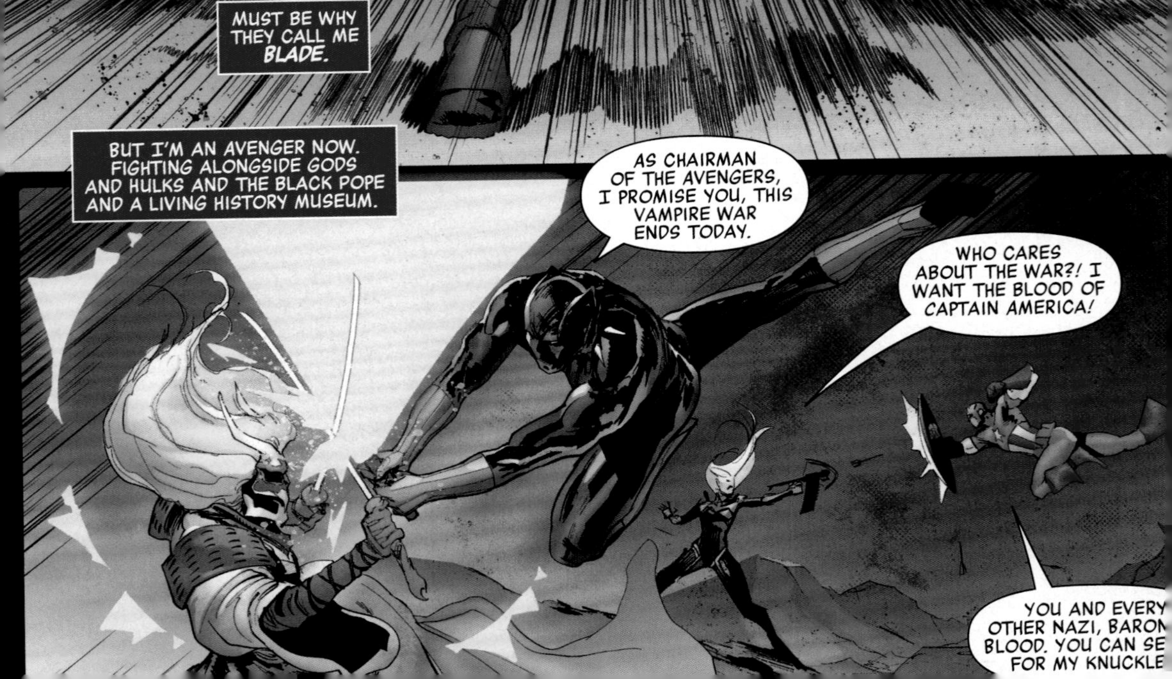
AS CHAIRMAN OF THE AVENGERS, I PROMISE YOU, THIS VAMPIRE WAR ENDS TODAY.
WHO CARES ABOUT THE WAR?! I WANT THE BLOOD OF CAPTAIN AMERICA!
YOU AND EVERY OTHER NAZI, BARON BLOOD. YOU CAN SE FOR MY KNUCKLE

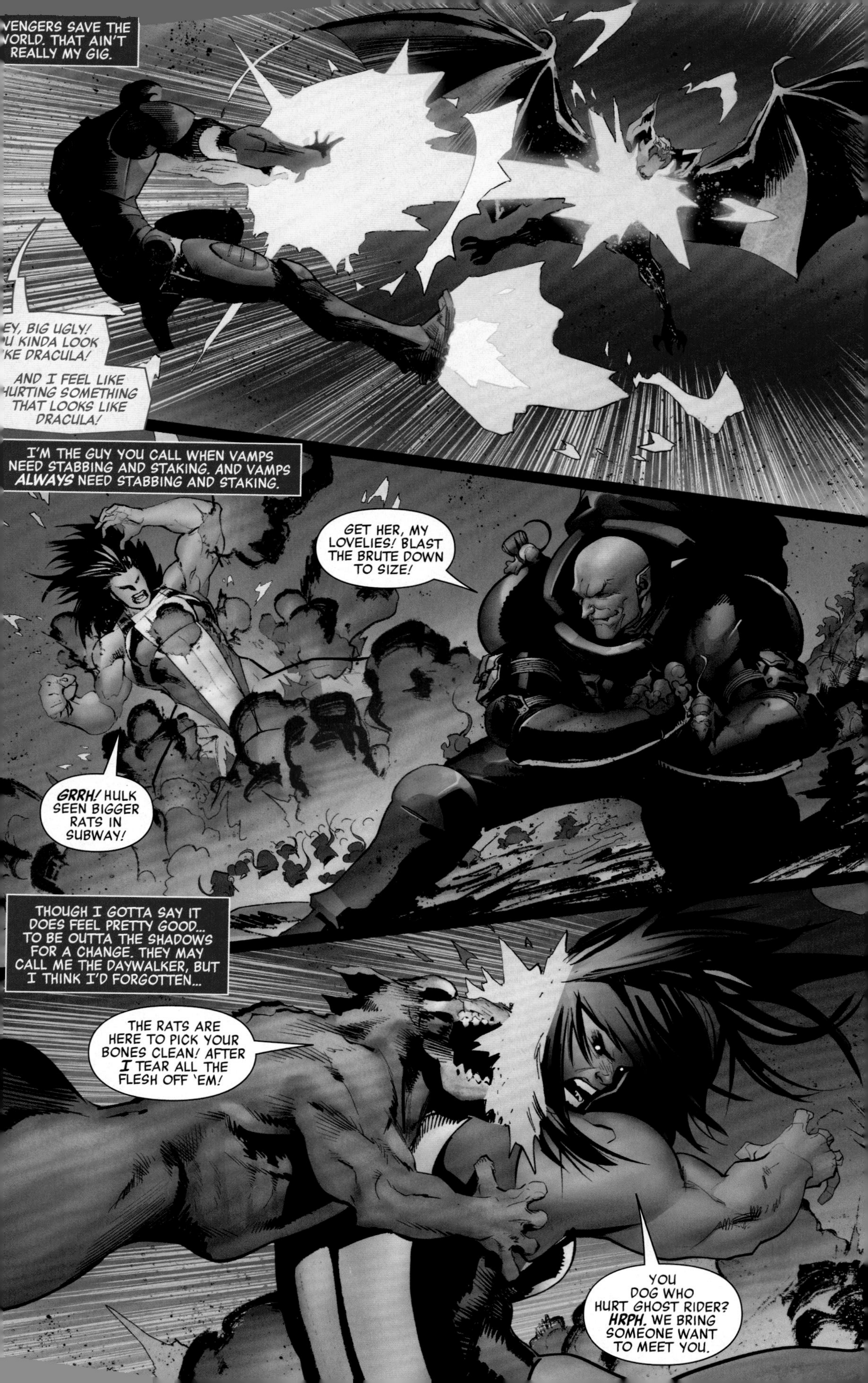

VENGERS SAVE THE WORLD. THAT AIN'T REALLY MY GIG.
EY, BIG UGLY! U KINDA LOOK KE DRACULA!
AND I FEEL LIKE HURTING SOMETHING THAT LOOKS LIKE DRACULA!
I'M THE GUY YOU CALL WHEN VAMPS NEED STABBING AND STAKING. AND VAMPS ALWAYS NEED STABBING AND STAKING.
GET HER, MY LOVELIES! BLAST THE BRUTE DOWN TO SIZE!
GRRH! HULK SEEN BIGGER RATS IN SUBWAY!
THOUGH I GOTTA SAY IT DOES FEEL PRETTY GOOD... TO BE OUTTA THE SHADOWS FOR A CHANGE. THEY MAY CALL ME THE DAYWALKER, BUT I THINK I'D FORGOTTEN...
THE RATS ARE HERE TO PICK YOUR BONES CLEAN! AFTER I TEAR ALL THE FLESH OFF 'EM!
YOU DOG WHO HURT GHOST RIDER? HRPH. WE BRING SOMEONE WANT TO MEET YOU.

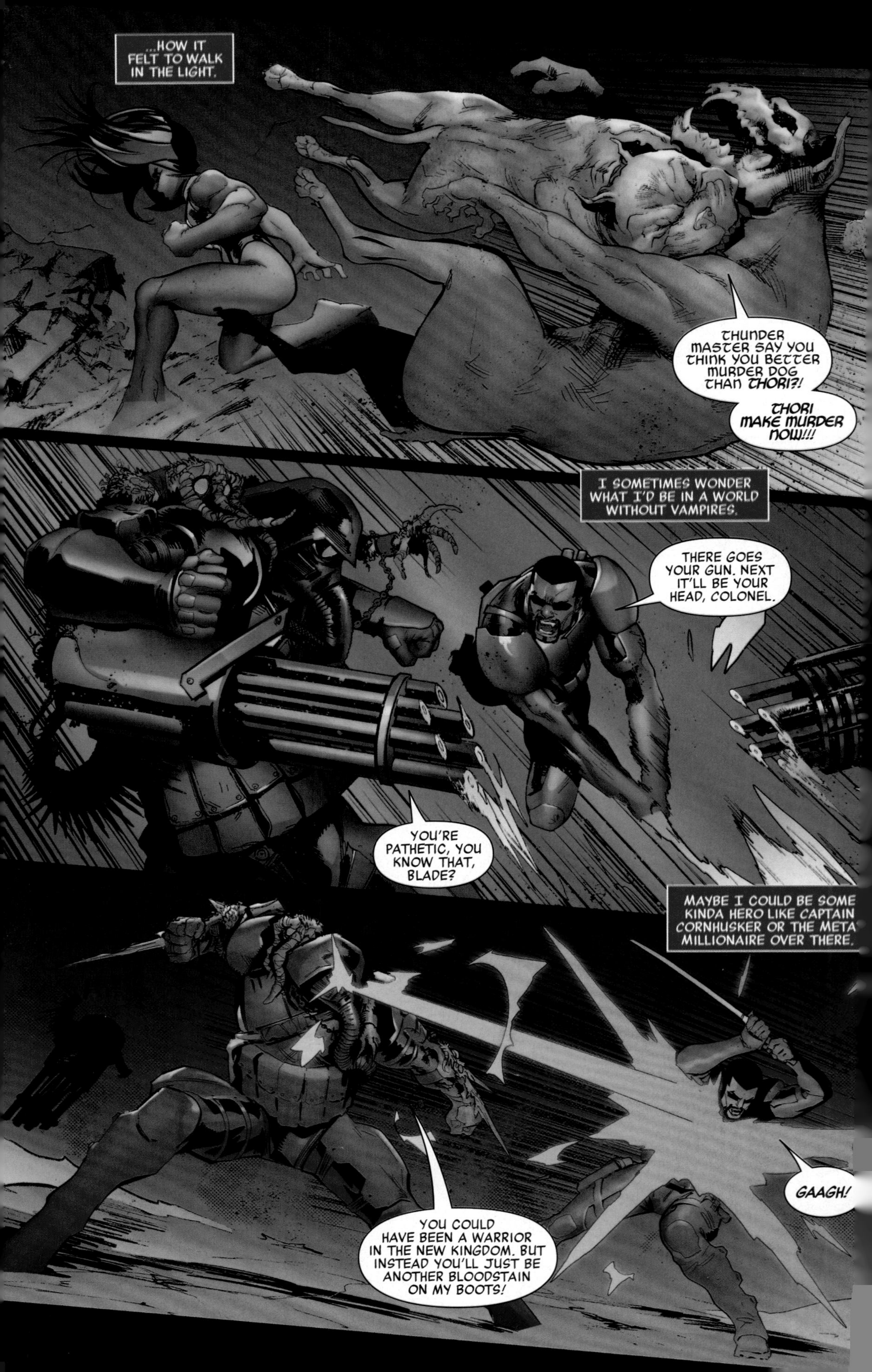
...HOW IT FELT TO WALK IN THE LIGHT.
THUNDER MASTER SAY YOU THINK YOU BETTER MURDER DOG THAN THORI?!
THORI MAKE MURDER NOW!!!
I SOMETIMES WONDER WHAT I'D BE IN A WORLD WITHOUT VAMPIRES.
THERE GOES YOUR GUN. NEXT IT'LL BE YOUR HEAD, COLONEL.
YOU'RE PATHETIC, YOU KNOW THAT, BLADE?
MAYBE I COULD BE SOME KINDA HERO LIKE CAPTAIN CORNHUSKER OR THE META MILLIONAIRE OVER THERE.
YOU COULD HAVE BEEN A WARRIOR IN THE NEW KINGDOM. BUT INSTEAD YOU'LL JUST BE ANOTHER BLOODSTAIN ON MY BOOTS!
GAAGH!

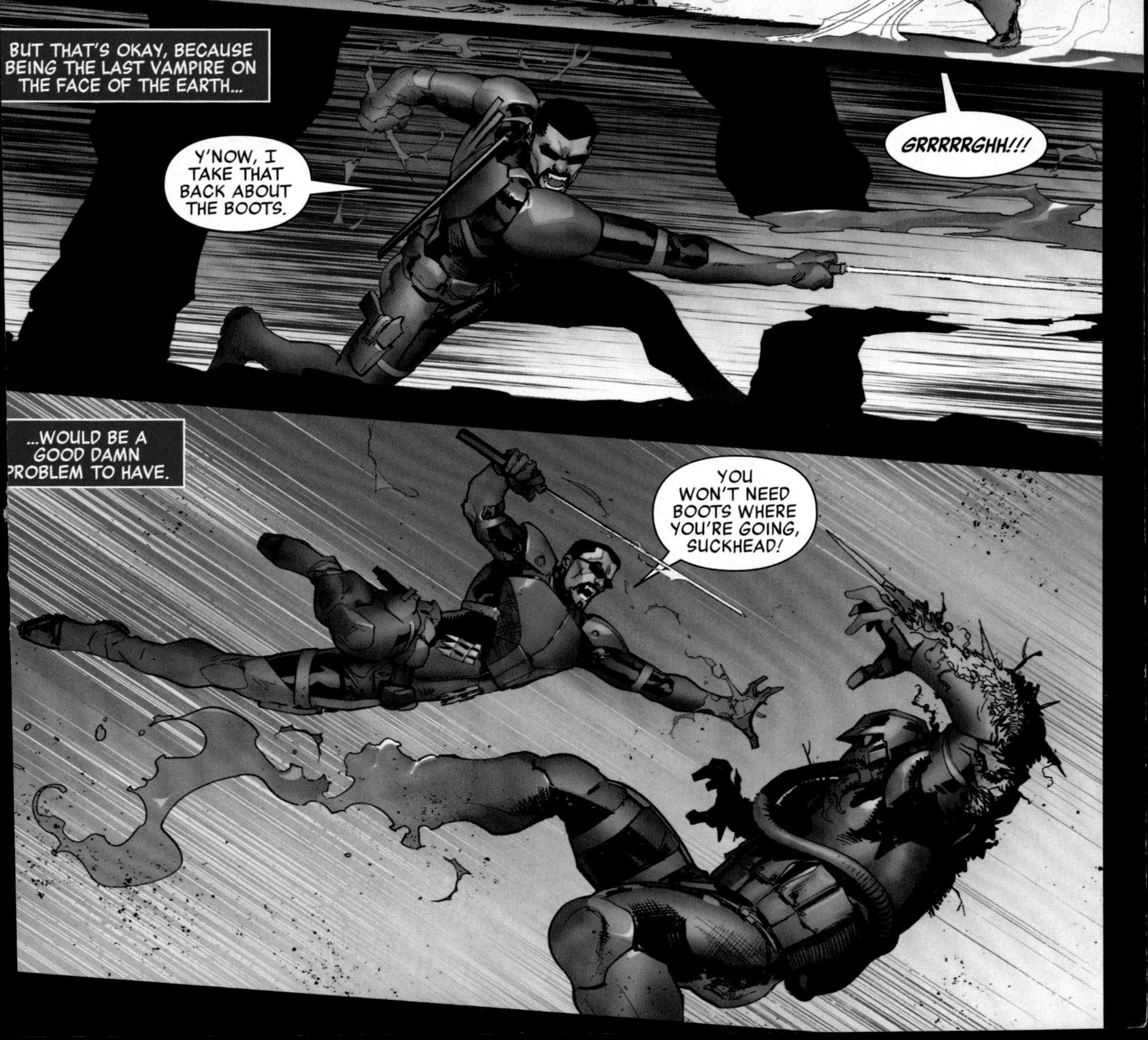
BUT THAT'S OKAY, BECAUSE BEING THE LAST VAMPIRE ON THE FACE OF THE EARTH...
Y'NOW, I TAKE THAT BACK ABOUT THE BOOTS.
GRRRRRGHH!!!
...WOULD BE A GOOD DAMN PROBLEM TO HAVE.
YOU WON'T NEED BOOTS WHERE YOU'RE GOING, SUCKHEAD!

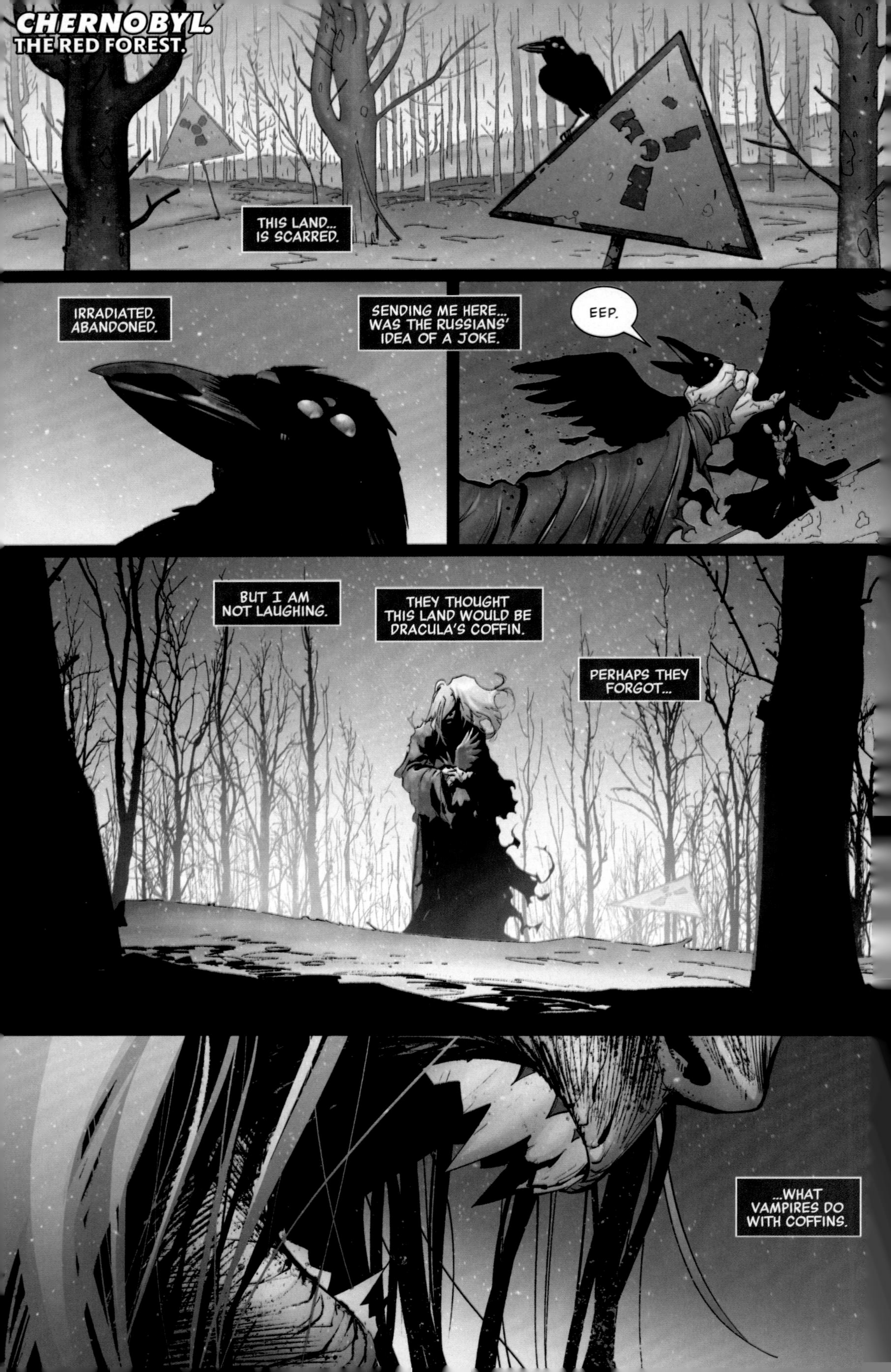
CHERNOBYL.
THE RED FOREST.
THIS LAND... IS SCARRED.
IRRADIATED. ABANDONED.
SENDING ME HERE... WAS THE RUSSIANS' IDEA OF A JOKE.
EEP.
BUT I AM NOT LAUGHING.
THEY THOUGHT THIS LAND WOULD BE DRACULA'S COFFIN.
PERHAPS THEY FORGOT...
...WHAT VAMPIRES DO WITH COFFINS.

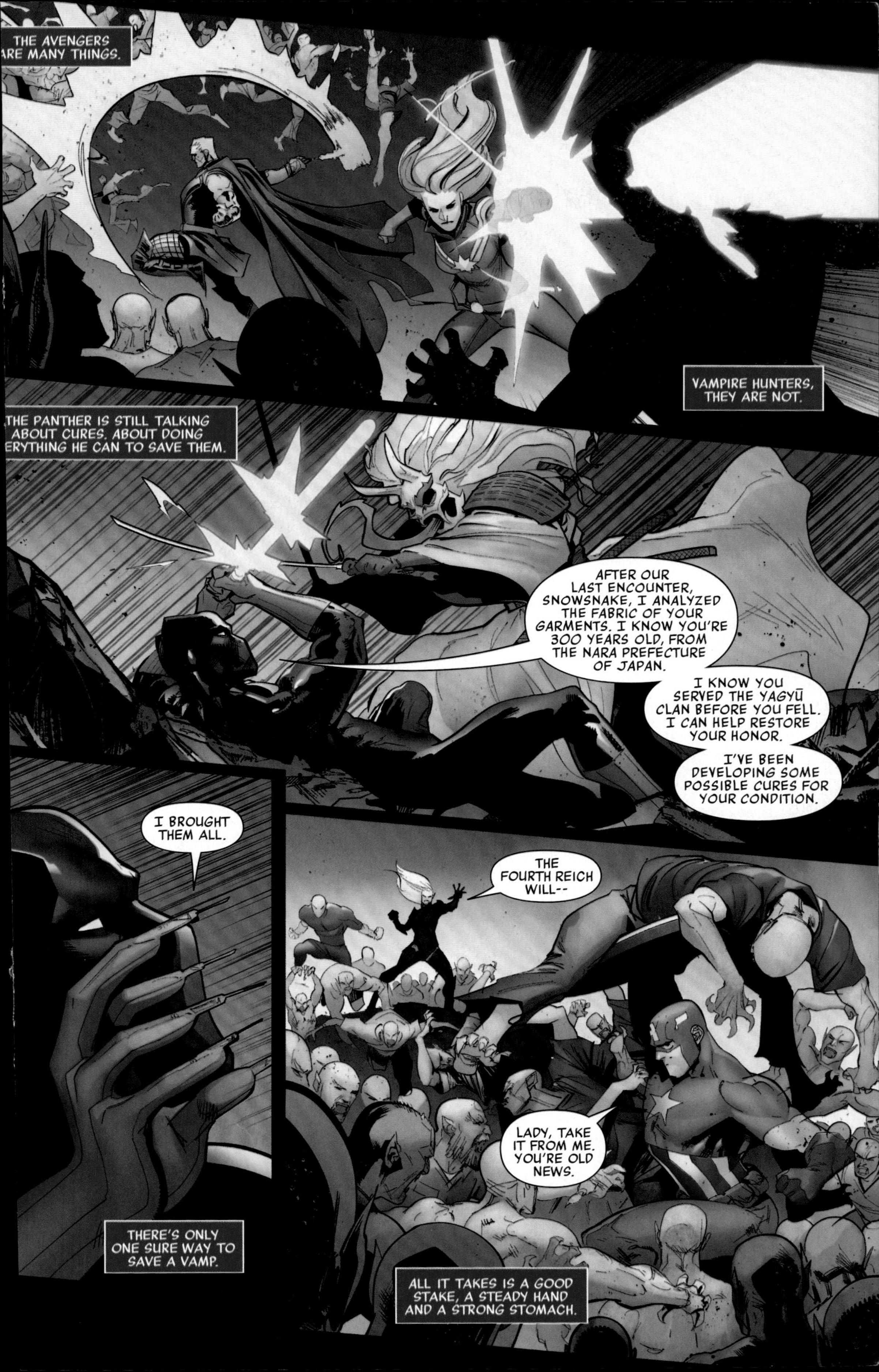
THE AVENGERS ARE MANY THINGS.
VAMPIRE HUNTERS, THEY ARE NOT.
THE PANTHER IS STILL TALKING ABOUT CURES. ABOUT DOING EVERYTHING HE CAN TO SAVE THEM.
AFTER OUR LAST ENCOUNTER, SNOWSNAKE, I ANALYZED THE FABRIC OF YOUR GARMENTS. I KNOW YOU'RE 300 YEARS OLD, FROM THE NARA PREFECTURE OF JAPAN.
I KNOW YOU SERVED THE YAGYŪ CLAN BEFORE YOU FELL. I CAN HELP RESTORE YOUR HONOR.
I'VE BEEN DEVELOPING SOME POSSIBLE CURES FOR YOUR CONDITION.
I BROUGHT THEM ALL.
THE FOURTH REICH WILL--
LADY, TAKE IT FROM ME. YOU'RE OLD NEWS.
THERE'S ONLY ONE SURE WAY TO SAVE A VAMP.
ALL IT TAKES IS A GOOD STAKE, A STEADY HAND AND A STRONG STOMACH.

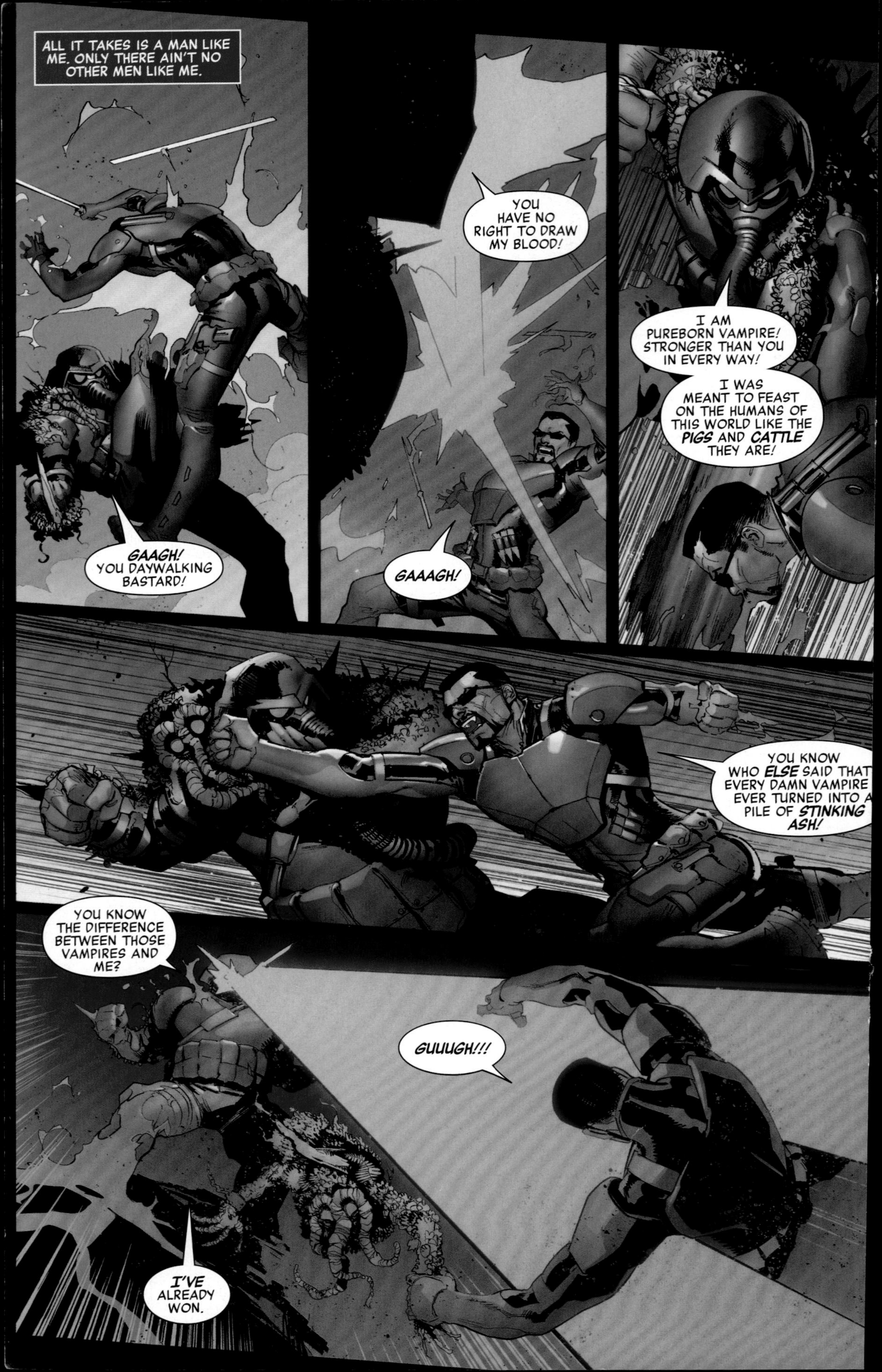
ALL IT TAKES IS A MAN LIKE ME. ONLY THERE AIN'T NO OTHER MEN LIKE ME.
GAAGH! YOU DAYWALKING BASTARD!
YOU HAVE NO RIGHT TO DRAW MY BLOOD!
GAAAGH!
I AM PUREBORN VAMPIRE! STRONGER THAN YOU IN EVERY WAY!
I WAS MEANT TO FEAST ON THE HUMANS OF THIS WORLD LIKE THE PIGS AND CATTLE THEY ARE!
YOU KNOW WHO ELSE SAID THAT? EVERY DAMN VAMPIRE I EVER TURNED INTO A PILE OF STINKING ASH!
YOU KNOW THE DIFFERENCE BETWEEN THOSE VAMPIRES AND ME?
GUUUGH!!!
I'VE ALREADY WON.

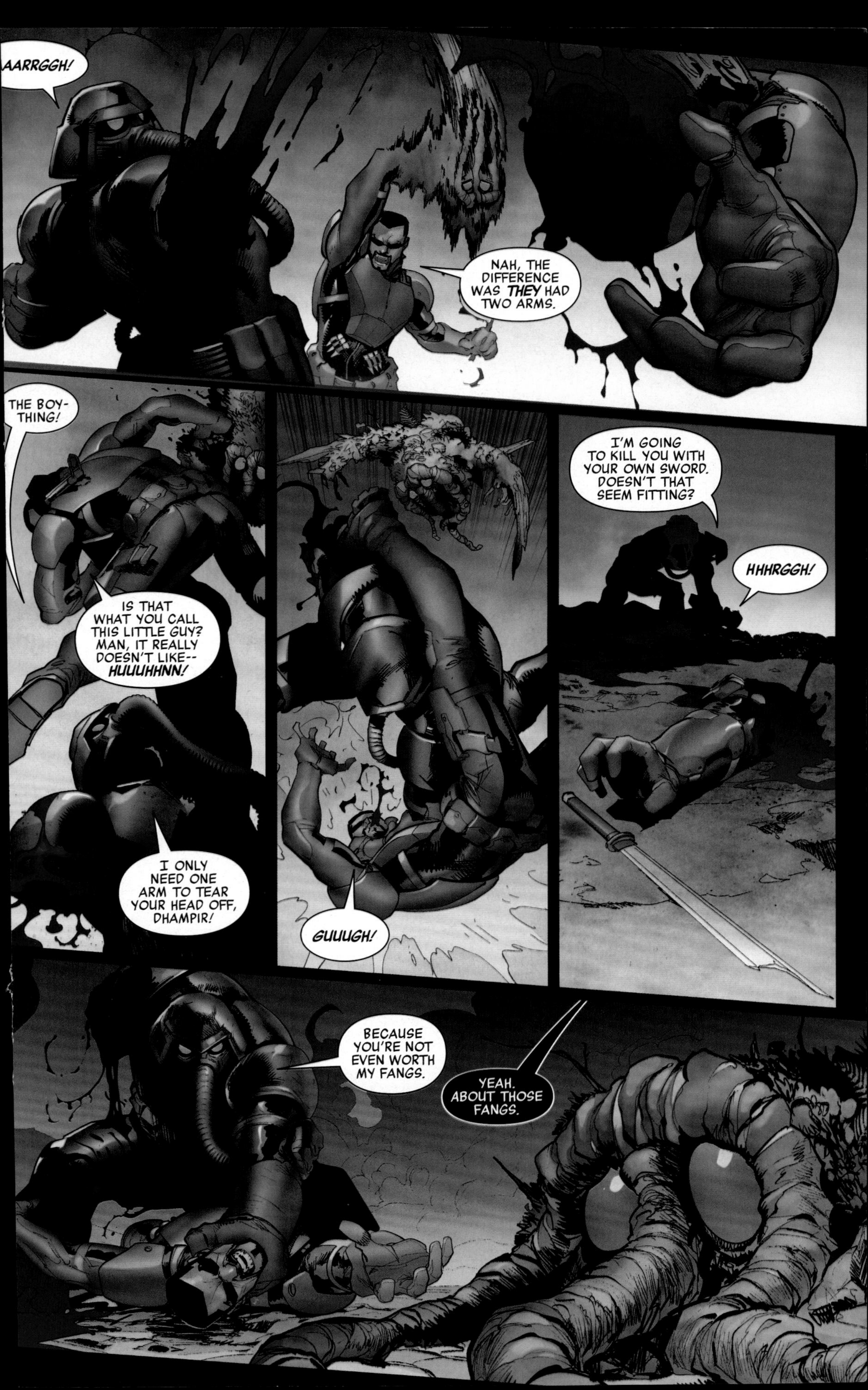
AARRGGH!
NAH, THE DIFFERENCE WAS *THEY* HAD TWO ARMS.
THE BOY-THING!
IS THAT WHAT YOU CALL THIS LITTLE GUY? MAN, IT REALLY DOESN'T LIKE-- *HUUUHHNN!*
I ONLY NEED ONE ARM TO TEAR YOUR HEAD OFF, DHAMPIR!
GUUUGH!
I'M GOING TO KILL YOU WITH YOUR OWN SWORD. DOESN'T THAT SEEM FITTING?
HHHRGGH!
BECAUSE YOU'RE NOT EVEN WORTH MY FANGS.
YEAH. ABOUT THOSE FANGS.

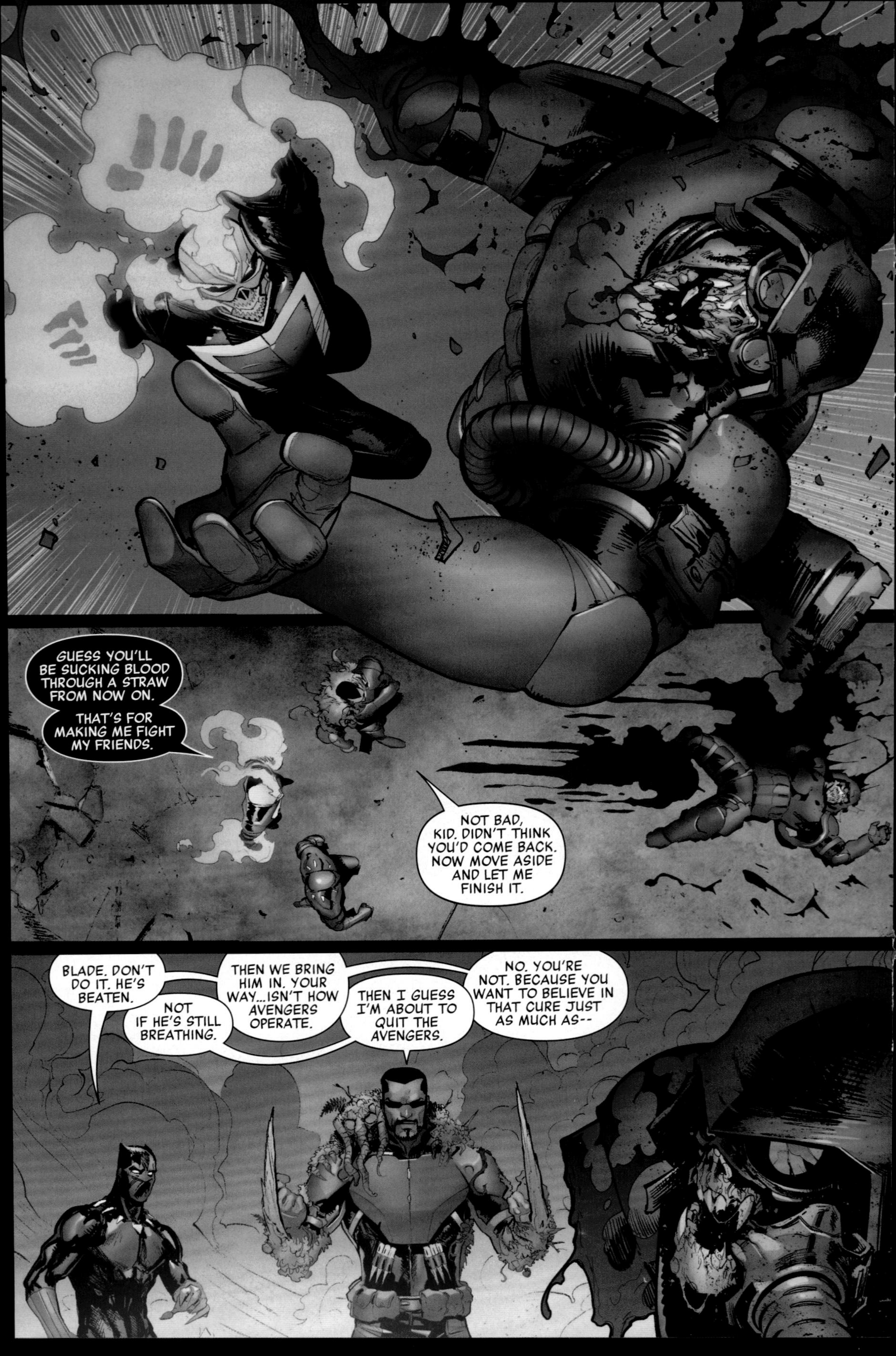
GUESS YOU'LL BE SUCKING BLOOD THROUGH A STRAW FROM NOW ON.
THAT'S FOR MAKING ME FIGHT MY FRIENDS.
NOT BAD, KID. DIDN'T THINK YOU'D COME BACK. NOW MOVE ASIDE AND LET ME FINISH IT.
BLADE. DON'T DO IT. HE'S BEATEN.
NOT IF HE'S STILL BREATHING.
THEN WE BRING HIM IN. YOUR WAY...ISN'T HOW AVENGERS OPERATE.
THEN I GUESS I'M ABOUT TO QUIT THE AVENGERS.
NO. YOU'RE NOT. BECAUSE YOU WANT TO BELIEVE IN THAT CURE JUST AS MUCH AS--

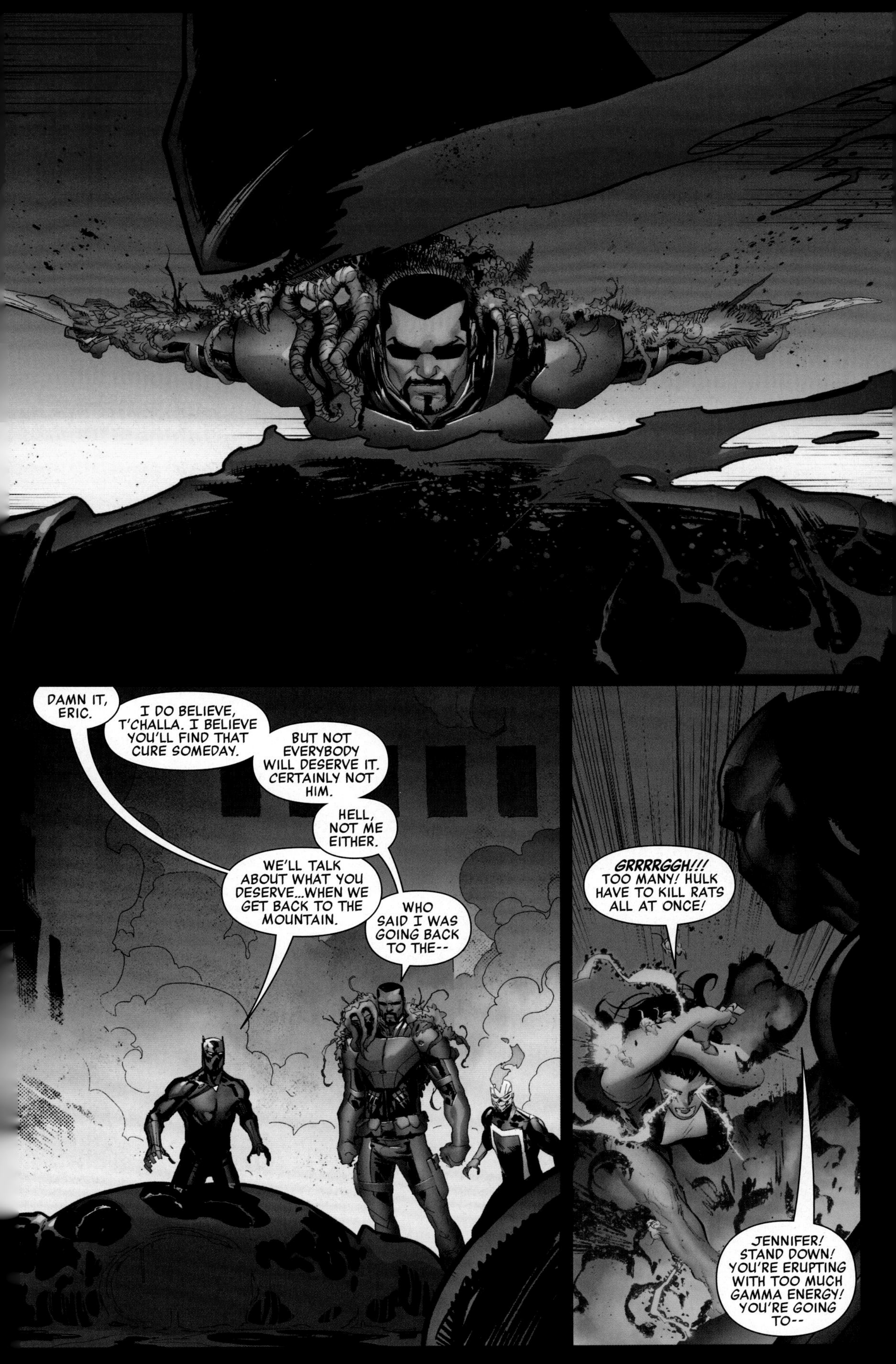
DAMN IT, ERIC.
I DO BELIEVE, T'CHALLA. I BELIEVE YOU'LL FIND THAT CURE SOMEDAY.
BUT NOT EVERYBODY WILL DESERVE IT. CERTAINLY NOT HIM.
HELL, NOT ME EITHER.
WE'LL TALK ABOUT WHAT YOU DESERVE...WHEN WE GET BACK TO THE MOUNTAIN.
WHO SAID I WAS GOING BACK TO THE--
GRRRRGGH!!! TOO MANY! HULK HAVE TO KILL RATS ALL AT ONCE!
JENNIFER! STAND DOWN! YOU'RE ERUPTING WITH TOO MUCH GAMMA ENERGY! YOU'RE GOING TO--

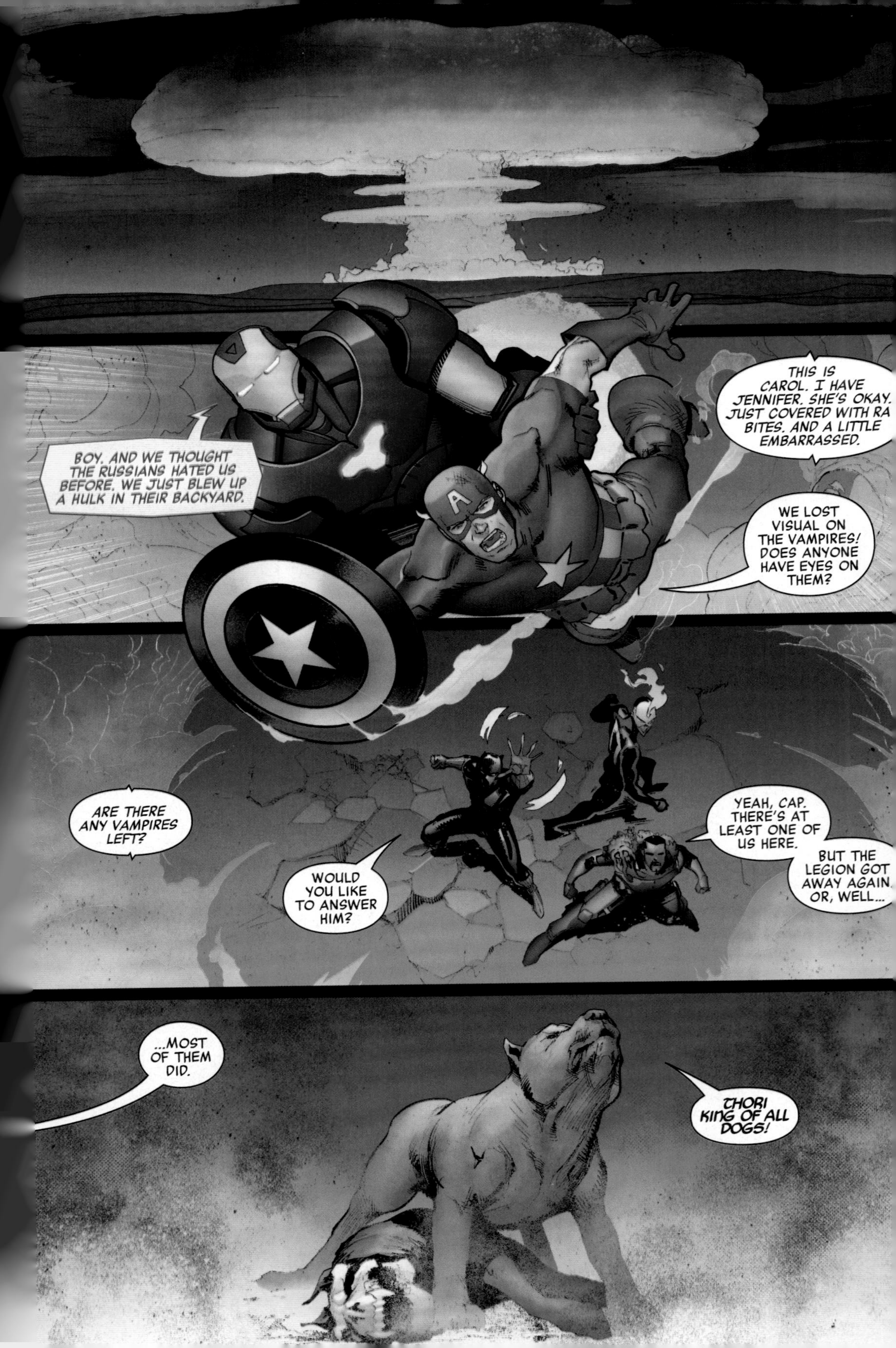
BOY. AND WE THOUGHT THE RUSSIANS HATED US BEFORE. WE JUST BLEW UP A HULK IN THEIR BACKYARD.
THIS IS CAROL. I HAVE JENNIFER. SHE'S OKAY. JUST COVERED WITH RA BITES. AND A LITTLE EMBARRASSED.
WE LOST VISUAL ON THE VAMPIRES! DOES ANYONE HAVE EYES ON THEM?
ARE THERE ANY VAMPIRES LEFT?
WOULD YOU LIKE TO ANSWER HIM?
YEAH, CAP. THERE'S AT LEAST ONE OF US HERE.
BUT THE LEGION GOT AWAY AGAIN. OR, WELL...
...MOST OF THEM DID.
THORI KING OF ALL DOGS!

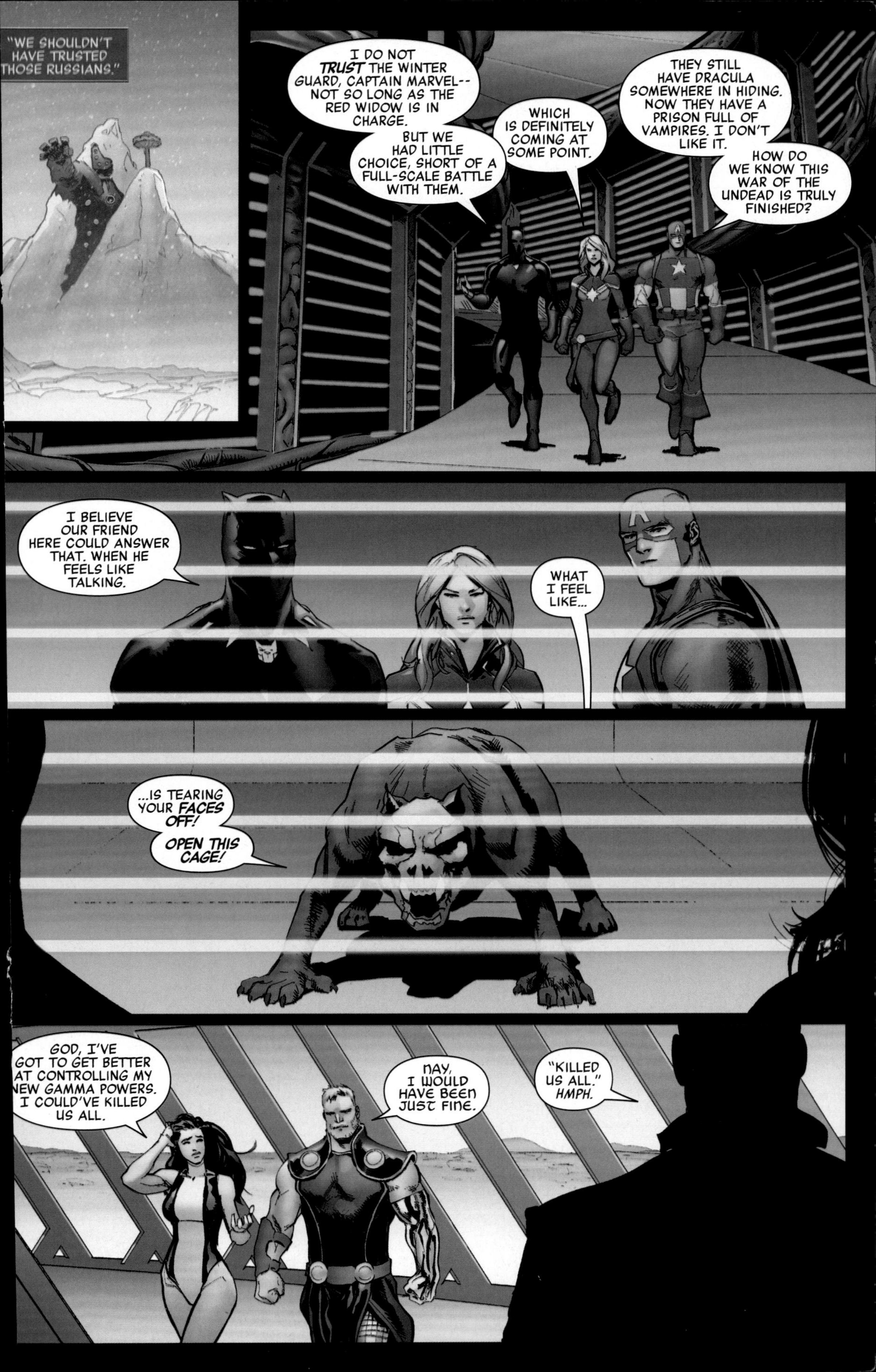
"WE SHOULDN'T HAVE TRUSTED THOSE RUSSIANS."
I DO NOT TRUST THE WINTER GUARD, CAPTAIN MARVEL-- NOT SO LONG AS THE RED WIDOW IS IN CHARGE.
BUT WE HAD LITTLE CHOICE, SHORT OF A FULL-SCALE BATTLE WITH THEM.
WHICH IS DEFINITELY COMING AT SOME POINT.
THEY STILL HAVE DRACULA SOMEWHERE IN HIDING. NOW THEY HAVE A PRISON FULL OF VAMPIRES. I DON'T LIKE IT.
HOW DO WE KNOW THIS WAR OF THE UNDEAD IS TRULY FINISHED?
I BELIEVE OUR FRIEND HERE COULD ANSWER THAT. WHEN HE FEELS LIKE TALKING.
WHAT I FEEL LIKE...
...IS TEARING YOUR FACES OFF!
OPEN THIS CAGE!
GOD, I'VE GOT TO GET BETTER AT CONTROLLING MY NEW GAMMA POWERS. I COULD'VE KILLED US ALL.
NAY, I WOULD HAVE BEEN JUST FINE.
"KILLED US ALL." HMPH.

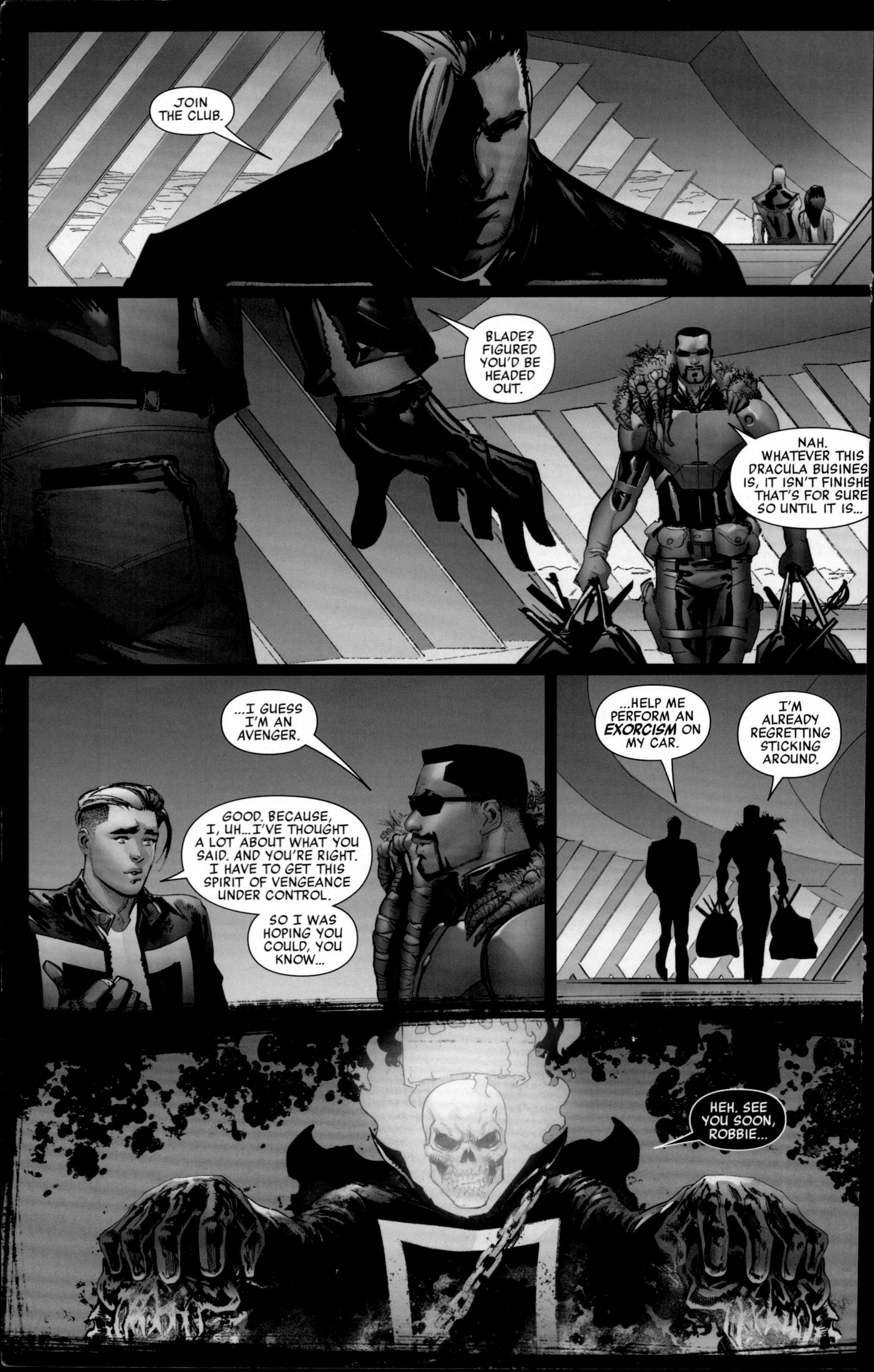
JOIN THE CLUB.
BLADE? FIGURED YOU'D BE HEADED OUT.
NAH. WHATEVER THIS DRACULA BUSINES IS, IT ISN'T FINISHE THAT'S FOR SURE SO UNTIL IT IS...
...I GUESS I'M AN AVENGER.
GOOD. BECAUSE, I, UH...I'VE THOUGHT A LOT ABOUT WHAT YOU SAID. AND YOU'RE RIGHT. I HAVE TO GET THIS SPIRIT OF VENGEANCE UNDER CONTROL.
SO I WAS HOPING YOU COULD, YOU KNOW...
...HELP ME PERFORM AN EXORCISM ON MY CAR.
I'M ALREADY REGRETTING STICKING AROUND.
HEH. SEE YOU SOON, ROBBIE...

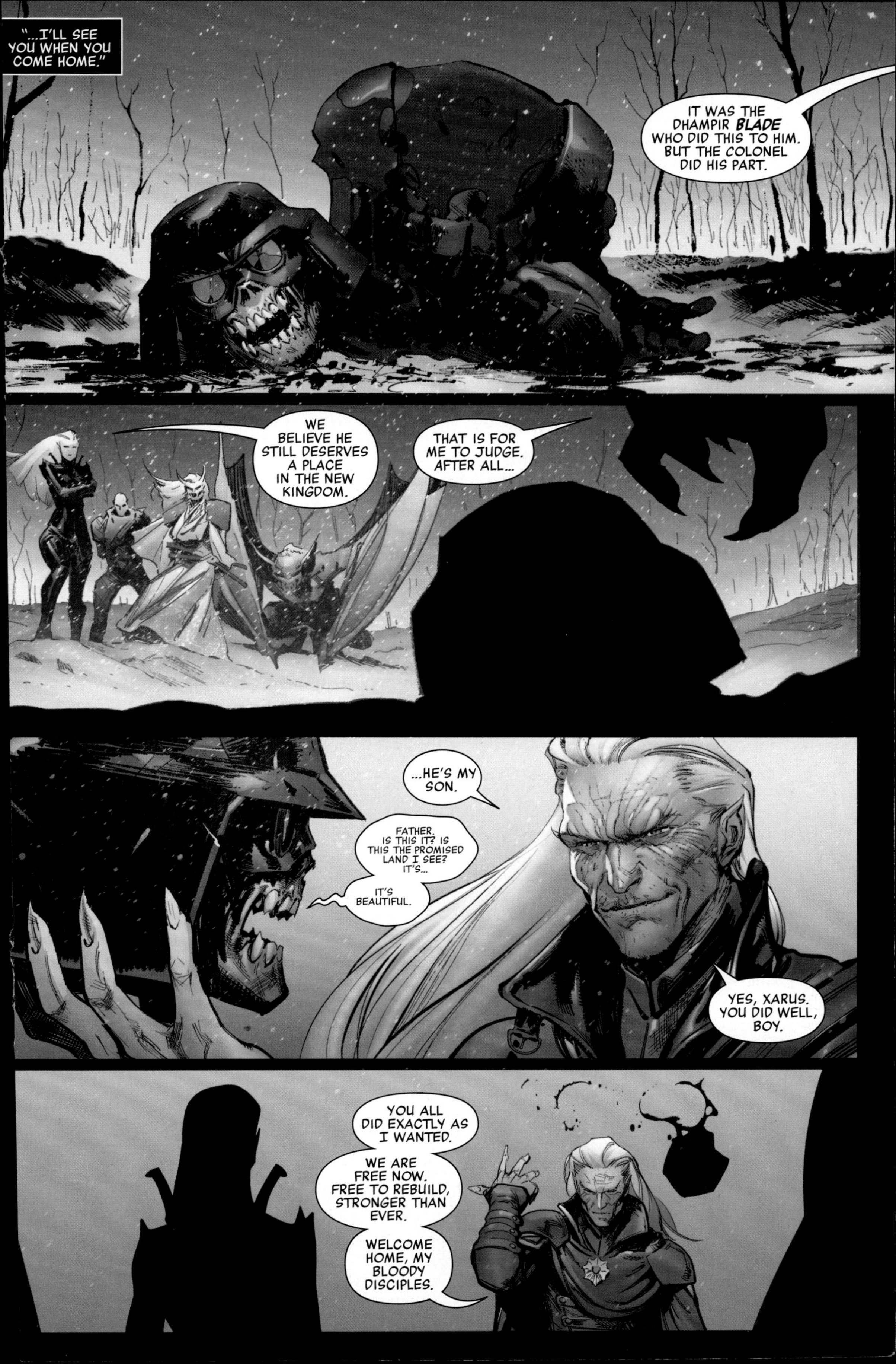
"...I'LL SEE YOU WHEN YOU COME HOME."
IT WAS THE DHAMPIR BLADE WHO DID THIS TO HIM. BUT THE COLONEL DID HIS PART.
WE BELIEVE HE STILL DESERVES A PLACE IN THE NEW KINGDOM.
THAT IS FOR ME TO JUDGE. AFTER ALL...
...HE'S MY SON.
FATHER. IS THIS IT? IS THIS THE PROMISED LAND I SEE? IT'S...
IT'S BEAUTIFUL.
YES, XARUS. YOU DID WELL, BOY.
YOU ALL DID EXACTLY AS I WANTED.
WE ARE FREE NOW. FREE TO REBUILD, STRONGER THAN EVER.
WELCOME HOME, MY BLOODY DISCIPLES.

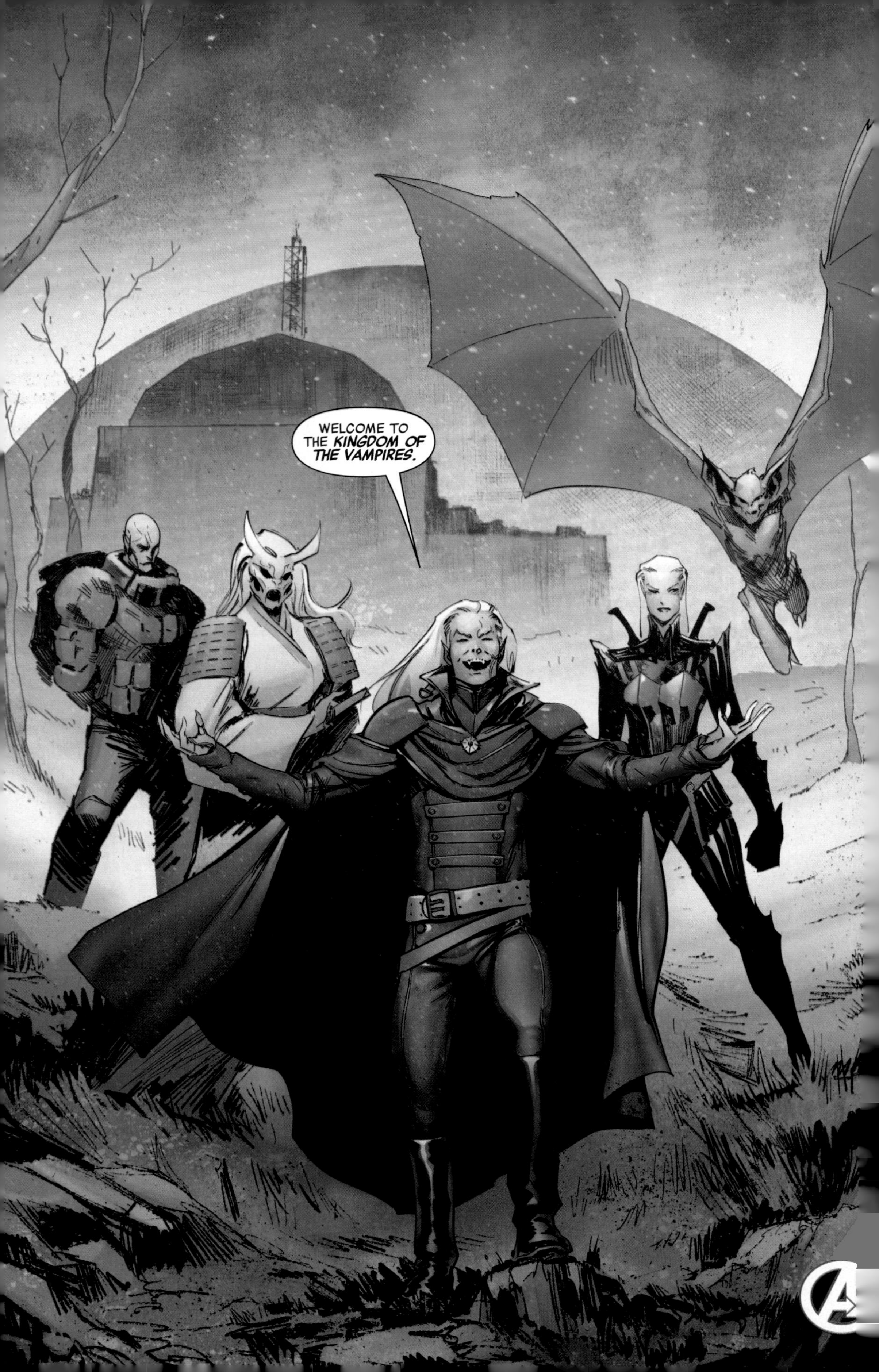
WELCOME TO THE KINGDOM OF THE VAMPIRES.

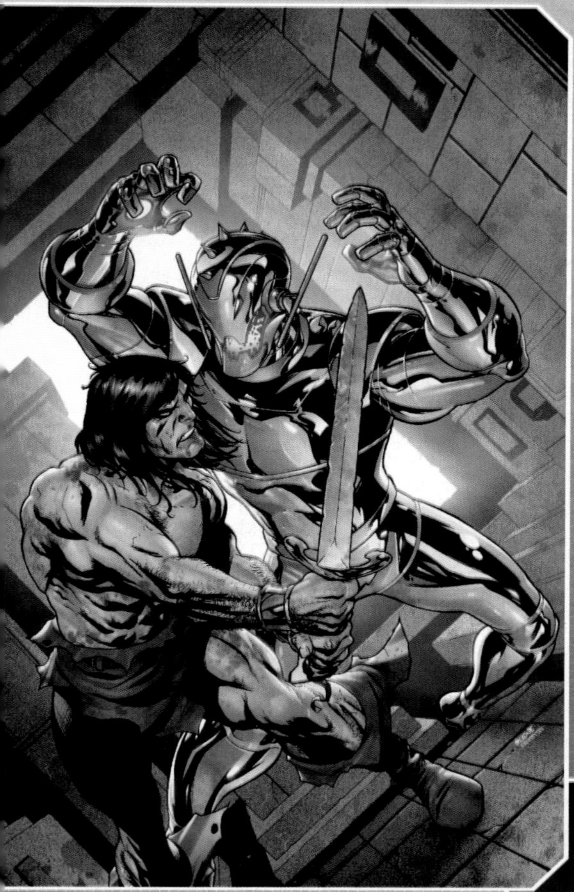

IKE MCKONE & JESUS ABURTOV
13 CONAN VS. VARIANT

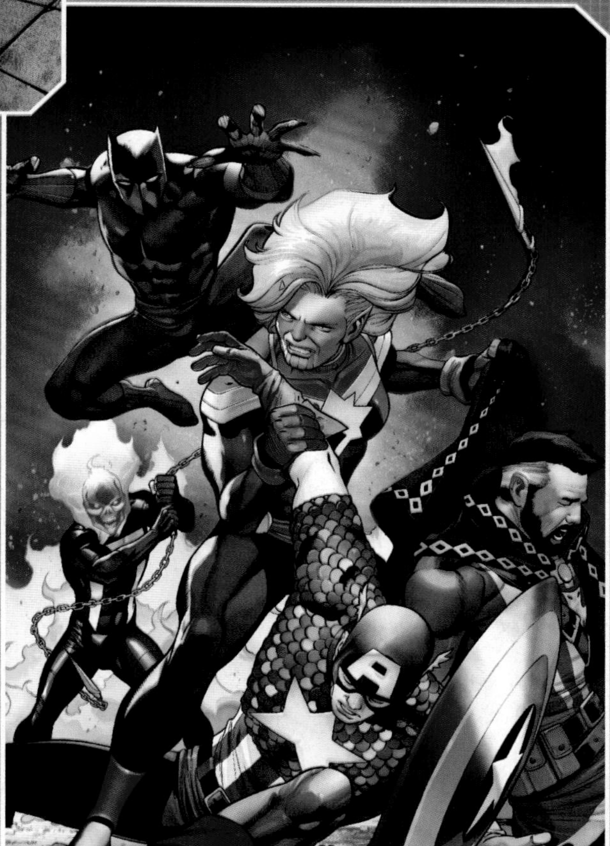

CARLOS PACHECO, RAFAEL FONTERIZ
& DAVID CURIEL
14 SKRULLS VARIANT

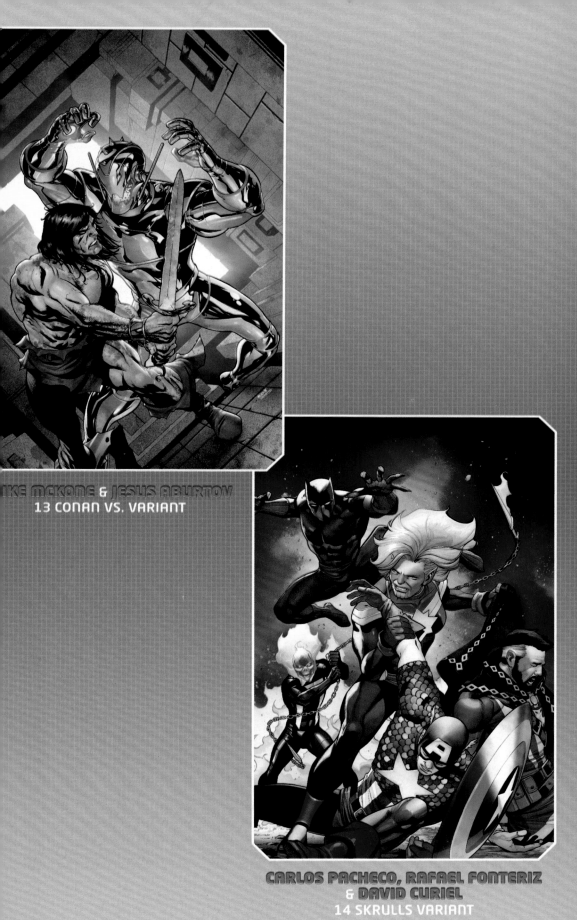

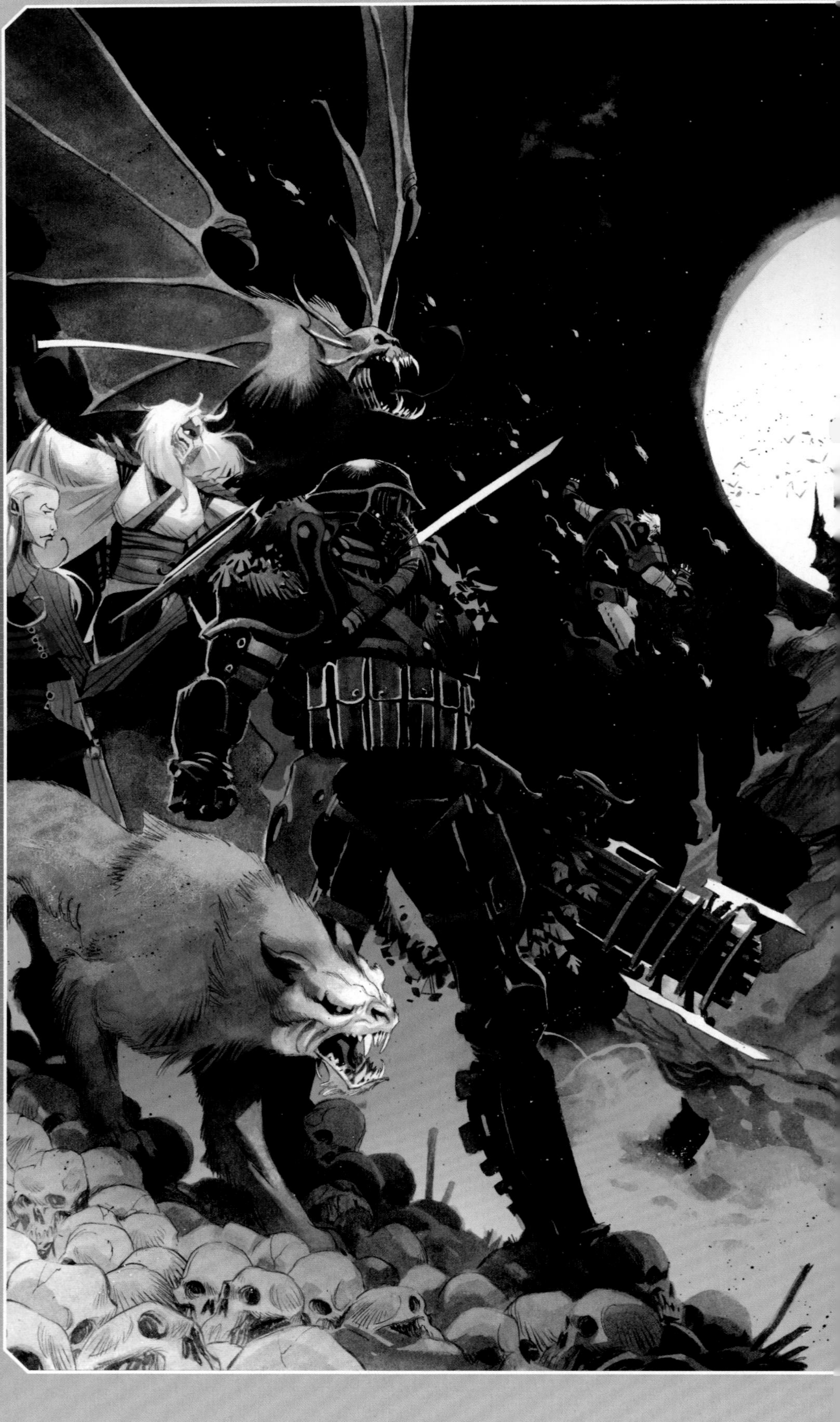

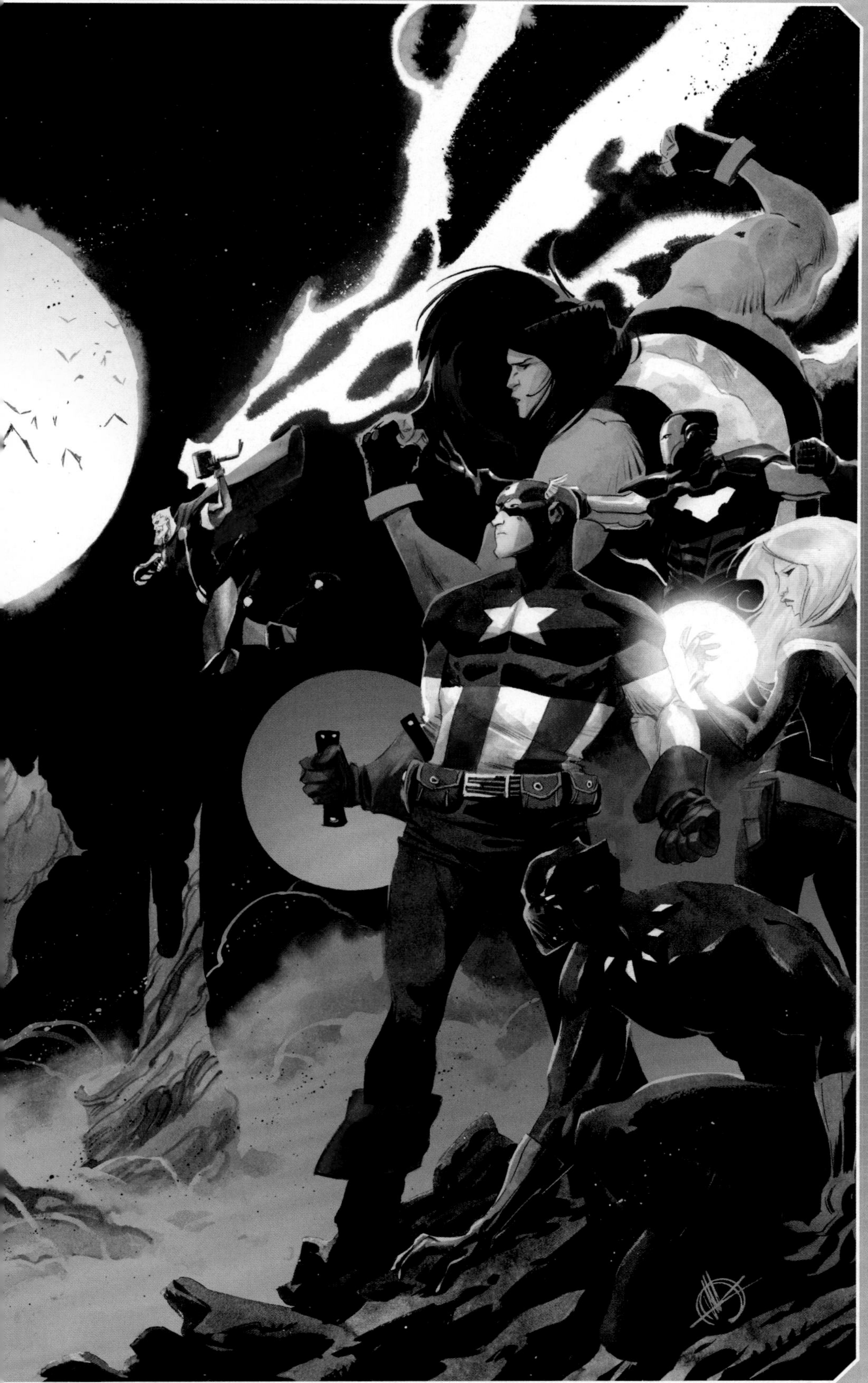

MATTEO SCALERA & RAIN BEREDO
14 VARIANT

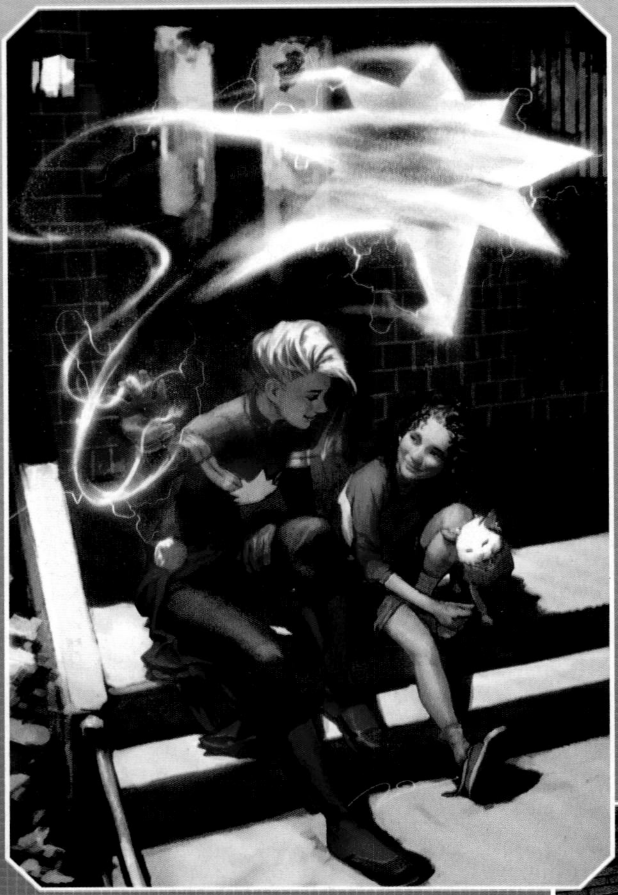

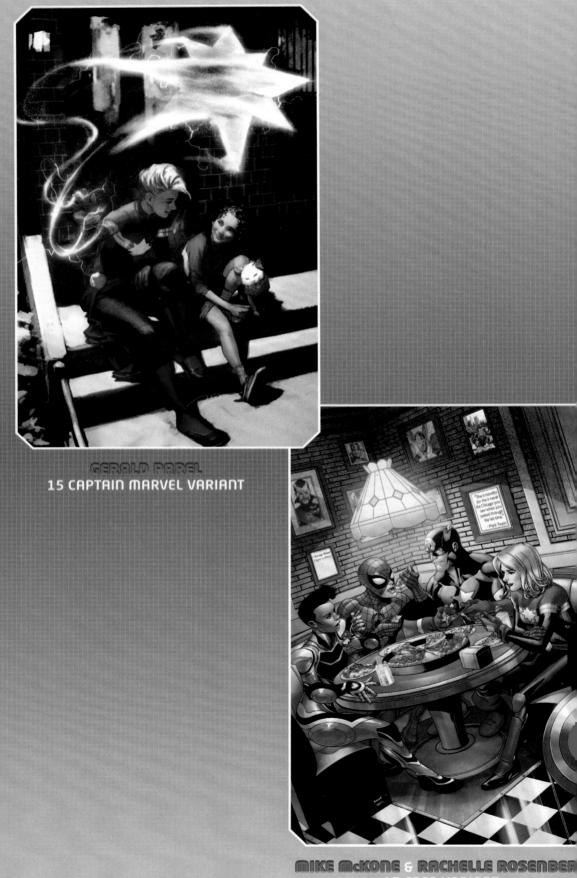

GERALD PAREL
15 CAPTAIN MARVEL VARIANT

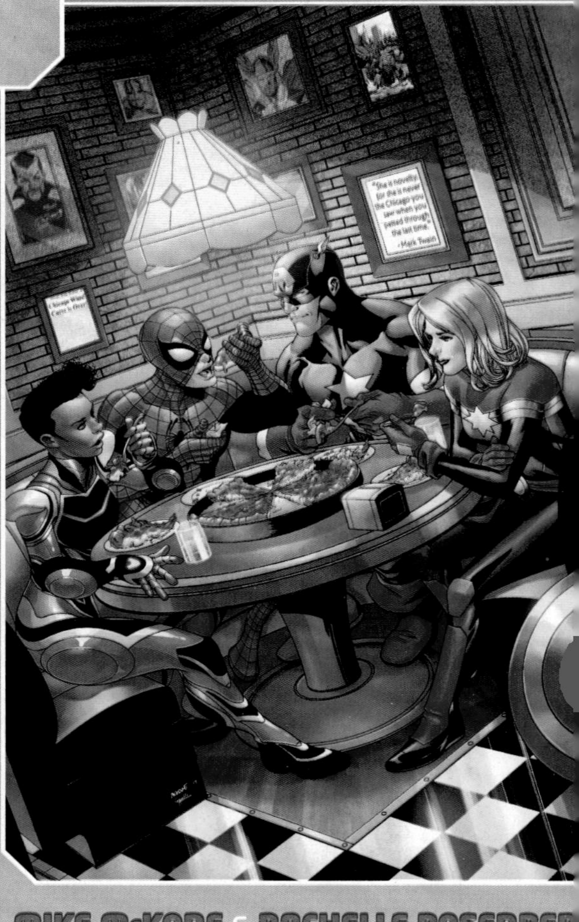
"She is novelty, for she is never the Chicago you saw when you passed through the last time."
- Mark Twain

MIKE McKONE & RACHELLE ROSENBER
17 C2E2 VARIANT